Language Arts and Literacy for Young Children

Terry S. Salinger
Educational Testing Service

Merrill, an imprint of
Macmillan Publishing Company
New York

Collier Macmillan Canada, Inc.
Toronto

Maxwell Macmilan International Publishing Group
New York   Oxford   Singapore   Sydney

To Audrey D. Williams

Macmillan Publishing Company
866 Third Avenue, New York, NY 10022

Collier Macmillan, Canada, Inc.

This book was set in Palatino.

Administrative Editor: David Faherty
Production Coordinator: Constantina Geldis
Art Coordinator: Lorraine Woost
Cover Designer: Jolie Muren

Photo credits: pp. 5, 34, 204, 229 by Terry Salinger; and p. 272 by Merrill Publishing/ Bruce Johnson.

Library of Congress Catalog Card Number: 87-61947
International Standard Book Number: 0-675-20552-2
Printed in the United States of America
Printing: 3 4 5 6 7 8 9   Year: 1 2 3 4 5

Preface

This book began to take shape in 1970 when I faced my first first-grade class, wondered why I had decided to become a teacher, and picked up a book to read to them. That class of 17 contained "street kids," inner-city children who had had no kindergarten and came from severely impoverished homes. Oh, how they loved to be read to! A feisty first grader named David, who hurled a piece of paper onto my desk and dared me *not* to be able to read what he had written, gave this book further impetus, even though I myself was a long way from beginning to write it.

Whole language, natural approaches to instruction, *emerging literacy*—these terms are all jargon until one actually observes the intensely intellectual methods young children use to explore the way reading and writing work. To young children, reading and writing are merely extensions of listening and speaking, more advanced and more structured forms of the communication strategies they have been refining since birth. This oversimplification may seem naive, but it is also powerful because it attests to children's interest in and conviction that they can master literacy. The power of whole language is that children take charge of literacy learning in ways similar to their strategies for learning to speak and listen with understanding. To children, there is one vast continuum of communication skills. This book discusses the knowledge teachers must have to enter into that continuum and build upon children's curiosity and need to communicate. The emphasis is on what children do and how teachers can strengthen children's natural explorations of speaking, listening, writing, and reading.

The book is divided into 14 chapters. The first two discuss the growth of oral language as the beginning of a communication continuum that progresses through the acquisition of literacy skills. Chapter 3 extends the discussion of oral-language growth to children's awareness of the social conventions of language use: how individuals use language to request, question, wheedle, tell stories and jokes, and so forth. Chapter 3 also includes instructional strategies for strengthening listening and oral-language skills. Chapter 4 presents informa-

043357

tion on children who speak dialects of languages other than English and stresses that these children experience the same developmental process as native English speakers.

Chapter 5 summarizes some of the recent research on children's acquisition of literacy skill and suggests ways teachers can implement the resulting "whole language" approach in their classrooms. This chapter makes the point that early childhood teachers should view literacy growth as part of a developmental continuum that begins with oral-language acquisition.

Chapter 6 discusses the development of handwriting skills; Chapter 7 presents information on spelling. In both chapters, theory and practical classroom strategies are presented so that readers gain an understanding of what children actually learn themselves about handwriting and spelling and insight into what teachers can do to strengthen emerging skills.

Chapters 8–10 trace the development of composition skills—authoring, as opposed to handwriting. Again, theory and practice are blended, and developmental stages are illustrated with samples of children's work. Chapters 11–13 concern reading growth from preschool through early elementary grades. The emphasis is on whole language strategies that can be implemented in preschool and continued as part of a developmental continuum to mastery of reading skills. Chapter 14 discusses the role of computers, especially word processing, in enhancing young children's emerging literacy skills.

Activities at the end of each chapter challenge readers to seek deeper understanding of the concepts and instructional strategies presented in the book. Many of the activities require observations in school settings. Appendix 1 lists children's books for early childhood classes, and Appendix 2 discusses the role of parents as partners in helping children strengthen literacy skills.

Many people have influenced this book directly and indirectly. Categorically, students come first: those remembered from my own public school teaching and my early childhood undergraduate and graduate students, who have enthusiastically but not uncritically embraced the theory and methods presented here. Others of special importance are Nancy Klein Rosenberg, Nora Ellen Rosenberg, Richard Ward, Maralee Gorter, and Carolyn Kidder. The comments and suggestions of the following reviewers are greatly appreciated: Janet K. Black, North Texas State University; Jana M. Mason, University of Illinois at Urbana-Champaign; C. Charis Sawyer, University of Kentucky; Sherry Schilling, Saddleback College; and Thomas D. Yawkey, The Pennsylvania State University. Special thanks go to Sallie Schott for her thoughtful comments on the manuscript, to Alice Sneddon, my long-enduring typist, and to Connie Geldis at Merrill and Susan Stites, for their care in guiding the book toward publication. Lastly, thanks to Dick Cole, my husband, an aquatic biologist who has learned to read invented spelling.

Terry S. Salinger

Contents

7

Spelling: Invented and Beyond 107

8

The Beginnings of Composition 129

9

The Process Approach to Composition 155

10

Composition Growth in Early Primary Grades 175

11

The Beginnings of Reading   199

12

Moving Toward Skilled Reading   221

13

Reading, Writing, and Thinking   247

14

Computers in Early Childhood Classes: Increasing Literacy Growth   271

1

The Beginnings of Language

Ask the parent of an infant or toddler; ask a preschool teacher. Ask them how young children acquire language skills. Quite probably the answer will combine personal stories and psychological theorizing about the way children rapidly gain control over the language they hear around them. Ask the same question of psychologists or linguists who have studied child language acquisition, and they will mention the vast amount of research that has been carried on for more than a century.

New babies cry from reflex, but even the very youngest infants attend to language around them. Infants as young as 3 days can distinguish between their mother's and similar voices. At about age 1 month, infants begin to exhibit differentiated crying; that is, different emotions can be detected in their cries and different intonation patterns can be easily distinguished. Between 6 and 8 weeks of age, babies begin to show contentment by cooing and laughing, causing delighted caregivers to engage all the more enthusiastically in what are still one-way conversations. At this point, any utterances that sound like specific syllables are purely the result of chance. This behavior will continue to approximately 20 weeks.

At roughly 16 weeks of age, babies begin purposeful **vocal play.** They repeat single syllables with vowel- and consonant-like sounds to amuse themselves and show contentment. At about 25 weeks, this play merges into babble. Babble consists of the same kinds of repetitions, but as they mature, babies use distinct vowel and consonant combinations and exhibit a wider awareness of intonation patterns. Babies experiment with the sound structures of their language as they repeat syllables, but they still have no sense of meaning of individual words and still use gestures and actions for communication. A baby may, for example, hold up her arms to indicate that she wants to be lifted or look back over her shoulder as she crawls away as if to say, "Follow me!"

Somewhere between 7 and 9 months, babies' short-term memory capabilities increase, and they can attend to objects and ideas for longer periods of time.[1] Increased short-term memory allows babies to process linguistic information differently. "Expressive jargon" or "jargon babbling" appears as babies repeat oral strings of sounds that often actually sound like sentences.

Babies seem to use expressive jargon to communicate, although demands and requests will most likely still be made by shrieks, eye contact, or a hand gesture. Children mimic the pitch and intonations of the language they hear around them as early as 8 months: They lower or raise voice levels depending on purpose (demanding, protesting) and situation (cuddling, joking). They seem also to be sensitive to different pitches and voice patterns, such as mock or real anger in a parent's voice, and mimic them appropriately.[2] Adult response to the babble does not change the content but encourages children to produce more language and longer strings of sounds.

Children's utterances sound like talking but still lack real words or grammatical structure. Preverbal communication can be thought of as placeholders for what children actually mean. The term **placeholder of meaning** refers to the nonstandard strategies children develop to express themselves. In this case, pseudo-communications "hold the place" of actual speech and express the meaning children want to communicate to those around them.

RESEARCH ON LANGUAGE GROWTH

Researchers have documented this developmental sequence and continue to propose, question, and examine factors that motivate and guide language learning. Theories about language acquisition have resulted from long hours spent observing young children and even longer hours spent analyzing transcripts of children's tape-recorded speech. The children who served as subjects in these studies came from diverse backgrounds, races, and economic levels, but all were studied in the natural surroundings of their homes, neighborhoods, play groups, or daycare centers.

Common theories of language learning maintain that children who hear speech around them will learn to speak. Worldwide, children begin to use oral language at roughly the same age, after passing through definite stages of cooing, babbling, and experimenting with speech sounds. Even before it can be readily understood, children's emerging oral language reflects the sounds, sentence structure, vocabulary, and social use of the language(s) they hear. Both the maturation of children's bodies and the development of their minds influence language growth.

Theorists accept that oral language emerges without direct instruction from parents or caregivers, but they disagree on several interesting issues. They debate whether babies possess an innate potential for language learning or learn to speak primarily through imitation. They question the extent to which language and thought interact before babies can actually speak, and also puzzle over the importance of adult models in shaping beginning speech. Understanding these issues (and why they are debated) can be beneficial for teachers who want to provide the best possible environment for very young learners.

Innate Potential and Imitation

Researchers agree that infants have an innate neurological/biological/mental potential for learning language, and for many years this was the only major commonality in discussions of language acquisition. Even though they accepted the concept of **innate potential,** theorists could not agree on the extent to which children learn language through imitation and the positive reinforcement of their efforts to communicate verbally. One group of theorists, called **behaviorists,**[3] stressed the importance of imitation and reinforcement. The behaviorists maintained that babies imitate what they hear and learn to respond to environmental stimuli, such as parents' voices or their own names. Smiles and cuddles positively reinforce desirable vocalizations; adults' scowls or other gestures negatively reinforce or extinguish undesirable behavior. Being understood and having one's needs met or failing to be understood serve as positive and negative reinforcements as well.

Another group, the **cognitivists,** proposed that a language-specific, innate ability motivates infants to listen to the language around them and to try to make sense of what they hear. This explanation maintains that one of the "shared physical and mental characteristics of all humans" is that infants have "a start on 'knowing' what a language is in its basic design . . . on cracking the particular linguistic code of [their] speech community" (Lindfors, 1980, p. 105). The innate potential for language learning is this head start on learning how to speak, and it is so strongly a part of healthy infants' make-up that virtually nothing can stop its functioning.

Until the early 1960s, the behaviorist perspective was the most widely accepted explanation of how children learn to talk. Arguments against this explanation contended that imitation alone cannot explain how young children produce a wide range of original statements and understand sentences they have never before heard. Positive and negative reinforcement alone do not explain what motivates children's language growth because parents and caregivers routinely reinforce the content or "truth value" of youngsters' statements, rather than correcting structure or form. Yet, without direct correction, children learn the accepted grammar of their language communities.

For practical purposes, it is not a question of whether babies imitate what they hear around them. Of course they do, just as they imitate behaviors, often to the delight of people who then reinforce babies' efforts through warm responses. Much more significant is that babies use imitation thoughtfully and as only one of several strategies to figure out the way language works. At first, babies "play" with the sounds they hear around them; later, they consciously attempt to imitate and test what they have come to realize is meaningful communication.

LANGUAGE AND THINKING

How much and in what ways babies think—and especially think about language—are important questions. The behaviorists' stimulus-response theory of learning leaves little room for thinking, but the cognitive psychologists have presented the view that infants actively explore their world and process information that they themselves gather.

In *Language and Thought of the Young Child* (1955), Jean Piaget maintained that infants think constantly about their world, and thought—termed *sensori-motor* because it is tied to movement and sensations—develops before babies are capable of speech. Observations of siblings and adults communicating help infants to categorize experiences and to realize eventually that words are used as symbols for objects, emotions, and desires. This realization marks the beginnings of **symbolic-linguistic functioning** and makes preverbal infants *want* to learn to use language to communicate verbally with others.

In *Thought and Language* (1962), Lev Vygotsky, a Russian cognitive psychologist, theorized differently about the role of thought in children's acquisition of language. He maintained that dialogue between infants and adults models the grammatical form and vocabulary of what he called *external speech*. From attention to these models, children develop their own whispered or silent monologues, which Vygotsky named *inner speech*. Whispered inner speech, developing before oral skills, makes children capable of real thought. Language and concept learning continues as children explore the world and "talk to themselves" about what they are experiencing and learning.

Importance of Language Models

"If language learning is innate," a student once asked, "why do children need other humans in order to learn to talk?" The behaviorists would answer that other humans reinforce the baby's efforts; Piaget would say that adults support linguistic growth; Vygotsky would maintain that models provide the form and structure of language.

In a way, all responses are correct. Language models give babies something to think about. Adults and older children willingly engage in "conversations" with infants, whose smallest attempts at language usually win smiles and attention. Those around babies use **motherese:** They shorten and simplify sentences, use contextual examples such as holding up an object, exaggerate intonations, and work constantly to keep infants involved in what may well be one-way conversations.[4] *Motherese* is far from nonsense syllables; it is simplified in grammar and word choice but not altered in sound structure from usual adult communication.

Parents often state that even very young babies *seem* to try to control interactions, for example, by turning the head toward a voice, smiling and gurgling at a song, or holding up some toy that seems always to elicit a specific chant.

Babies *seem* to gaze intently, almost with furrowed brow, when they want an adult to use shorter sentences, repeat a pleasant sound, or exaggerate intonations. These "cute" behaviors are actually babies' purposeful attempts to control communication in order to get the linguistic information they want: They want to hear sounds, intonation, and voice patterns so that they have the auditory raw material from which to construct their own sense of language.[5] They also seek social raw material by observing the way those around them combine language, gestures, facial expression, and voice levels to communicate. By watching, listening, and seeking information, babies discover how communication works. Expressive jargon reflects the sounds, pitch, and intonation of this raw material.

THE FIRST WORD AND BEYOND

From the consonant and vowel sounds strung together in expressive jargon will emerge a child's actual first word. Very few children combine real words and expressive jargon, as the emergence of words as markers for people and things seems to indicate a major cognitive leap forward. There is strong evidence that the age at which this happens is fairly consistent worldwide. The actual first word is an utterance used consistently in response to or request for some object or person. Parents would like their offspring to refer to one of them with the

important first word, but Church (1961, p. 62) pointed out that the [ma] and [da] sounds "are ingredients in most babies' babbling, and it is likely that adults hear them as words." What the first word actually will be differs among children but seems most often to represent something upon which a child can exert a force, which he can suck or grasp or bite or squeeze. The very nature of children's thinking processes during this time does much to account for the first word choices and, indeed, for the words chosen by young children to include in their first vocabulary or personal lexicon. One researcher stated that "children learn the names of things they can act on . . . as well as things that can act themselves such as dogs and cars. They do not learn the names of things in the house or outside that are simply 'there' " (Nelson, 1973, p. 31). Children also seem to select words that are easy to pronounce and whose meanings are simple, straightforward, and unambiguous.

Single Word Sentences

Single-word utterances—formed by using those words children have accumulated in their beginning vocabularies—are often called **holophrases.** Each single-word expression represents a thought and must be interpreted in the context in which it is uttered. This context includes people and things, as well as the child's intonation, facial expression, and gestures. Children may also use what they think is a name of a situation to clarify their assessment of what is happening. A child, observing his mother chew gum for the first time, watched her carefully and finally asked "Teeth?" to summarize what he was seeing. When she showed him how she could put the gum under her tongue, he confidently commented, "Hide!"

Adults and older children quickly learn to interpret a child's holophrastic speech and accompanying gestures, and they respond to demands and expressed needs. They also expand on children's one-word utterances and provide valuable models for the next stage of language development. Thus, a child might say, "Apple?" The intonation should cue the adult to the child's *requesting* rather than *naming* the apple, and the adult might respond, clearly and slowly, "Yes, this is an apple. It's a fruit. Would you like a piece? Here's a piece of apple for you." Such expansion seems to become second nature to those who care for young children, almost an instinctive behavior in helping children learn to communicate with words.

These early sentences appear to be of three types and reflect what children are learning about the interpersonal contexts of language. The first type of utterance is an interjection, an expression such as "Hi," "Gee," or "Bye." Social in nature, these sentences show children's attempts to communicate or to express their emotions. The second category contains commands issued to other people or to the child himself. Such commands do not have to be actual verbs, as "Up" accompanied by raised arms is a fine substitute for "Please pick me up." When children issue commands to themselves, they are essentially commenting on their intention to do something. The final category is denominations, or naming. Children may see an object and name it, name an object to initiate conversation with an adult, or utter a name questioningly to check on their vocabulary.

Telegraphic Speech

After mastery of one-word, holophrastic speech, children learn to use two-word and three-word sentences. These sentences are called **telegraphic speech** because, like those who write telegrams, children use as few words as possible to express their ideas. Telegraphic speech is characterized by present-tense verbs and the absence of conjunctions, articles, prepositions, most pronouns, and verb markers such as "to be" or "to have." Some children use the pronoun *I*; others use *Baby* or *me* as the subject of their sentences. Telegraphic speech, while full of gaps, hesitations, repetitions, false starts, irrelevancies, and made-up words, does have an apparent orderliness and grammar of its own. The structure of telegraphic speech foreshadows the grammar rules that are accepted in the child's linguistic community.

Telegraphic utterances seem to be constructed from two categories of words.[6] One category includes high-frequency words whose meanings are relatively stable for learners. They have been called *anchor words*, and the idea of these words as anchors upon which youngsters can depend may be helpful in remembering how language evolves at this age. Examples of anchor words are *tonight, allgone, 'nuther,* or *give.* The following episodes illustrate how these are used: One child used *time* as an anchor word. She had extracted the word from expressions such as "dinner time" and "bed time." She used the expression one evening when she heard her father come home and gleefully cried, "Daddy time!" Her parents and I made a great fuss over her. The connection between the attention (positive reinforcement) and her statement was not lost on the child, because the next day, sitting in a car with me and a bag of fragrant, fresh bagels, she turned to me, gave me a knowing and shrewd look, held out her little hand, and said confidently "Bagel time!" This time reinforcement was a snack.

The second category includes literally all the other words the child knows, although sometimes a word can function in either role. Manipulating categories of words to form such expressions has been termed the "most salient and psychologically challenging feature of sentence construction productivity" (Brown, 1973, p. 143), and indeed, this state of language mastery truly demonstrates the intellectual power of young learners.

Telegraphic utterances serve six major functions. They state: (a) recurrence, (b) nonexistence, (c) location, (d) agent-action, (e) action-object, and (f) possessor-possession. Like holophrases, these statements demand context for interpretations, but they clearly demonstrate that children understand that language is controlled by specific, logical rules. Figure 1.1 shows examples of telegraphic utterances and interpretations.

Situation: Baby in high chair with cereal bowl

Utterance	Interpretation
more cereal (stirs in bowl)	"I want more."
more cereal (makes face)	"No more cereal."
eat cereal	"I will eat my cereal."
allgone cereal (stirs in bowl)	"I want more."
allgone cereal (pushes bowl away)	"No more cereal."
bye-bye cereal (pushes bowl away)	"No more cereal."

Situation: Baby snuggled in father's lap

more story	"Read more."
no bed	"I don't want to go to bed."
baby teddy (hugs teddy bear)	"This is my teddy bear."
daddy sweater (rubs father's arm)	"This is daddy's sweater."
mommy **bye-bye**	"Mommy isn't home."
mommy **home** ? (shows concern)	"When is Mommy coming home?"
mommy **home** ! (shows delight)	"Mommy is home!"

Anchor words are boldfaced.

FIGURE 1.1
Samples of telegraphic speech.

Just as they helped children with expansions of holophrastic utterances, adults and older children model more extensive language in response to telegraphic sentences. They fill in missing auxiliary verbs, articles, prepositions, conjunctions, and inflections (past tense, plural markers) so that expansions reflect the way most language users in the children's environment speak. It is uncertain whether children understand the meanings of these extra words at this point, so the adults' role is the dual one of modeling correct wording and teaching word meanings. Sensitive, observant parents and caregivers learn the amount of expansion to provide to guide children's learning.

Intellectual Activity: Sensorimotor Period

It has been stressed so far that infants have an innate potential for language learning and that they bring to their learning strong cognitive or thinking skills. Piaget termed these thinking skills *sensorimotor* because children from birth to about age 2 depend on action and sensory and motor experiences to gather information about their world.[7] So-called action schemes, such as sucking, grasping, or dropping, dominate this period. Babies apply these actions to different objects, then observe and think about the results. This is the preverbal or sensorimotor thought already mentioned. That babies do think and make sense of such actions is illustrated by the gradual progression of behaviors. For example, babies move their hands far beyond an object they wish to grasp but learn gradually to reach out the exact amount, grasp the object efficiently, lift it, drop it, and eventually even pick it up from the floor. Babies learn also that objects exist when they are out of sight (object permanence) and begin to understand that symbols can be used to represent concrete objects. This emerging awareness of what Piaget called *symbolic functioning* is essential for language growth.

Transition to Early Preoperational

Near age 2, children move to the second of Piaget's developmental stages. Called preoperational, this stage will last until approximately age 7. Like children in the sensorimotor stage, children over the age of 2 are *egocentric* and think that they are the center of the world. They make judgments and form ideas based on their own narrow perception of the environment. Whatever they see is the only reality for children during this developmental stage. Preoperational thinking differs from sensorimotor thinking in that children begin to internalize events and to use symbols: Thought becomes verbal as children's dependence on concrete objects and experiences lessens.

The early preoperational period is marked by rapid, dynamic growth in language, as children build on the observations made during the sensorimotor stage. In the years from birth to age 3, children form and seek answers to questions about the way language sounds and how it is put together. They also want to know what different words mean and how language is used socially. Children discover answers themselves, partially through thoughtful use of adult models and partially through systematic and powerful discovery procedures.

Language and Concepts

Language skills and concepts grow simultaneously during this period, and the 50 or so words children possess by their second birthday label their increasing number of concepts. During this period, children frequently generalize specific linguistic or conceptual information to cover many different situations. A child whose mother sewed extensively learned "Cut!" as the signal for such sharp or dangerous objects as pins and scissors. He often picked up a pin and merely said "Cut!" before putting it down safely; but sometimes he jabbed away at a pin cushion, while gleefully yelling "Cut! Cut!" He showed his understanding of the concept when he encountered a cactus for the first time. Pricking his finger on a spine, he appropriately said, "Cut" before bursting into tears.

Another child might acquire the word *dog* easily because of a family pet and then generalize the word for other dogs, guinea pigs, cats, or goats. In this case, the label denotes an emerging concept, that of four-legged, furry, animate creatures. This behavior is termed overextension. This same language learner, familiar with her tail-wagging, licking, barking companion, might find it difficult to accept a stuffed animal, although realistic in appearance, as a member of her specific "dog" concept. However, told that the stuffed animal was a *woof-*

woof, she could readily accept this term (even though it was used for the family dog's barking) and possibly even establish a new conceptual equation: "Woof-woof" means "stuffed animal." This behavior is termed underextension. By age 20 months, children can usually learn to use new words for old concepts (dog, puppy), can form new concepts to match newly presented words (dogs make noises called barking), and can use words to categorize new situations (cats make noise too, is that also called barking?).

Problems in Language Acquisition

This book is about children who develop normally, who will build enthusiastically upon their innate abilities for language learning. Some infants do not develop language skills with the apparent effortlessness that has been described so far. A few words about these children are appropriate now.

For many language-disordered children, language acquisition progresses in the same manner as in normal children but at a much slower pace. Such developmental delays can include difficulties in forming ideas about the concrete world.[8] These infants do not make sense of their experiences as rapidly as do normally developing babies and are slower in reaching the level of symbolic-linguistic functioning that allows them to understand and use language to represent their thoughts. Given time and rich experiences to explore and think about, such language-disordered children will usually catch up.[9]

Hearing-impaired infants can hear neither themselves nor others adequately. Because they cannot benefit from the adult reinforcement and models that teach so much to hearing children, verbalization develops slowly and awkwardly, if at all. Yet, even totally deaf children can learn to use and process language with American Sign Language, whose structure is as complex and varied as that of English, or through a combination of signing and whatever auditory-vocal communication they are capable of mastering.[10] The importance of early childhood programs for hearing-impaired children is obvious, for through such programs, children can learn appropriate communication methods, experience environments rich in objects and ideas about which to think, and learn to use their emerging language skills in purposeful interaction with other people.

Speech problems may impede normal language development and even cause reading difficulties. Central nervous system disorders are rare but can undermine infants' abilities to produce or understand language. Mental retardation may also slow or inhibit language growth.

A WORKING MODEL OF LANGUAGE GROWTH

Even within normal development, healthy children exhibit a wide range of differences. Some speak early; others, much later. Some use complete sentences almost immediately, others persist in monosyllabic utterances. Some children seem fascinated by language, engage in extensive verbal play, singing, and chanting; others are quieter, taciturn, and seemingly reluctant to speak. As with any developmental characteristic, these differences in language growth are normal and are not tied to differences in intelligence. Talkative children are not necessarily smarter than their quieter peers; what differs is oral production, not the underlying cognitive abilities. All children have experienced similar discovery processes in attempting to make sense of language, and lack of profuse oral communication does not necessarily indicate intellectual weakness.

Knowledge of language acquisition and the interaction of language and thought cue early childhood teachers to children's developmental processes and provide a working model upon which to build in explaining the way language grows and develops throughout childhood. By recognizing that, from their earliest babbles and squeals, children are trying to communicate, adults are better prepared to respect children's striving toward linguistic mastery. Awareness of how active a role children play in mastering oral language enables teachers to structure early childhood environments to facilitate children's exploration with concepts and language. Finally, appreciation for the cognitive abilities of young learners helps teachers see mastery as the tremendous accomplishment it is.

Don Holdaway (1979), a New Zealand teacher and author, has summarized how young children control their own learning. "To put the matter very simply," he wrote, "the child's own system acts as an amazingly sensitive teaching machine" (p. 23). This teaching machine functions in different ways throughout children's development, but is probably never more active than when children learn to use language.

SUMMARY

The three essential components of language are the innate growth abilities for or inclination toward language learning with which human babies are born, the babies' own strong thinking skills that impel them to form concepts about the world, and the language models they hear. We can think of these components as the biological/genetic, the cognitive, and the social aspects of the infants' environment. The interaction of these three components produces the dynamic, intellectually active world in which infants live, a world of constant learning and cognitive change. Just as babies explore objects by touching, smelling, poking, tasting, and seeing them, they try out the sounds of human speech. Just as they make sense of color, shape, tastes, size, and other concrete aspects of the world, they learn abstract characteristics of language: sounds, sentence structures, functional uses of language, and word meanings. For healthy, neurologically sound babies, the learning is natural and easy. It is only from the vantage point of adulthood that the task seems so monumental.

REVIEW QUESTIONS

1. Be sure that you can define each of these terms:
   behaviorist
   cognitivist
   holophrases
   innate potential
   motherese
   placeholders of meaning
   symbolic-linguistic functioning
   telegraphic speech
   vocal play
2. The chapter states that researchers on language acquisition studied children from different ethnic and economic backgrounds. How does this increase the validity of their findings?
3. How can crying be considered a child's first sign of language?
4. What role does motion or movement play in young children's learning to communicate with those around them?
5. This chapter discusses Nelson's research about children's first words. Based on her research, what *other* words might you expect to find in the first 50 words a child speaks? Justify your suggestions.
6. Interview at least two infant or toddler caregivers or parents of children under age 15 months. Ask them for their theories about language and concept development *and* for practical observations about what children learn during the first 15 months of life. Do the theories and practical observations coincide? Are the theories behaviorist or cognitivist? What were the babies' first words?

NOTES

1. Lindfors, J. W. (1980). *Children's language and learning.* Englewood Cliffs, NJ: Prentice-Hall.
2. Sachs, J. (1985). Prelinguistic development. In J. B. Gleason (Ed.) *The development of language* (pp. 37–60). Columbus, OH: Merrill.
3. Skinner, B. F. (1957). *Verbal behavior.* New York: Appleton-Century Crofts.
4. Lindfors, *op. cit.*
5. Sachs, *op. cit.*
6. Brown, R. A. (1973). *A first language: The early stages.* Cambridge, MA: Harvard University Press.
7. Furth, H. G. (1970). *Piaget for teachers.* Englewood Cliffs, NJ: Prentice-Hall.
8. Bloom, L., & Lahey, P. (1978). *Language development and language disorders.* New York: John Wiley & Sons.

9. Cicourel, A. V., & Boese, R. J. (1972). In C. B. Cazden, V. P. John, & D. Hymes (Eds.) *Functions of language in the classroom* (pp. 32–66). New York: Teachers College Press.

10. Bloom & Lahey, *op. cit.*

2
Making Progress with Oral Language

The child, that "amazingly sensitive teaching machine," moves quickly to new levels of language skills. After learning to string words together into two- and three-word sentences, children expand basic forms into detailed, sophisticated patterns. This chapter discusses language development throughout the preschool years, beginning with toddlers.

WHAT THE CHILD IS LIKE

Two aspects of this age group are especially important. First, toddlers are in transition from the sensorimotor to the preoperational stage of development, and their behavior may show characteristics of both stages. The desire, indeed, the need, to move still dominates toddlers' lives. Their energy is boundless as they explore wider circles of their environments.

The preoperational stage, as mentioned in Chapter 1, is often divided into two substages, preconceptual and intuitive. The preconceptual stage, from age 2 to 5 years, is marked by short attention spans, hasty judgments, hypothesis formation, constant exploration, and increased autonomy as children venture farther away from parents and trusted caregivers.

The second important aspect, a major component of Piaget's theories, is that children (at this and at other stages) think differently from adults. They are only beginning to understand that symbols can stand for objects and that words themselves are symbols. They are only beginning to experience the mental images and inner monologues that mark sophisticated thought processes, and they are only beginning to be able to think through situations before acting. Preschoolers are egocentric and believe that the world revolves around them. Abstractions such as height, weight, or color are still fuzzy, even though children may have words for these ideas.

Linguistic Play

Children continue to learn primarily through play and manipulation of their environment. They play with elements of language to test ideas about how it works, and they are especially encouraged to do this when their environment demonstrates the many uses of oral language. Self-initiated **language play** is a good example of children acting as "teaching machines." Children commonly play with sounds, word order, word meanings, expressive noises, timing, pitch, intonation, and turn-taking in speech. Alone, they play with language to amuse themselves or to practice what they are discovering about oral skills. When they are with other people, children may try to amuse, question concepts, test the power of language, or check their assumptions about how it all works. A 3-year-old boy demonstrated this as he sat with his 6-year-old sister, Nina, and me. His aunt had moved in with the family shortly before my visit, and he was uncertain about my place in the family structure. He chanted "Auntie Jane" several times in reference to his aunt and was told she was out. Turning to his sister, he questioned "Auntie Nina?" and laughed. I represented a challenge: "Auntie Terry?" As his sister and I tried to explain, his mother entered, and he was able to turn his confusion into a joke. Laughing loudly and confidently, he yelled "I know! I know! Auntie Mommie!"

Rhyming is another common form of language play. Children discover that they can form strings of rhyming words, which become chantlike, moving from real words (often names) to rhyming nonsense words. Acutely aware of rhyme, children frequently make barely audible rhymes in response to what other children or adults say. This behavior may frustrate or anger adults but should be accepted as yet another sign of children's playful experimentation. Children who watch *Sesame Street* or who ask or are told about spelling may become aware of beginning sounds. Far from being ready to read as such, they are learning some basic and important information about how language works. Knowing a sound, children may turn the monosyllable itself into a chant. Intoning "bah, bah, bah" can occupy many hours or lead to new forms of rhyming behavior. Children may even begin to identify and play with other words that begin with the same letter.

Children play with sound, especially accent and pitch. I overheard a child of 2 years, 5 months break off his fluent conversation with his mother to intone the following monologue during landing at a large metropolitan airport: "We're at the *airport*. We're *at* the airport. We're at the air*port*. We're at *the* airport. We're *on the ground*. We're at the *airport*. . . ." The child tested more than 20 variations before tapering off and resuming his conversation with his mother about changing planes and continuing their trip home.

Adults should support and encourage this kind of behavior. Listening to books and records and tapes with rhythmic, interesting language and learning songs and poems are pleasurable for young children and provide adults with opportunities to stimulate and share language play. Children's own songs or poems deserve adult praise; they reinforce language learning, and praise increases self-esteem and conveys a message that language exploration is a valued pursuit.

Through language play, their own experimentations, conversations with adults, and sheer trial and error, children learn about the world around them and the language needed to discuss, describe, and think about what they experience.

Production of Longer Sentences

Between ages 2½ and 3, children who have mastered the process of combining two words into a coherent, telegraphic utterance move to the next stage of language development. Brown (1973) wrote that "In this period . . . a set of little words and inflections begins to appear: a few prepositions, an occasional copular *am, is,* or *are,* the plural and possessive inflections on the noun. All these, like an intricate sort of ivy, begin to grow up between and upon the major construction blocks, the nouns and verb, to which **[telegraphic speech]** is largely limited" (p. 249).

Language changes occur along a normal, developmental continuum. The average number of words or place-holding word-substitutes in a child's utterances is a better measure of language development than chronological age. Children progress along this continuum at their own pace, often at different rates within the same family. Weir (1966), who studied the preschool language skills of her three sons, wrote that her middle son at 2 years, 5 months "had not mastered what his older brother had or younger brother would be able to do at a comparable age" (p. 159). This son, Weir wrote, was the least aggressive and least verbal of her children but also the most creative and the most dependent. Many families have witnessed similar differences.

WHAT CHILDREN LEARN ABOUT SEMANTICS

Growth in vocabulary and understanding of word meaning is rapid during preschool years, approximately two to four words per day between 2 years, 5 months and 4 years, 5 months.[1] How verbal children are at 3.5 indicates to some degree how verbal they will be as adults. Some children do seem to learn vocabulary faster than others, partially because of their environment and partially because of some individual heightened attention to language. Such children, psychologists speculate, may have a "special cognitive aptitude" for language learning. This aptitude is not necessarily indicative of intelligence. Parents, caregivers, and teachers should be aware of this and avoid labeling children with strong verbal fluency as more intelligent than their peers. Children's growth in vocabulary is not correlated to their abilities to form new concepts and expand existing ones, and adults must be careful not to evaluate the growth of a child's conceptual base only by her ability to name or talk about concepts.

Learning About Concrete Concepts

Beginning at birth and continuing through childhood, children learn about things in their environment through their senses and through direct physical interaction. As vocabularies increase, children are able to talk and think about concrete objects in more precise terms. With appropriate experiences, they can, for example, hear the words *horse* and *dog* and be able to understand and express the differences. Children might say that the major differences are that one is bigger and lives outside, but that is progress from their initial use of the word *dog* for all four-legged creatures. Part of children's growth has been learning how to form increasingly broad categories for what they see and encounter. Knowledge about specific categories and use of precise labels grow with experience, although accurate use of specific labels may lag behind understanding of the innate characteristics of whatever children experience.

In addition to learning from direct experiences with objects and from discussion and labeling during these experiences, children learn through vicarious experiences provided in books and other media. Thus, a child learns about dogs, fish, and birds at home, farm animals and squirrels during a ride in the country, elephants at the zoo, and whales from a children's book read to him at home or in school. The level of understanding about whales may be minimal, but when the child is taken to an aquarium and sees a live whale, he can say with confidence, "I know about them from a book!"

Understanding Abstract Concepts: Color

It is much more difficult for children to think about abstractions, which cannot be touched, manipulated, smelled, tasted, heard, or seen. Color is an example of such a concept. Children, from infancy, are attracted to color, but colors themselves are initially embedded in the objects they see.[2] Children learn that things have different colors and that colors have labels, but they do not immediately differentiate color from object. For example, children might consider redness an integral part of fire engines and might then name all red vehicles fire engines. Shown a red color chip, the same children might not be able to say "red" with any assurance, and a yellow fire engine would not be recognized for what it is.

Children must learn three concepts: (a) Things have color, (b) colors have names, and (c) each color has its own name. The third concept is a linguistic one, an aspect of the way language functions. A child confidently responding "yellow" when asked the color of a red ball demonstrates mastery of concepts a and b. She knows that ball has a color and knows yellow as a color name; the answer seems appropriate. A child responding "Yellow? . . . no, I mean red" is demonstrating more advanced conceptualization. In either case, an answer of "red" is not necessarily correct; it may be a good guess and should be checked with "Oh, the ball is red. Can you find me something else that is red?"

Shapes, Letters, Number Names

Children's ability to learn terms such as *circle, heart, square,* and the names of letters and numbers is similar. What they are mastering is the idea of naming and the association of specific shapes or figures (letters and numbers) with the names. It is not uncommon for children asked "What shape is this?" to respond "circle" to a triangle or to guess their way through several shape names. They may not be able to specify the shape of a ball, fit an abstract shape into a foamboard or wooden puzzle, or draw a circle, because the terms are still embedded in concrete representations such as cookie, moon, or pancake. However, asked to draw a cookie, children can readily do so, often with embellishments such as chocolate chips or raisins.

The same behavior is true for naming "letter names" and "number names." Having learned the names themselves, children still have to conquer the abstractness of these ideas. Children who can say the alphabet or count to 10 have not necessarily understood the purpose of letters or realized that what they are reciting can be seen around them as environmental print. Equally, they may have memorized number names and not understood quantity at all.

Spatial Relationships

Children also have difficulty with terms such as *here, there, on top of, into, behind,* and *in front of.* These words represent context-dependent, spatial and temporal concepts—distance, time, space. Pointing, children may say either "here" or "there," and they will not differentiate the terms or the distance when adults use one term or the other. A child who puts a book "here" (close by) rather than "there" (farther away) has not deliberately disobeyed; he has acted upon his own level of understanding of the words. Children need situational clues to understand these words in others' speech and need concrete experiences and demonstrations to understand implied meanings.

Causality

Words and expressions indicating causality and responsibility are also difficult for preschoolers. "Why" questions are children's attempts to grasp the underlying causes of events and phenomena they experience. Because they cannot conceptualize cause-and-effect relationships fully, they assign causality inappropriately, often by attributing some human-like capacity to inanimate objects. Turkle (1984), for example, found that youngsters considered computer games like Speak and Spell "sort of alive" because they "cheated" and did not "let" players always win. Things happen, children also believe, because they have to happen; if events occur close together in time, they *probably* have a causal relationship.

Opposites

To understand opposites, children must conceptualize oppositeness, the existence of two related states that are directly opposed to each other along a continuum—a difficult proposition for those just beginning to feel comfortable with abstractions. Children must identify states of being, learn appropriate labels, remember which label goes with which state, and then apply them when needed. As with color, knowledge of the concept may precede use of the correct label; sometimes, too, children may misuse labels completely because they have formed incorrect rules about what words or pairs of words actually mean.

INSTRUCTIONAL IMPLICATIONS: CONCRETE AND ABSTRACT CONCEPTS

As children learn more about concrete concepts, they search out appropriate labels for what they know. Caregivers support this search by providing labels, by structuring experiences, and always by talking about what children are doing and seeing.

Children begin to understand concepts through three kinds of experiences. The first kind is direct interaction with concrete objects or personal experiences. Children learn about dogs by seeing dogs, about books by handling books, about singing by singing. The best preschool environments are those in which children *do* many things, handle many different familiar and unfamiliar objects, and engage in conversations about what they see and do.

The second level of experience is with pictorial representations of objects and experiences. Photographs, drawings, cartoons, or other representations are more abstract than concrete objects (even though children can hold them and trace around outlines of what they see). Because they are more abstract, it is harder for young children to extract information from pictures; learning to do so takes maturation and experience with many concrete objects. As they introduce pictures to children to develop concepts and vocabulary, early childhood teachers should provide as many back-up concrete experiences as possible. A unit on plants, for example, should start with a demonstration of real plants so that children can see and feel leaves, stems, and soil. Real seeds should be planted, ideally in a transparent container so that roots will be visible. Houseplants, garden plants, flowers, vegetables, bushes, and trees can all be experienced in one form or another. To expand the concept, children may examine pictures of strange and exotic plants that do not grow in their area.

Being able to extract information from pictorial material is a necessary skill for learning from books. A child of 2 might look at an early childhood science book and enjoy the pictures, but a more advanced child will often study the same pictures and surprise those around him by commenting on how the "bush in that yard had leaves just like the ones I saw in a book." Even without reading skills as such, the child has learned to gain information from a printed source.

Experiences with abstractions represents the third means by which young children can and do learn about concrete objects. This is not the same as learning about abstractions, which was discussed above. In early childhood classes, abstract representations of information usually take the form of "teacher talk" or lectures. Children listen to the teacher, try to understand, and attempt to gain information without an object or picture as a representation. They must think about something they cannot directly experience. Unless children have had appropriate background experiences, they will either not understand what a caregiver is saying or will misunderstand as they try to tie the new information to something they already know.

Reading to children about unfamiliar topics without first providing ample experiential background can also present an abstract representation, from which most children will gain little useful information. A book about the desert will make little sense to inner-city children; however, a well-illustrated picture book about desert plants used as suggested above, along with a total unit on plants, can do two things. First, such a book will give children a beginning understanding of the desert and of its strange-looking plants. Second, they will realize that cacti are only samples of the concept *plants* and that the total concept is much broader than they thought.

Caregivers can help children expand vocabularies, strengthen concepts, and clarify abstractions by their own modeling, expansion, and questioning. **Modeling** is the caregiver's own use of correct terminology and clarifying statements. If a child refers to his yellow slicker with a new color word *purple*, the caregiver would model appropriate use by replying, "No, your slicker is yellow, like the counter by the sink." If another child called her dark blue sweater purple, the caregiver might reply, "No, it's blue. Blue and purple sometimes look almost alike. Let's find something purple so you can see the difference." Here, the caregiver is using **expansion** to clarify vocabulary and concepts.

Questioning can help too, so long as it leads to meaningful communication. The teacher might ask, "What color is your sweater?" When the child responds "red" incorrectly, the teacher should reply, "Well, no, it's not red. Do you want me to tell you the color? The sweater is green." From here the teacher might use expansion to help the child generalize the color word to other green objects. The danger with questions is that many caregivers "interview" or "quiz" children and do not follow up on information children provide about what they know. In the interchange about the sweater, an interview would have had an abrupt "No, it's green" in response to the child's wrong answer.

WHAT AND HOW CHILDREN LEARN ABOUT SYNTAX

During all the preschool years, children form and test grammatical rules, accept those that help them convey their messages, and reject those that seem wrong.

What children hear may not be standard grammar, but this is of no importance to young language learners. They take in the patterns of their distinct language community and process those patterns as their own.

Roger Brown proposed (1973) a sequence of morphemes that children master as they learn to produce longer sentences. By morpheme, Brown meant any word part or word that could be added to a word or inserted into a sentence to convey a particular meaning. The first morpheme children learn, according to Brown, is -ing, which allows them to form the present progressive form of verbs: *I am eating, she is talking,* and so on. This allows children to utter longer, more varied sentences.

Children next learn to use *in* and *on* and then to form regular plurals with *s*. Use of *s* leads to **overgeneralizations** such as "mices," which children unravel later. Understanding the concept of irregular past tense verbs comes next: Children recognize that some verbs do not form the past tense with -ed or *d* and gradually learn which ones fit into these categories. Nonstandard forms like "runned" will still appear until children have totally mastered this aspect of English. Possessives (e.g., brother's, Richard's) come next, followed by the ability to use the verb *to be*. Prior to acquisition of the possessive and *to be* morphemes, children have slurred over sentences such as "It *is* my sister's doll." Children who speak certain dialects will continue to slur these morphemes in oral production (see Chapter 4). Children master these morphemes on their own initiative; they are not imitating the language users around them. Children's mistakes "which externalize the . . . search for the regularities of English syntax" (Brown & Bellugi, 1970, p. 90) are the strongest evidence of children's own control of this process.

Children are capable of imitating adult speech at this point and often do include phrases and expressions they have copied with no comprehension of total meanings. Imitative speech rarely captures the totality of what an adult has said and usually omits words children consider unimportant. The word order of an imitated utterance reflects the original, but the total utterance rarely extends beyond four words. Children cannot, however, imitate constructions that they themselves would not be able to produce. For this reason, direct correction of grammatical errors will not hasten children's mastery. Rather than corrections, adults should use modeling or expansion, as in this dialogue:

Child:	I bringed cookies for snack.
Teacher:	Oh, you brought cookies. What else did you bring?
Child:	Milk.
Teacher:	You brought milk and cookies. Did you bring anything else?
Child:	I bringed a napkin too.

The verb *to bring,* as used above, represents work toward mastery of irregular past-tense morphemes. With regular verbs, one adds *d* or -ed to present tense verbs, but *to bring* forms its past irregularly with *brought*. To be successful in distinguishing between "bring" and "brought" children must realize that verb forms include markers of both *action* and *time* and that *bring* and *brought* refer to the same action *at different times: Bring* refers to an action in the present, while *brought* is past. Additionally, verbs seem to form their past by adding *d* or *-ed*, but some verbs are irregular. *Bring* is an irregular verb. This is a lot of information for a child to comprehend, but gradually the connections are made. Weir (1966, 1970), who tape-recorded many of her sons' private monologues, reported that her children spent considerable time practicing such forms. She said that the most common stimulus for this kind of practicing (as opposed to practicing rhymes or other sound patterns) was correction of a faulty grammatical form by an older sibling. Her own corrections and models carried much less impact on her young sons' learning!

OTHER WAYS OF FORMING SENTENCES

Children also test specific patterns of sentence organization, all of which require some change in word order or some addition or deletion of words in any straightforward simple statements. Major patterns are: (a) **question formation,** (b) **negation,** and (c) **passive formation.** Mastery of each of these represents increased competence and linguistic sophistication.

Questions

The ability to understand and form questions develops early in most children because so much of the verbal interaction between them and adults consists of questions. Children recognize the rising intonation patterns of these utterances, and while they realize that questions seek information, they are not at first sure what kinds of information are sought. Thus, a child, when asked, "Who's reading?" might respond, "A book." Or a child, when asked, "What color is this?" might reply, "My sweater" because she had not yet learned that specific question formula, let alone knowing the concept of color (as already discussed).

Children learn to comprehend questions in three stages.[3] First, they learn what, where, and yes/no questions. Next, they can understand questions that ask who, whose, and what _____ do (as in "What did you do to your toy?"). Finally, they can comprehend the complexities and relative abstractions of why, how, and when questions. Yet, children who have figured out the kind of informational exchanges required by certain kinds of questions may still be a long way from being able to produce the utterances themselves.

Their stages of question production begin, as would be expected, with the simple device of raising the intonation at the end of a statement with normal word order. Early attempts at rearranging word order to form questions are awkward and often accompanied by exaggerated intonational markers. Children might say, "Why not me can't swim?" or "What I did with doll?" or "Where I should put book?" The achievement in these sentences is clearly the selection of the appropriate interrogative word and the placement of the word at the beginning of the sentences. As children form more elaborate rules for question formation, they adjust their utterances to reflect increasing competency.

Negation

Understanding of negation marks a step in children's quest for autonomy and self-expression. The first verbalization of negatives is with *no* or *allgone* as anchor words in holophrastic speech ("no milk," "allgone cookie"). These clearly show nonexistence, the category of negation acquired first. In learning to make negative statements, children must also learn to express rejection (other than by pushing something away) and denial (other than by shaking the head). To be able to express negation meaningfully, children need to remember first of all what another person has said. Next, the child must judge that a statement is wrong. To do this, the child has to have realized that she and the other person *both* have points of view and that these can, in fact, differ. Finally, the child must devise and be able to express verbally the differences of opinions, reasons, and possibly her alternative suggestions,[4] as for example, in the following scenario.

Parent:	It's time for bed.
Child:	No. [Thinking: It's too early for bed; I want to stay up.]
Parent:	Yes, it's time for bed.
Child:	I don't want [to] go [to] bed.
Parent:	Why not?
Child:	Not sleepy.
Parent:	That's too bad. It's time for bed.
Child:	No bed! Not sleepy! Too early!

Denial is the most difficult negative utterance for children to master.[5] To understand and to use denial correctly, children must be able to conceptualize a *symbolic referent*, that is, whatever is denied is not present before the child or is there in a changed form. For children in the preoperational stage of development, this understanding is difficult to grasp. Another scenario follows.

Parent:	Did you break your toy?
Child:	No. [Meaning: That's not the toy I used to have. My toy is in one piece.]
Parent:	You were the last one to play with it. Are you sure you didn't break it?
Child:	No, I didn't. [Meaning: I don't know what she's talking about. That isn't my toy.]

The child does not understand the changed form of the toy and cannot recognize his own responsibility for the change that has taken place.

Children learn to form negatives in stages.[6] The first stage is simply to place *no* at the beginning of a sentence. Next, children will insert *no, not, can't,* or *don't* within a sentence. Thus, depending on their developmental level, children might say "Baby can't touch," "Today no sun shining," "I'm not hungry," or "I can't see." Next, children separate the words *can* and *do* as distinct units of meaning (morphemes) from the contracted forms *can't* and *don't* used commonly in negation. Children can comprehend the different uses and can produce correct sentences with all forms, and at this point, *can* and *do* begin to appear at the beginnings of children's questions.

The next level of understanding finds children using double negatives. Rather than imitation of incorrect use they have heard, these double negatives are another form of overgeneralization, deriving, probably, from children's idea that if one negative is good, two undoubtedly will be even better. Finally, children learn to understand and use such indeterminant words as *anything, anyone,* or *any,* as part of negative statements. It is important to remember that understanding of these rather *fuzzy* words takes considerable time and develops over the entire preschool and often early primary period.

Passives

The passive construction is rare in children's spontaneous speech and is also difficult for them to understand.[7] In a passive construction the subject of the sentence receives the action of the verb with or without an actual agent specified in the utterance. Examples are: The sweater was made by my grandmother; the sweater was made in a factory; the boy was hit by the swing; or the boy was hit by his sister. As would be expected, children come to understand passive constructions through several stages. The easiest for them to understand are sentences in which an agent is stated and the inanimate subject renders the action irreversible, as in "The sweater was made by the grandmother." The relationships here are straightforward. It is more difficult when there is no agent to account for causality, as in, "The sweater was made in a factory." Initially, children may have trouble attributing human-like intent to inanimate objects acting on humans, as in, "The boy was hit by the swing." Finally, the most difficult constructions express reversible action, with animate agents and receivers of action. In "The boy was hit by the girl," children may not be able to differentiate agent and receiver to answer "Who was hit? Who did the hitting?"

The difficulties with passive constructions arise from children's dependency on the rule they have formed about word order: Whatever comes first in an utterance does the action expressed in the verb. Passive constructions violate this rule and are easiest to misconstrue when the first subject of the passive statement is animate and is actually capable of performing the action of the verb. Children frequently use forms of the verb *to get* to form passive constructions.[8] Thus, "He gets hit," or "He got hit," or even "He gots hit" are equivalent depending on context to "He is being hit," "He was hit," or "He has been hit."

INSTRUCTIONAL IMPLICATIONS: GRAMMAR AND SENTENCE STRUCTURE

The best way to teach preschoolers to use "good" standard grammar and to produce interesting, varied sentences is to be a good model. Correction, especially laced with impatient judgment, will not work until children are developmentally ready to understand and produce some particular grammatical or structural feature of oral language.

Teachers need to remember the responsibility they have to be good models, to use language in a correct yet creative way. Too many early childhood teachers oversimplify their oral language. Their speech is correct but dull, artificial, and condescending. Children, better than anyone else, know that language is dynamic; and teachers need to model interesting, varied ways of stating ideas, wishes, commands, questions, and statements.

Children's literature can also provide language models, especially if teachers read with enjoyment and appreciation for the flow and cadence of the written text. Selecting books carefully and preparing oral reading adequately allow teachers to use children's literature as another means of enhancing children's grasp of oral language.

Expansions versus Corrections

As already mentioned, adults almost unconsciously expand upon children's statements and elaborate to fill in ideas, missing words, and primitive sentence structures. This behavior works better than correction in helping children acquire standard language patterns.

When teachers say "You're wrong; say it this way," children often interpret well-meaning corrections of grammar as personal assaults. Alternative behaviors work better and help children retain their self-esteem. Suppose a child says, "We don't have no way to paint with no brushes." The teacher might respond by the statement "Oh, you don't have *any* way to paint because you have *no* brushes. I'll get some." If nonstandard constructions such as this double negative persist, teachers might comment more directly, "In school we would say 'I don't have any way to paint because I have no brushes'; I'll get you some now." This response suggests that there are ways of speaking in school and outside of school but does not pass judgment on the way the child obviously speaks at home.

Learning that one should adjust word choice and sentence formation to suit particular situations is known as learning different *registers* of speech. Teaching children to accept and act upon this important concept of language use is more valuable than having them memorize but not understand extensive lists of grammatical principles. Gradually, children come to realize that a formal, standard language is used in school. First, they can understand the teacher's use of the language, and eventually they will be able to use it, too. Children do not have to "give up" their vernacular, home language when they enter school but will need to develop competence with school language as used by teachers and as encountered in books.

SUMMARY

During the period discussed in this chapter, children discover the power of language for communication with those around them. They also discover the intricacies of their language structure as they experiment with word choice and sentence structure to communicate their thoughts. They learn the rules of their language community so that by the time they are ready for school, they will have mastered most of the structural conventions of speech.

REVIEW QUESTIONS

1. Be sure that you can define each of these terms:
   expansion
   language play
   modeling
   negation
   overextensions
   overgeneralizations
   passive formation
   question formation
   telegraphic speech
2. Children's beginning understanding of concepts is often referred to as *fuzzy*. What do you think *fuzzy* means in this context?
3. What kinds of problems can arise between children and early childhood caregivers because of children's fuzzy conceptualizations?
4. Why is correction usually not an effective way to help children achieve standard language use?
5. Children learn constructions such as questions, negations, and passives relatively slowly. What implications are there in this fact for preschool teachers and parents?
6. Visit a preschool or daycare center and spend time talking to children. Do you have any difficulty understanding them? Do they understand you easily? Observe the teacher carefully. What special language skills does he or she have? What skills does the teacher seem to be lacking? What are the strengths and weaknesses of the "language environment"? Does it seem to support children's language learning, and if not, how could it be better?

NOTES

1. Pease, D., & Gleason, J. B. (1985). Gaining meaning: Semantic development. In J. B. Gleason (Ed.) *The development of language* (pp. 103–138). Columbus, OH: Merrill.
2. Church, J. (1961). *Language and the discovery of reality.* New York: Vintage.
3. Lindfors, J. W. (1980). *Children's language and learning.* Englewood Cliffs, NJ: Prentice-Hall.
4. Keller-Cohen, D., & Gracey, C. A. (1979). Learning to say *NO:* Functional negation in discourse. In O. K. Garnica & M. L. King (Eds.) *Language, children, and society* (pp. 197–212). Oxford: Pergamon Press.
5. Bloom, L. (1970). *Language development: Form and function in emerging grammars.* Cambridge, MA: MIT Press.
6. Klima, E. S., & Bellugi-Klima, U. (1971). Syntactic regularities in the speech of children. In A. Baradon & W. Leopold (Eds.) *Child language: A book of readings.* Englewood Cliffs, NJ: Prentice-Hall.
7. Tager-Flusberg, H. (1985). Putting words together: Morphology and syntax in the preschool years. In J. B. Gleason (Ed.) *The development of language* (pp. 139–171). Columbus, OH: Merrill.
8. Menyuk, P. (1969). *Sentences children use.* Cambridge, MA: MIT Press.

3

Listening, Speaking, and Social Conventions of Language

During their early childhood years, children learn to produce, understand, and use language. Observing and being part of this tremendous growth are rewarding for parents and teachers. Although language learning on the whole occurs naturally, spurred on by children's own explorations of communication, several aspects of language processing respond to direct and indirect teaching. Figure 3.1 defines the many aspects of language use that children learn before they enter school.

PRAGMATICS

As children learn about receptive and expressive oral language, they also learn about the structure and conventions of their social world and about the relationship between language and those conventions. These relationships are often called **pragmatics** and include how to give directions, make requests, tell jokes and stories, make up songs, offer explanations and evaluations, assume new roles through voice changes and talking funny, pass judgments verbally, and initiate, maintain, and end conversations.[1] Children learn about pragmatics directly from adults and through their own observations, practice, and play. Scaffolding and modeling are means by which adults teach children to use language in specific ways. Models have been mentioned before; scaffolds are interchanges in which adults at first utter entire "scripts" and gradually allow children to fill in parts of those scripts as they master necessary skills. For example, adults sing or recite nursery rhymes, songs, or game chants; but gradually children themselves can add more and more words of the specific script. As they do so and find their accomplishments lavishly praised, they are also learning the specific convention of reciting poems, singing songs, or accompanying games with

Receptive language—language that children take in, first listening, later reading

Expressive language—language that children give out, first speaking, later writing

Inner speech—language for private, inner monologues, helps to regulate behavior and moderate thinking

Holophrases—one-word statements

Telegraphic speech—two- or three-word statements

Questioning—forming questions, both directly and indirectly; first accomplished by raising voice at end of statement; direct questions require rearrangement of word order; indirect questions are embedded in statements

Passive verb constructions—placing the recipient of an action as the subject of a sentence

Negation—forming negative statements; first formed by adding *no* or *not*; later structure requires use of morpheme (unit of meaning) and possible reordering of word in statement

Name (nomination)—giving objects, people, or events names, referring to them verbally, other than by pointing

Conversations—verbal interactions of two or more people, involving oral turn taking

Commands—telling someone (or self) to do something; uses imperative form of verb, with no subject, e.g., "Go!"

Directives (requests)—asking for something or some service verbally, rather than by pointing or other physical sign

Stories—relating incidents in a specific sequence; involves understanding progression of stories through so-called story schema

Listening—taking in information receptively

Hearing—lowest level of listening, responding to auditory stimuli

Listening (as technical term)—second level of listening: organizing and sequencing sounds

Auding—highest level of listening: appreciating and comprehending what is heard

FIGURE 3.1

Language uses and variations which children learn prior to school entry: summary, review, and definitions.

chants or other verbal formulas. They can easily generalize the skill to learning new scripts.

Models serve similar purposes but are usually less "scripted" than the rhymes, songs, or chants mentioned above. As language skills increase, adults' models expand to provide a running account of youngsters' activities. These accounts may include such questions as "What are you going to do next?" or comments like "Oh, I like the way you drew that shape," which encourage children to continue their activity and also help them realize the structure of talking about an action. From such commentaries, children learn the basic conventions of descriptive and explanatory speech.

Teachers of children in preschool, kindergarten, and early primary grades should use the same techniques to help children master the language conventions of the early childhood classroom. Children whose oral production in school-like situations is disappointing may not know the specific conventions of show-and-tell time, explaining about one's vacation, or describing a birthday party. Teachers can provide the appropriate models by telling about their own vacations, or bringing something themselves for show and tell. Gradually, children learn that verbalization is expected in games, in response to questions, in requests to have needs met, and in seeking information. In the close proximity of a family, most children learn to form and express their wishes and to reply to questions verbally, although most adults know of situations in which older siblings do the talking for the youngest family member. Teachers, through nods, smiles, and verbal prods, approximate the family interaction, and "[if] the child learns that the blocks or toys with which he is playing are related to a response the teachers will expect of him, he seems to learn to process the experience he has in a more systematic way" (Pease & Gleason, 1985, p. 122). Unless preschool teachers remain observant, shy, timid, or even overly independent children can escape this lesson in social use of language and also miss the important cognitive experience of perceiving situations, ordering thoughts, and finding and then uttering the words required to represent their ideas.

Direct instruction is also beneficial. Here, adults direct the child to ask, say, or tell some particular linguistic formula. This is how adults usually teach appropriate social language and manners. For example, adults insisting "Say 'Thank you,' " "Say 'Bye-Bye,' " "Ask them, 'May I please . . . ?' " or "Say 'Excuse me, please' " are demonstrating direct instruction. Adults want children to understand and internalize the underlying purpose of these sociolinguistic conventions, but often children merely memorize some verbal formula. A common example of such memorization is those children who have equated saying "I'm sorry" or some attempt at "I apologize" with easy forgiveness when they have hurt another child or broken a rule.

Teachers must remember that the social conventions of language that children bring to school reflect the values and customs of their homes and communities. Children who curse or use socially inappropriate terms for bodily functions do not, in all probability, realize that they may be offending the teacher. Some children may not understand that the language is unacceptable, while others may even be amused and titillated to hear these words coming from a peer; others may be deeply offended (without really knowing why) and can be cruel in rejecting the speaker. Teachers who hear children using offensive language must be firm but not judgmental in their insistence that "We don't use that term in school," with the goal of broadening children's vocabulary choices and knowledge about language use. A different tack, firmer and more insistent, must, of course, be taken with children who knowingly use offensive language for effect. Because these children have learned the pragmatic reality that some words offend some people, their behavior is deliberate and should be treated like any other discipline problem.

Language Play

Language play can be a means for children to express hostile, resentful, or outrageous ideas without incurring parents' or caregivers' anger. Play, after all, is play and not to be taken seriously. Geller (1985) reported such a playful verbal episode among preschoolers.

Daniel: [sitting with several other children peeling carrots] Wouldn't it be funny if these carrots were poison! [He laughs.] Wouldn't it be funny if there were no teachers! [He laughs harder.]

Molly: [sitting at the playdough table] I'm going to make a big cake . . . with lollipops over it . . . all colors . . . big ones.

Teacher: Molly, that sounds beautiful.

Molly: [with gusto] And they are all poison! (p. 10)

Often such responses within a normal context mean a child is attempting to repress some negative feelings.

Children younger than age 3 are too egocentric for such conversations, but after this age, playing with language for its own sake becomes part of children's explorations of their world. **Pragmatic language play** as part of social interactions includes conversations, word play, and rhyming. Children seem to teach and quiz each other on what they know about language and bring fantasy, nonsense, role playing, and deliberate practice of various discourse conventions. Children change their voices, word choice, and sentence structure to assume new roles (teachers should listen to how *they* sound when portrayed in these situations!) or simply to sound funny. Children try to sound grown up or babyish depending on the role they assume in dramatic play.

Names

Names also become the object of this playfulness as children misname objects and coin new names for each other and for real and imaginary people. Names that are illogical or that verge on the scatological are especially satisfying to preschoolers because they so dramatically violate normal language conventions. Garvey (1977, pp. 39–40) reported a conversation that illustrates this behavior well. It will sound familiar to anyone who has spent time eavesdropping on young children:

Conversation
Female (5.7)   Female (5.1), on [play]
                                               telephone

1. Mommy, mommy, I got new
   friends called Dool, Sol, Ta.

2. Dool, Sue, and Ta?

(Both laugh)

3. Those are funny names,
   aren't they?

4. No, it's Poopoo, Daigi,
   and Dia . . . Diarrhea.

(Both laugh)

The laughter in conversations such as these marks the interactions as play. Ritual insults, mock threats, and outrageous comparisons are other examples of this kind of linguistic play.

Directives and Requests

Preverbal infants point, gesture, slap, smile, scowl, and so forth to indicate choices, requests, and directives. All these motions can be accompanied by squeals, cries, and other noises. Words like *want, more,* and *allgone* express desires in both holophrastic and telegraphic speech. This progression from nonverbal placeholders of meaning to verbal expressions may occur faster in people-oriented children, but the sequence seems to be common across all linguistic communities.

The imperative verb form (e.g., "Give me a cookie," with the subject *you* understood) appears in children's conversations at about age 3. It may or may not be accompanied by the "magic word" *please*, which can be heard in speech of children as young as age 2. Studies have indicated that children know the power of the word *please* and differentiate its use.

Stories

Children show what they know about stories through verbal accompaniments to dramatic play and through their own storytelling. Adults' comments on children's actions are the initial models for sequenced stories and, by 18 months, children begin to recite their own commentaries on what they do. These commentaries reflect a narrative format (sequence, description of actions, etc.) and, coupled with children's sense of story, become the basis for their own storytelling. By age 3, children can create characters verbally and describe their actions; by age 4, they can attribute motives and feelings to their creations.[2] With an audience, children may tell highly elaborated stories, complete with ghosts, devils, make-believe, ritual insults, and quotations with appropriate changes in voice. Two or more children may collaborate and tell a joint story with well-orchestrated turn taking. Where there is a family tradition of oral storytelling, as in a group of part-Hawaiian children studied by Kernan (1977), the stories may be quite adult in their discussion of sex, marriage, and childbirth. Even without the model of oral storytelling, many children include these themes as a reflection of what they have seen and heard on television. Children also frequently

incorporate comedy routines and commercials from radio and television into their stories. Indeed, the media should not be discounted for the influence they have on children's emerging sense of language and the world in general.

Importance of Pragmatics

As children learn about pragmatics, they learn much more than when to say "Please": They learn that language may be contextual and decontextual. **Contextual language** consists of verbal interactions based on the shared knowledge and shared experiences of speaker and listener, i.e., the discussion of people or things in the immediate environment or other topics of common interest and mutual familiarity. The ability to produce and comprehend contextualized language develops over time, as children participate in the routines and rituals of their society. **Decontextual language,** on the other hand, conveys meaning with relative independence from any specific context; words themselves convey meaning to receivers who understand how decontextualized language functions. Stories in a book are good examples of decontextualized language, because the characters and settings exist only in written two-dimensional form. Television and movies also represent decontextualized language and situations.

The need to understand decontextualized language extends beyond comprehension of stories or media. School language in general, both oral and written, is decontextualized in that teachers and students do not necessarily share mutual assumptions and experiences and also in that content and topics are relatively abstract and not directly present. School "conversations" such as instructions or direct lessons usually rest on no firm base of mutual understanding. What teachers say may not make sense to a young child who is unfamiliar with the jargon of school. Equally, what books have to say to beginning readers may seem equally meaningless unless children enter school with a scaffold of decontextualized language from which to develop school-related scripts.

Children must form the scripts necessary to understand decontextualized language if they are to succeed in school. They must be able to understand direct and indirect questioning, requests, and instructive lectures; they must be able to conceptualize language as a way of discussing abstractions or people and objects that are not present or are imaginary; and they must be able to discover sequential and causal relationships in what they hear and read. Research has indicated that children who have been encouraged to develop narrative commentaries on their own routine behaviors and who have had exposure to many different kinds of narrative literature develop home-based scripts that easily expand to the school-related scripts needed in instructional interactions. Research has further indicated that not all children come to school so prepared and that those who lack these scripts are at an academic disadvantage because they have to learn broader language skills.[2] Children who do not develop this competency may not progress to their full intellectual potential.

Children have traditionally learned about language conventions in the home; however, as more children are entrusted to preschool programs, the task of helping youngsters learn the complex functions of language will be shared by teachers.[3] The one-on-one interaction of the home is impractical for early childhood classrooms. Teachers must find alternative means, therefore, for modeling language use and for expanding children's awareness of linguistic conventions. Both direct and informal instruction and learning experiences that stress listening and speaking skills can help children develop the needed skills for school success.

The pragmatic language skills discussed so far in this chapter do not really constitute a part in the early childhood curriculum: They are learned through observation, from direct and indirect instruction arising from specific classroom situations. The rest of this chapter discusses the way children learn to listen and speak in purposeful ways and the kinds of classroom activities that will strengthen these skills.

LISTENING

Listening behaviors are essential in oral language development. Infants hear voices and sounds around them and learn to entertain themselves by babbling, and they are remarkably sensitive to pitch, tone, and stress in oral language. As children grow, they increasingly delight in songs, music, and rhymes and clearly use their listening to good advantage. Within capabilities determined by their receptive vocabularies and experiences, they are using various forms of listening skills.

There are several **levels of listening** skills. The first, often called *hearing,* is responding to an auditory stimulus by recognizing that there is a sound and possibly identifying the direction from which it came. The second level, frequently labeled *listening,* includes organizing and sequencing sounds, determining time lapse between sounds, and identifying whether a sound has been heard before. The infant who recognizes his mother's voice amid other sounds and voices is using this skill. The highest level of listening skill, sometimes called *auding,* includes listening with appreciation and comprehension. Listeners form associations with past experiences, perceive organizational patterns, criticize the message, or respond pleasurably, imaginatively, or angrily. Specific activities can be used in an early childhood classroom to help children refine their auditory appreciation and learn other sophisticated listening comprehension skills.

Some Concerns About Listening

More than maturation and specific instruction determine children's listening abilities. Some people prefer to learn through an auditory modality; that is, from birth, they prefer to receive information by hearing and are more attentive than others to auditory cues. Children who are "auditory learners" develop and display strong, dependable listening skills early in life. They would rather hear than look at a book, like to sit very close to a record player. They may seem to be day-dreaming as the teacher speaks but later show that they had been listening very attentively.

Also important are individual's **auditory memory** capabilities—the amount of auditory information people can store in their brains and retrieve for later use and the ease with which they can do this. Young children who can sing a TV commercial perfectly, learn all the words of a song the first time it is sung, or recite poems along with the teacher display strong auditory memory abilities. They have had no other means of taking in this information—they have not read it—and are able to get the whole auditory message out of their memory quickly and thoroughly. While tied to this learning modality to some extent, children can learn to strengthen auditory memory.

Auditory perception and acuity are also important in children's listening skills. **Auditory perception** refers to children's ability to distinguish one sound from another, blend sounds together, and sequence and repeat sounds they have heard. This auditory perception is an essential component of learning to spell and read. **Auditory acuity** is the ability to distinguish between sounds on the basis of pitch, tone, and loudness. Teachers must remember, however, that individuals hear sounds differently depending on the speech community from which they come. A common test of auditory acuity is to ask children to distinguish between "minimal pairs" such as pen and pin, which differ only in one sound. In some dialects, however, the short *e* and short *i* are voiced in the same way, as though the words were homophones.

Between 5% and 10% of all children have hearing impairments, the most severe of which is deafness. Children who have complete hearing loss can be taught to communicate through speech or sign language, but the less severe impairments may go undetected. It is often the early childhood teacher who first associates a child's behaviors with hearing difficulties, and teachers should be alert to those children whose voices are unnecessarily loud, who cup their ears or lean toward speakers, or who seem never to respond to their names or other comments. Testing is often advisable and is essential early in the child's school life so that she can make sense of the total school experience with no loss of instruction or self-esteem. Colds, allergies, and sinus problems, especially chronic difficulties, can also impair a child's auditory acuity.

Instruction in Listening Skills

Adults provide the first instruction in listening skills. As adults carry on pseudo-conversations with preverbal infants, the infants learn to track voices and respond to intonation and pitch. Noise-making toys help them to distinguish one sound from another and to select toys that make favorite sounds.

In school, games or routines strengthen listening skills. Clapping games are one example, as children listen to a pattern of claps and try to reproduce it. Children may also be given simple oral directions such as "touch your head" or "walk to the window." With older children, patterns may be lengthened and directions made more complex. Such activities are offered as games, not lessons, and teachers are observant of children's levels of "auditory fatigue." Rhymes and songs to be memorized also develop listening skills. Children must attend to the auditory message and store words and music in their memories.

Commercial and Teacher-Made Materials for Listening Instruction

Many commercial materials are available for listening instruction, and other materials can easily be made. Maria Montessori (1964, 1967) considered listening instruction as part of the "education of the senses." She developed a series of 13 bells hung on a wooden frame and used in sets of two to teach sound discrimination. She also suggested using little whistles and small boxes filled with different materials that produce different sounds when shaken. Materials such as she suggested, drum sticks, and other musical instruments all are useful for listening instruction. Commercial records and tapes, along with teacher-made tapes, can be valuable, too. Records of different kinds of sounds—farm animals, woodland sounds, city sounds, and so forth—can be described, labeled, and classified. Listening in order to describe and classify the different auditory attributes is fun. Songs like "The Wheels on the Bus" and "Old Mac-Donald's Farm" further support the instruction. A record player or tape recorder that can be attached to multiple headphones provides the core of a listening center for any daycare center or early childhood classrooms.

Some Words of Caution

Listening exercises can be frustrating if the children do not know what is expected of them. Teachers should make sure that all children understand what listening involves. Teachers should begin listening instruction by defining expected behaviors and insisting upon relative silence. Children should understand good listening manners. Repeating the rules and expectations before each lesson keeps children alert to the special behaviors required of them.

Everyone will be frustrated if children are asked to perform tasks beyond their capabilities. Children should understand that the procedures in listening tasks are : (a) listening to the auditory stimulus, (b) organizing it mentally, and (c) reproducing it in some way (by clapping or following directions, for example). If teachers ask children to hold in their memories more complex auditory patterns or longer strings of words than they can possibly remember, the goal of increasing listening skills will be thwarted.

INSTRUCTIONAL ACTIVITIES FOR SPEAKING AND LISTENING

Although oral language development during the preschool years seems to move forward under its own momentum, direct instruction in specific kinds of speaking belongs in a well-formulated early childhood language arts curriculum. By their very nature, exercises that refine oral language skills also develop listening skills. These activities should allow children to use all their senses whenever possible; touching, tasting, and smelling give children something to *talk* about. Activities should encourage children to move, whether it is wiggling a finger, getting up and down, or dancing across a floor. Whenever possible, children should see a written copy of what they are hearing, memorizing, or reciting. Even if they are not yet able to read, seeing the graphic image helps children make connections between what is heard and said and the written symbols of language. Finally, as much as possible, activities should include play and should encourage thinking and problem solving. No tasks should be beyond children's cognitive abilities. Teachers should make sure that children understand fully what is going on in any instructional sequence. This statement may sound so obvious as to be almost silly, but its implications are very important for all early childhood instruction. Children want very much to please their parents and teachers. Without understanding the true nature or purpose of a lesson, they will often "fake" behavior or imitate what they see others doing in order to gain caregivers' approval and affection. This faking can then influence their emerging concept of appropriate school behavior. Children should know that what they do is *supposed* to make sense. They should feel comfortable enough to ask for clarification if they do not understand what is going on. Teachers themselves should use questioning strategies, comments, and praise throughout a lesson. These techniques model comprehension monitoring, help children stay alert and attentive, and allow the teacher to check on those who may not be understanding the current lesson.

Rhymes, Poems, Jingles, and Finger Plays

Nursery rhymes, counting rhymes, poems, jingles, songs, and chants from games can all build listening and oral language skills. Children's natural playfulness embraces the words and sounds, and the funnier they are, the better. The words become even more effective learning material when children are invited to manipulate the sounds by imitating teachers' exaggerated readings or devising their own funny voices to personify a familiar chant or poem. Children should be encouraged to make up and present their own jingles, rhymes, and poems. Good listening manners can be practiced as children recite their poems in turn. Children who do not want to participate in such performance should never be forced to do so but should be invited to recite their poems or chants privately to a favored adult. Needless to say, all efforts of this sort must be accepted enthusiastically and with lavish praise. Children who speak more than one language should use their dominant language with teacher-translations provided for the rest of the class. The self-confidence these activities encourage, as well as the knowledge about language, is invaluable.

When children begin to write their own stories and poems, they may read them to small groups and to their whole class. Peer response—a technique to foster writing growth, which will be discussed in Chapters 9 and 13—depends on children's willingness to share their writing with others and to listen attentively and objectively to what peers have written. The roots of these oral reading and listening skills are firmly planted in preschool and kindergarten experiences where children share their own oral compositions and accept the efforts of others.

Finger plays are fun, too, and encourage auditory memory and clear speaking skills. Finger plays require that children coordinate words, often in rhymes, with actions. The most basic finger plays have children moving their fingers—clapping, walking up and down their arms, wiggling fingers, hammering, sewing, and so forth. With more complicated ones, children move their faces, arms, or whole bodies. Children can participate even before they have learned the actual verses by merely following along with the movements. Early childhood teachers can use finger plays to develop vocabulary and concepts (for example, "Ten Little Indians" reinforces number awareness) and to help children release pent-up energy.

Conversations, Dialogues, and Discussion

Young children's group conversations and discussions should be kept short. Teachers should maintain eye contact with children and should position themselves as much as possible at the children's level. A focused topic—for example, What We Did on Our Trip to the Farm—works well to help children learn to listen to each other, not repeat what they have heard, and stick to a specific topic. If the conversation is about an object or animal present in the room, children should be allowed to handle it.

Some children may not learn the conventions of carrying on conversations in their homes. If teachers realize that particular children are experiencing trouble functioning in a conversational situation—large or small group or individual—it may be possible that children simply do not know what is expected. Teachers should make an extra effort to engage these children in frequent, focused conversations that model appropriate behavior.

Teachers must try to keep children on task, involve as many children as possible, and anticipate boredom or silliness. While accepting anything that is said, they should also restate, clarify, and comment on what is presented. These teacher behaviors maintain momentum. A teacher leading a discussion with 4-year-old children might say, "Yes, Steven, Lois told us about the cows, too, but you told us their color. You said they were black and white. We have also talked about the pigs we saw; Jimmy said they were big, and Rachel said they were cute. Who can tell us about something else? I remember that the farm also had ducks. Who remembers seeing them? Oh, lots of you saw them. Ana, would you tell us what you thought about the ducks?"

Older children benefit from longer, more open-ended discussions and can actively participate in group problem solving. Children might suggest ways to decorate their classroom for a holiday, improve the storage system in the painting area, or make presents for Mother's Day. Even if none of the suggestions proves practical ("No, we can't paint the room orange for Halloween"), the process of brainstorming together is beneficial. Group problem-solving sessions in primary grades give children opportunities to think through practical problems and evaluate solutions. Writing activities can easily follow such brainstorming sessions to round out the experience.

Wordless Picture Books or Other Picture Stimuli

Wordless picture books and single pictures that tell a story can encourage children to interpret visual material, sequence and express their ideas, and make up extended stories. As individuals tell what they have seen in a picture or compose narrative for a wordless picture book, their peers listen, evaluate, comment, and add their own ideas. Visual learners, those who learn best by observing and who are most sensitive to visual stimuli, will enjoy these kinds of activities. The visual learners may well see more in the pictures than some of their peers and can offer unique and perceptive comments to the class discussion. Children's words can be combined to form a dictated chart story to further enhance prereading skills. Teachers merely transcribe what the children have said on a chart tablet and read the story back for shared enjoyment. Questions about what was dictated enhance listening comprehension. Open-ended books or pictures are best because they encourage children to draw upon their imaginations and past experiences to compose creative, meaningful oral language. Numerous wordless picture books are listed in Appendix 1.

Guided Imagery

Guided imagery can provide children with opportunities to listen appreciatively to stories, to exercise their imaginations, and to learn visualization skills. The traditional guided imagery experience is a sequential story of 10 minutes or so, which the teacher reads to children who listen usually in a relaxed posture with their eyes closed. Children are encouraged to fantasize to the evocative words and to practice visualizing the scenes that they hear. Teachers may also play music while they read or while children just relax, draw, or paint. Such suggestive music as classical, folk, or popular can also stimulate spontaneous dancing, as children listen and translate what they hear into movement.

Oral Reading and Storytelling

Who reads to young children or tells them stories is not important, so long as someone reads to them at least once a day. Aides, volunteers, children from an upper grade, or student interns can all be trained to be effective readers for young children. Parents or community members who are gifted storytellers often enjoy spending time in preschool or early childhood classrooms because audiences there are so receptive. I witnessed a kindergarten class in which one of the children frequently read to his classmates. The boy was an excellent and enthusiastic reader and seemed completely unaware how advanced his skills were. Having watched his teacher read to the class, he knew how to turn the book to show the pictures and even had a sense of how to pace his words. The teacher had introduced this boy's reading to the class as an exciting and different activity—"Today we have a real treat. I have asked Jimmy to read to you and I'll just listen"—and the children received their classmate's accomplishment with appreciation and support. Throughout the year, Jimmy read to the whole class at least once a week and often read to small groups as well. He gained a strong sense of himself and was able to introduce many children to favorite books and to his love of reading.

Directed Listening-Thinking Activity

Reading to children and sharing picture books with them are often cited as excellent ways to encourage love of literature, critical thinking, and appreciative listening. Reading is most profitable when teachers adopt an approach often called a "directed listening-thinking activity" or DLTA. With this approach, teachers read, question, and encourage children's thinking about the stories being presented. The basic lesson, which is as applicable to a discussion or instructional sequence as to storytelling or reading, has five parts: establishing background, setting purposes for listening, active listening (without interrupting the speaker), following up on what has been presented, and extending the ideas to relate the story, topic, or skills. Figure 3.2 outlines these steps more fully. While teachers should not dilute children's enjoyment of storytime by turning the experience into a didactic session of quizzing and right and wrong answers, careful, thought-provoking questioning before, after, and during reading can help children learn to listen attentively, purposefully, and critically. Chapter 13 presents another version of this approach, the "directed thinking about reading (DTAR) activity," in which children listen as well as read and think.

Questioning in a DLTA can also serve a diagnostic purpose. Because of language differences and experiential backgrounds, children will differ in their

---

Objective:
To encourage children to listen attentively and to interact thoughtfully with stories presented orally.

Assumption:
Teacher has selected the story to be shared carefully and has prepared to read the book with expression.

Procedures:
1. Call children to circle for story.
2. Show the cover of the book and read the title.
   "I'm going to read this book to you today. It's called *Rich Cat, Poor Cat** and it's by Bernard Waber. What do you see on the cover? What do you think the book will be about?"
   [Elicits that there is a plump, bejeweled cat and a thin one slinking by a garbage can; wants children to suggest that the book may compare their lives.]
3. Read a few pages (depending on amount of text per page). Show the pictures for each page, allowing children enough time to see them clearly.
4. Ask children to make predictions based on what has been read. Summarize or request summaries if needed to maintain story line.
   [Reads description of rich cats and of Scat, a street cat.]
   "Who can tell me what we've heard so far? What kind of pillow does it say Scat has? Would that be nice? Why not? Why do people call her Scat? Do you think she likes that name? What's going to happen?"
   [Elicits that rich and poor cats have been compared, that Scat has been described, and that Scat sleeps on cobblestones. Clarify term "cobble-

---

FIGURE 3.2
Directions for a directed listening-thinking activity (DLTA).

abilities to understand what is read to them. Some may show that they are not comprehending by fidgeting during storytime. Others may never indicate their lack of understanding. By questioning the children teachers can discover those who might not fully comprehend what they are hearing and thus can help to make future experiences more meaningful.

Movement Activities

Although many movement activities and pantomime involve wordless dramatizations, they still belong in any list of activities to strengthen oral language and listening skills. They are highly motivating because they capitalize on young children's need to move and be active. Movement activities, in general, begin with children's natural sense of rhythm and enjoyment of motions such as

---

stones" for those who do not know it. Discuss name "Scat" and entertain all guesses about the rest of the story.]

5. Stop again and repeat procedure after several pages.
   "Who can tell me about those rich cats? Did you hear what I read last? 'There isn't anything very special in Scat's life?' How does that make you feel?"

6. Continue process through significant sections of book, stopping to summarize and elicit predictions.
   "Well, what do we know about rich cats? Poor Scat, the book says that she is nobody's cat! Do you think that will be forever? What could happen to change it? Look at that picture of Scat; how does she look?" [Summarize and elicit guesses about Scat's life; allow children to suggest that she could get run over, could be taken to the pound, or could, ideally, be adopted; do not give away ending by overly responding to any possibility.]

7. Complete book with questions about how children liked it and which parts they liked best.
   "How many of you thought that would happen to Scat? How does she feel now? What do you think made the little girl and her mother take Scat home? How do you think Scat likes her new name?" [Elicit that Scat was adopted, that she probably feels happy, that the people were nice, and that Scat, now Gwendolyn, is finally a "rich cat." If no one notices, point out that the bejeweled Gwendolyn on the last page is the same as the picture on the cover. Let children respond to the book's content and make relevant comments about their own cats, neighborhood cats, pets in general.]

---

*Waber, B. (1963). *Rich cat, poor cat.* Englewood Cliffs, NJ: Scholastic.

FIGURE 3.2
(*continued*)

swinging, walking, stretching, or tumbling. Vocabulary is stretched along with young, supple bodies, as children understand and use specific terminology for their varied movements.

Pantomime is a more complex behavior and should be introduced only when children's observation skills have developed to the point that they can isolate and reproduce essential aspects of motion from the person, animal, or thing they will depict. Children may do pantomime singly or in coordination with a peer. If the class terrarium had a snail in it, for example, children should be encouraged to watch it carefully before trying to pantomime how it moves. They may even talk together about how the motion should be imitated, with the teacher directing the discussion to develop new vocabulary with terms such as *slither.*

Technically, pantomime is soundless; but children enjoy accompanying their movements by appropriate noises such as croaking, barking, and meowing. They should be allowed to do so. Music can also be used with children's pantomime either for specific animals (e.g., "The Flight of the Bumblebee") or as stimuli for more abstract movement as children sway, run, or gallop to specific musical pieces. "Peter and the Wolf" and *The Nutcracker Suite* are often used with young children but are by no means the only appropriate pieces of classical music. "Pictures at an Exhibition" and *New World Symphony* are also excellent because they present so many "scenes" or "situations" to stimulate movement. Characterizing the movement of objects (trees, cars going up a hill) and specific characters (a witch's walk, a clown or giant) hone observation, imagination, and movement skills even further.

But Keep It Fun!

Movement activities develop body awareness, self-confidence, listening and oral language skills, and vocabulary in all children; but they are especially important for children whose learning style or modality is tactile-kinesthetic. Just as auditory learners prefer to take in information through hearing, tactile-kinesthetic learners learn best through movement. Their movements in activities such as these reinforce vocabulary and strengthen thinking skills far better than would the teacher-talk and class discussion that best serve auditory learners. Similarly, auditory and visual learners will benefit from the practice of processing information through tactile means.

Still, directed-movement activities are harder than they appear because children must receive the directive and interpret its meaning, often by coordinating an action word (wriggle) with a qualifier (quickly) and a locator (across the floor). Next, they must draw from memory *how* to perform these actions physically and then actually perform them, ideally in a way that will not make them look too foolish. Because these behaviors involve linguistic, cognitive, psychomotor, and social functioning, they are valuable parts of an early childhood program, but they lose their effectiveness when perfection is required. They must remain fun—little bodies and minds stretching together—and never take on aspects of tests or judgments.

Dramatics and Improvisation

Spontaneous dramatic play, a natural part of early childhood that involves extensive movement, helps children learn about many pragmatic functions of language. Dramatics and improvisation as planned activities strengthen understanding of social uses of language as well and are excellent means for demonstrating the need for good speaking and listening skills. Structured dramatics activities are most suitable for children of at least age 4 because, to assume roles, children need to be able to "decenter" or move out of themselves into a new, specified identity and point of view. They must then identify and enact attributes of the character they will portray—voice, movements, emotions, and appearance.

This movement from oneself to a new character takes place when roles are assigned and parts are learned or when children are asked to improvise a person or animal. In either circumstance, children strengthen their abilities to present ideas orally, improve their enunciation, and develop poise and self-confidence. Improvisation is a good starting point for introducing children to dramatics. In improvising characters, children experience focused role playing and often can release emotion, express humor, and gain insight into conflicts or distressing situations by "trying" different roles and appropriate voices, movements, and characteristics without the effort of producing an actual play. Improvisation as a follow-up to story reading reinforces appreciative and interpretive listening skills and gives teachers a view to how well children have comprehended what they have heard. As in their spontaneous dramatic play, children also enjoy improvising a character from television or movies.

When teachers decide for the first time to produce a play with young children, they frequently do not realize what a complicated project they are about to undertake. Coordinating all aspects of a production requires time and patience, as shown by the experience of one of my students. During an internship in a second-grade class, she decided to write and produce a play for parents' night. The children, all Mexican-American, would transfer in third grade from bilingual to monolingual instruction. Instruction was conducted in both English and Spanish, and the intern decided to use both languages in her play. Her journal related how she decided on a topic:

> Journal Entry: The classroom teacher prompted the idea of using sections of the Mexican culture, as the students could more readily relate to the theme. . . . I began an outline and elaborated on a script so that I could present it to the children for feedback.[4]

Journal Entry: Introduced the idea of a play; conducted that as an oral speaking/listening lesson; discussed what is meant by "performing a play," various types of plays, and brainstormed about any specific type of play they would like to perform.

Journal Entry: Conducted another oral speaking/listening lesson in English (English as a Second Language). The theme was the concepts of bilingual/bicultural identity, ancestry, and family origin—how they relate. One student brought up the fact that he has been told of his Aztec ancestry. What more could I ask for? Naturally—what is a person to do? Capitalize! A play was born!

Other tasks are to assign parts to the most capable speakers and actors and to devise alternative parts or jobs for less capable or willing children. All children should be involved in some way, but no child should be forced to assume a role against his or her will. Because overall quality is a goal, teachers must be careful in assigning roles. Criteria for leading roles should include willingness to participate, good speaking voice, self-confidence, and reliability. The student intern noted:

Journal Entry: Children took turns speaking about their respective backgrounds, origins or grandparents, parents, and some traditions they practiced, while I took note of their speaking abilities. I needed two main speakers for the play. I admit this was a little sneaky, but effective for my purposes.

Teachers must plan costumes, sets, music, and children's stage movements. Children who do not want speaking parts can often participate in these tasks, especially in primary grades. Rehearsal is another chore. Children's ability to memorize will vary, as will their stamina for repeated practice. Children must understand the importance of their cooperation but not feel stressed or overly anxious. Clear explanations of expectations and ample teacher support are essential. Teachers must realize that it will take a long time to learn parts and to coordinate actions and that, even then, some children may go blank at the time of actual dress rehearsals or performances.

Journal Entry: Dress rehearsal! We worked on reciting loudly and distinctly and pronouncing properly. We practiced several times until they were able to do their parts on their own without my assistance. The students were a little nervous but excited.

Production time—at the very least, some children whose voices have resounded through a classroom or empty auditorium may be virtually inaudible because of stage fright. The end result of all the work may be less than anticipated. Teachers must not show frustration or lack of respect for the effort the children have put into the production, even if the entire play appears to fall apart on opening night. The processes that everyone has shared are the important aspects of producing a play: the planning, cooperation, coordination, problem solving, and specific language skills practiced for this new kind of speaking. The end results may also be wonderful:

> Journal Entry: Show Time! Relaxed and enjoyed the presentation. The kids were great! The parents seemed to enjoy it, too.

SUMMARY

Skills for listening and speaking are a standard part of early childhood curricula, but they remain just "subjects" to be taught unless teachers place them within the larger context of what children are learning about pragmatics, the social uses of language. Movement, dancing, dramatics, and verse are central to children's mastery of language skills during these years and must be included in activities designed to strengthen listening and speaking skills.

REVIEW QUESTIONS

1. Be sure that you can define each of these terms:
   auditory acuity
   auditory memory
   contextual language
   decontextual language
   directed listening-thinking activity (DLTA)
   levels of listening
   pragmatic language play
   pragmatics
2. The social uses of language or pragmatics vary according to social group. Why must early childhood teachers be aware of this?
3. What can early childhood teachers do to help children whose sense of pragmatics differs from that of most of the children in a class?
4. Pragmatic linguistic play may be offensive to teachers and to some children, but it is a natural part of learning about social uses of language. Suggest ways in which teachers should respond to this kind of play.
5. List as many values as you can for teaching listening skills. What kinds of problems might a child encounter if her listening skills are weak?
6. Find several wordless picture books and use them with young children. Contrast the stories told by each child. In what ways are they similar and different?
7. Learn several finger plays and use them with young children. How easily do the children learn the finger plays? Do they like them? Do they learn all the words? What do they do for words they do not know? What kinds of finger plays seem most popular?

8. Observe several early childhood teachers reading to children. Do they use a directed listening-thinking approach? Try the approach yourself with children ages 3, 4, 5, and 6. How does it work? What, if any, adjustments did you need to make for each age group?

NOTES

1. Cazden, C. B. (1983). Adult assistance to language development: Scaffolds, models, and direct instruction. In R. P. Parker & F. A. Davis. (Eds.), *Developing Literacy* (pp. 3–18). Newark, DE: International Reading Association.
2. Pelligrini, A. D. (1984). The effects of classroom ecology on preschoolers' functional uses of language. In A. D. Pelligrini & T. D. Yawkey (Eds.) *The development of oral and written language in social contexts* (pp. 129–144). Norwood, NJ: Ablex.
3. Tizard, B., Cooperman, O., Joseph, A., & Tizard, J. (1972). Environmental effects on language development: A study of young children in long-stay residential nurseries. *Child Development, 43,* 337–338.
4. Alba, Rose (1985). Process log of internship at Alta Vista Elementary School, El Paso, Texas. Used by permission.

4

Linguistically Different Children

The latest census found that more than 8 million school-aged children live in homes where a language other than English is spoken. This number increases with the addition of children who speak nonstandard **dialects** such as **Black English** or "code-switch" between two languages, as is common along the Mexico-United States border. Some of these children are immigrants; others, native-born, live in families where parents themselves speak another language. Many of these children are poor, have few experiences beyond their immediate communities, and do not see books or newspapers, especially in English; some live in areas where they may hear little English spoken around them. Families may differ widely but, barring neurological or other impairments, the children all have learned to use language and have learned it in the same intense, dynamic way as described in the previous chapters. Research has produced "overwhelming evidence to show that when both middle-class and non-middle-class children, no matter what their native language, dialect, or ethnic background come to school at the age of five or six, they have control of a fully-formed grammatical system" (Gumperz & Hernandez-Chavez, 1972, p. 84). They have gone through stages of preverbal concept development, gathered information about oral language, tried out the sounds they heard around them, and burst forth with a semantic and syntactic system that reflects their language community. The language children feel most comfortable with, the one they have learned from infancy and actually think in, is their *dominant* language. Whatever a child's dominant language, the cognitive process for arriving at a certain level of competency has been similar.

Children also understand the pragmatic aspects of language. They know that the purposes of language include communicating wants and needs, expressing emotions, and telling stories and jokes and that language, as a whole, encompasses both verbal and nonverbal production. Children's home cultures or societies have determined what they know about pragmatics. Classmates from different backgrounds may show respect through shyness or overt signs of affection, and even within the same broad ethnic groups, different subgroups will find certain behaviors acceptable and others not.

Accepting the equality of all children's self-motivated efforts at language acquisition is essential in developing programs to help each child achieve his full language potential. People who work with young children, especially with children of nonstandard language backgrounds, must not subscribe to what Cazden (1981) called "myths" about language. The first two myths are that some languages are better than others and that some dialects represent bad language use. These are false, because all languages and dialects are structured systems of expression with distinct semantic, syntactic, and phonological elements. Some languages are more complex than others, but complex is not synonymous with better. The third myth is that people who speak nonstandard dialects are stupid. This is false, because how one speaks is a social reality, not an intellectual one. The final myth is that learning a nonstandard dialect is not the same as learning a language. "Not the same" in this case means not as intellectually demanding. This, too, is false because dialects have been shown to have distinct structures, vocabularies, and systems of rules. The same is true for *pidgins*, combinations of two or more languages that have developed so that groups can communicate. In places such as Haiti or Hawaii, children often learn a pidgin first; in that case, the pidgin is called a *creole*.

LINGUISTICALLY AND CULTURALLY DIFFERENT CHILDREN

The term *linguistically different* refers to children who speak some language other than Standard American English. They have learned the syntax and semantics of the other language and know the social/pragmatic conventions of language use in their own community. In early childhood classes, linguistically different children may speak nonstandard dialects such as Black English, may have been born in the United States but have not learned English as their first language, or may be immigrant children who speak the language of their native country. California, New York, Florida, New Jersey, Illinois, and Texas serve the highest percentage of non-English-speaking children, but, linguistically different children can be found throughout the United States. Teachers need to be aware of strategies to meet the needs of these students, especially if no bilingual programs are available.

Indochinese Immigrants

Immigrants from Indochina include, most recently, Thais, Laotians, Vietnamese, and Kampucheans, as well as Chinese, Japanese, Koreans, and Filipinos. They bring many different religions and customs, and in some cases, long-standing between-group hostilities.[1] West cautioned (1983) " . . . teachers are sometimes baffled when [Indochinese] children refuse to interact or show some degree of hostility toward one another. . . . Children may not know one another's language [or] be of the same religion; their parents may have been in opposing armies; or they may harbor feelings of superiority, inferiority or resentment toward one another" (p. 84). Less outgoing, more modest in dress and behaviors, Indochinese children may have been socialized to listen politely to adults, may seem shyer and more reserved than other children, and may answer only when directly asked to participate.[2] Expectations of school may be for strictness, formality, and quiet, and the informality of good early childhood classes may be confusing to children (and to parents). Students may have difficulty merging into active, busy classrooms, and teachers must entice them with covert, subtle, and yet respectful signs of welcome.

Young immigrants may bring memories of recent suffering and terror, and teachers should not discount the effects that the immediate past may have on young lives. Teachers need to remember that "if children have known only war and fear, it is difficult for them to believe that peace and security will last" (West, 1983, p. 88). This "difference" in children's lives cuts across culture and language and necessitates teacher sensitivity and support as children enter school.

Spanish-Speaking Children

Recent immigration from Mexico, Puerto Rico, and Central and South America has filled classes with children whose first (and often only) language is Spanish. Additionally, many native-born children grow up speaking and hearing only Spanish at home and in their communities. Spanish-speaking families come from different socioeconomic backgrounds; but many immigrants are poor, illiterate, and, like the Indochinese, fleeing from some form of oppression. While there are basic similarities between groups, Spanish-speaking children show many cross-group differences, including background experiences, expectations for school, and dialects of Spanish that they speak. In some Hispanic families, children hear and use English and Spanish and become bilingual. Recognizing social contexts for using each language, they may learn to code-switch between the two. Code-switching should not be discouraged, especially in young children seeking to master two languages.

There are many differences in the languages Hispanic children bring to school with them. "The Spanish and English that the bilingual child brings to school may not be the standard language used by textbooks or by the teacher. A child acquires the particular variety of a language s/he learns at home. The variety of Spanish spoken at home, marked regionally and socially, is the one the child will learn. If the family also speaks English at home and the variety of English is strongly influenced by Spanish pronunciation or grammar, the child acquires that particular variety" (Ramirez, 1981, p. 226). It is possible for children in one class to speak several dialects, and teachers must remember to expand children's understanding of the range of Spanish-language skills. One theorist (Gonzalez, 1979) cautioned: "Although the use of the child's Spanish dialect variety is encouraged, this form should not be the only variety the child is exposed to . . . [T]he student should be made aware of other varieties of Spanish such as the Standard form. To deny the child this exposure is to limit communication skills, to hamper the ability to communicate in Spanish beyond the limits of the child's *barrio* or *colonia*" (p. 126).

Other Languages

Indochinese and Spanish languages are by no means the only languages children may bring to American classrooms. The diversity includes such eastern European languages as Russian, Rumanian, Polish, Hungarian, and Czechoslovakian; Iranian, Greek, Hebrew, and Italian; and creoles from Hawaii, Barbados, Haiti, Jamaica, and Trinidad. Each group may be broken down further into regional dialects, and individuals speaking the same language may have widely differing cultural backgrounds. Although groups of people may choose to live together in "ethnic" neighborhoods, so that schools have a concentrated population of children speaking the same language, this is not always the case.

Black English and Other Dialects

Black English (BE) differs from Standard American English (SAE) primarily in phonology and syntax; but the two are more alike than they are different. Many blacks do not speak BE, and some whites, notably in the rural South, speak a similar dialect. BE is systematic and rule governed;[3] and teachers working with BE speakers can, with practice, understand children's speech. Many young BE speakers learn to understand SAE from exposure to media and people outside their immediate linguistic community, and BE does not seem to hinder acquisition of beginning reading and writing skills, as long as teachers understand children's dialect and the underlying principles of literacy acquisition.[4]

The major difference in pronunciation between SAE and BE concerns the ends of words. BE speakers frequently do not articulate the final consonant sounds of words, especially, *r, l, t, d, s,* and *z*. *Th* may or may not be voiced, as in *muvver* [mother], *toof* [tooth], or *brudder* [brother]. The *g* in *-ing* is usually dropped. Consonant clusters may be simplified, resulting in weakened possessives, verbs endings, or plurals, as in, *Bob friend, He swim,* or *ten boy*. Words ending in the consonant clusters *sk, sp,* or *st* form plurals by adding *-es*, so that *desk* (pronounced "des' " in the singular) becomes *desses* in plural. Initial consonant clusters are often shortened, for example: *three* becomes *tree*, or *shrimp* becomes *srimp*. Vowels may differ regionally even among BE speakers; words that do not rhyme in SAE may rhyme in BE, as in these pairs: *steer/stare, tour/tear, Tom/time, boil/ball, fire/far,* or *pin/pen*.

Pronunciation influences syntax in BE, so that *she walks* and *Bob's friend* become *she walk* and *Bob friend*. BE deletes forms of the verb *to be* whenever English could use a contraction, or uses *be* to show habitual action, for example, "We are (we're) in the second grade," becomes "We in the second grade," and "Mom is generally home by noon," becomes "Mom be home by noon." Compound past-tense verbs are formed with *done*; for example, "Sue has finished her homework," becomes "Sue done finish' her homework." Double negatives are standard.[5]

Other English dialects are strongly marked by regional language differences in phonology, syntax, and semantics. Different words for different objects, events, and concepts can be confusing even when one is discussing everyday events. Talking about bringing a "bag lunch" for a picnic provides a social context for the children used to referring to bags as "sacks" or "pokes"; but if a storybook or reader introduces the term without context, the child may be thoroughly confused. Equally, the child who states that he forgot his "poke" may draw blank stares from a teacher.

Phonological differences and regional accents can make children hard to understand and can cause laughter and ridicule. Teachers need to model acceptance of dialectical differences and often must work hard themselves to understand children's speech. Teachers also need to monitor their own speech, for often their dialects or particular speech patterns are different enough from their students' to cause confusion and lack of communication. Teachers' responsibility toward nonstandard speakers is to expand listening and speaking skills so that children can communicate more efficiently beyond their homes and neighborhoods. With preschoolers, listening skills may be the target; in kindergarten and early primary grades, increasing children's range of expressive language may be the goal.

Social Contexts of Language

In addition to oral production, children have learned varied uses and social conventions of language. Different environments encourage different behaviors; teachers, as the experienced adults in a classroom, need to learn as much as they can about the social meaning of children's use of language so that their interpretation of what children say and do can be as accurate as possible.

LEARNING MORE THAN ONE LANGUAGE

Increased immigration and political action have focused attention on children's need to learn English as a second language. Heightened political awareness has led to understanding the educational needs of young Black English speakers. Discussions of second language learning and of standard versus nonstandard dialects inevitably raise serious political and ethical issues, including the question of allowing children to maintain cultural identity while entering mainstream society. At present, political, social, and cultural debates rage over the general issue of **bilingual education** and the merit of individual models of bilingual instruction. This chapter is not about bilingual education; it is about the language learning of children who do not speak SAE. What follows addresses the needs of these children within a monolingual-English classroom, although many of the strategies can easily be used in a bilingual, early childhood setting.

Bilingualism/Bidialecticalism

Many children become bilingual before they enter first grade, when they learn to understand and speak at least some aspect of two languages, live in a bilingual community where they can learn both languages naturally, and when languages are learned at the same time. Becoming bilingual in no way interferes with other normal cognitive functioning.[6] Bilingualism seems to occur most readily when there is societal approval for speaking two languages or where children perceive the need to communicate with peers and adults in a second language. This learning, it seems, is natural, an outgrowth of children's interest in language and desire to communicate. Children may not even realize that they are learning two languages, especially if parents do not interfere in the process or force children to speak one language or the other. With increased awareness of pragmatics, children will learn, for example, to use one language with grandparents and another with the babysitter.[7] Errors abound in these beginning efforts but do not block communication. The essential point to remember about children who become bilingual in this way is that their environment supports use of both languages. They do not perceive themselves accomplishing anything unusual; they are merely learning to communicate within their particular communities.

Young speakers of BE and other dialects use the media and their larger communities as models of SAE. From exposure to SAE models, children become essentially *bidialectical*; they gain command of two "dialects," BE and SAE, although in early childhood grades, their command of SAE may be primarily receptive.

Bilingual Education

Formalized bilingual education seeks to help children with limited English proficiency (LEP) master oral and written English. Children are considered to be LEP when they understand some English but their skills are not strong enough for active participation in instruction conducted in English. There are an estimated 3.6 million LEP school-aged children in this country, 80% of whom are Hispanic. With the high Hispanic birthrate, the number is growing constantly.[8] Historically, there have been several models of bilingual education, and much of the present national debate concerns local autonomy in selecting a model to use.

One model of bilingual education insists that, while in school, children use only the mainstream, target language. "This approach artificializes education to the extent that it identifies it with a variety [of speech] that is not functional in the life of the community. It threatens the viability of the students' primary community and of its primary [support] networks to the extent that it implies that *only by leaving his native speech repertoire behind can the student [succeed]*" (Fishman, 1977, p. 13, italics added). This approach can be disastrous for young learners because it denies them the means of socializing, communicating, and expressing themselves. A more permissive approach allows for instruction in both English and community languages, where "the school is viewed . . . as a place in which local speech, local folklore, local history, and local authenticity have their rightful place" (Fishman, p. 15). Many bilingual/ bicultural programs affirm "local authenticity." Other programs use the first language for the beginning years of school to teach basic skills and concepts. Teachers increase their use of English as children's skills grow, continue to use the first language as needed for explanation, and allow children to respond in their first language. Still others immerse children as quickly as possible in instruction in English, with the first language used for concept development, emotional support, and conversation. **Second language learners** do not compete instructionally with English-dominant students but instead use English purposefully with other language learners.[9] There is one final category: English as a Second Language (ESL). This is a "pull-out" service; children attend an intensive course of ESL instruction for an hour per day or several times per week.

Most programs use children's cultural backgrounds as a core for the curriculum and aim for a transition to monolingual instruction without loss of first language skills or cultural identity. A common goal of these programs should be students' sense of themselves as competent language users. Teachers' acceptance of children's communicative efforts, full as they may be of errors, affirms young learners' natural approach to language and encourages them to continue experimentation with oral language in purposeful ways.

Discrimination

In discussing children who speak nonstandard language, it is necessary to discuss discrimination. Teachers may not view themselves or their behaviors as discriminatory, but research repeatedly reveals that many teachers instruct minority children with a slower, more deliberate style, enunciating each word correctly "as if to avoid any verbal sign of emotion, approval, or disapproval. Children [in such classes] were expected to speak only when called upon, and the teachers would insist that each question be answered before responding to further ideas. Unsolicited remarks were ignored even if they referred to the problem at hand. Pronunciation errors were corrected whenever they occurred, even if the task had to be interrupted. The children seemed . . . distracted and inattentive . . . and answered in a style that approached in artificiality that of the teachers" (Gumperz & Hernandez-Chavez, 1972, p. 103). The same teachers, with nonminority students, used open-ended questions and stimulated discussion and interaction. Assignments for minority students in these classes were rigid drill and practice activities that differed substantially from those given to their peers.

If the community from which children come does not value schooling, youngsters may approach formal learning with trepidation and an impending sense of doom. These feelings can comprise a "culture" of their own apart from any national or ethnic group, a culture that teachers must acknowledge and work to overcome. Teachers who understand language acquisition and child development will seek and build upon children's strengths rather than allowing language or economic differences to dictate behaviors or expectations. One researcher summarized positive teacher attitudes well (Bernstein, 1972): "If the culture of the teacher is to become part of the consciousness of the child, then the culture of the child must first be in the consciousness of the teacher" (p. 149).

Learning the Language and Culture of School

No matter what their backgrounds, all school entrants must adjust to the language and culture of school. "Schools represent a special sub-culture, embodying attitudes and values—and even a special type of language—to be found nowhere in the open society beyond" (Holdaway, 1979, p. 17). Children must learn special kinds of sharing and turn taking, patience, walking and waiting in lines, and subordination of the self to a group identity. Children who attend preschool encounter this culture early and adjust; those who enter school at kindergarten or first grade find themselves less comfortable with the "society" of school. Children must also learn to talk *about* language and other symbol systems, as in math, and to talk and think about abstractions such as "the sounds letters make." Learning to communicate in these ways is like learning a new dialect of English for native speakers and is even more difficult for second language learners.

Children must also learn about "book language." The first step is realizing that book language is based on oral language. Book language can sound alien to nonstandard speakers, and teachers may initially need to "translate" their oral reading to make stories sound right, so that children can identify with and take pleasure from literature. Books with predictable story lines or repetitive sentence structure or chants help, too, because children can quickly understand the rhythm of the language. Wordless picture books encourage children to create their own stories, as well. Don Holdaway, who has worked with nonstandard speakers in New Zealand, maintains that children from different cultural and linguistic backgrounds often gain their first comfort with school through literature.

CLASSROOM PRACTICES TO ENCOURAGE STANDARD ENGLISH

One year my first-grade class in Brooklyn, New York, included two English-speaking Japanese children, a Chinese-speaking new arrival from Hong Kong, an English/Chinese bilingual student who did not speak the other child's dialect, a Haitian who understood my French but replied in creole, several English-dominant white children, and the rest blacks and Hispanics, some of whom spoke Spanish better than English. This situation might be most probable in New York, Los Angeles, Chicago, or other large cities, but variations are possible anywhere in the country. Indochinese languages, Spanish, BE, and Haitian creole are but a few of the languages and dialects that teachers may encounter within regular, mainstream classrooms.

The Dilemma: Timing, Procedures, and Responsibility

Children should learn to communicate in and recall standard, mainstream English, but they should also maintain the use of their first language and appreciation for their cultural heritage. The early childhood years, when children are so actively gaining communication skills, is an ideal time to acquire a second language or to master SAE.

The crucial term here is *acquire;* children should be encouraged to extend their natural pursuit of language toward new goals and to apply strategies similar to those used in first language acquisition. Neither rote memorization of English vocabulary and sentence forms nor abrupt attempts to change dialect patterns will produce long-term, meaningful language growth. Children must view new or standard language patterns as useful additions to their communicative skills if language expansion is to be more than an artifact of "getting along" in school.

Realistic Expectations

The process of learning a new language or dialect is often slow, with initial periods of silent observation and reflection. When children begin to speak, their utterances will be filled with mispronunciations and nonstandard expressions and words. Teachers often overcorrect oral production, until even secure children may question their skills, intelligence, and worth. Modeling, rather than overcorrection, is the effective strategy. Indeed, "[if] we concentrate our educational efforts on 'correcting' [children's] phonology and their grammar (hopefully) without simultaneously eliminating verbal behavior altogether, we may end up with children who speak in well-enunciated, 'grammatical' sentences but who have nothing to say" (Horner & Gussow, 1972, p. 192). Or, at least, they may have nothing to say in school!

As with first language learners, receptive language will develop first. Children will be able to understand teachers and peers before they themselves begin to verbalize. Listening and doing as asked, responding nonverbally or with smiles, or responding with a monosyllabic utterance are all signs of progress in language mastery and should be welcomed with praise.

Assessing What Children Know

Standardized tests are repeatedly criticized for providing limited measures of young children's language skills. This criticism is especially valid for second language learners and nonstandard dialect speakers. Teachers themselves gather background information and assess concept development, language skills, and socialization. If teachers understand children's language, they can converse with them directly or eavesdrop as they interact with others or talk to themselves. Asking children to repeat patterned sentences or rhymes gives information about receptive and expressive language. If the repetition leaves out some words but makes sense, if it translates SAE into BE, or if it adds words in the first language, teachers know that children have understood the sentence and have processed it mentally.

Teachers also must assess how much information children can extract from regular classroom situations (e.g., clean up time, lining up for lunch) or from nonverbal behavior (e.g., scowls, frowns, smiles). Parents can sometimes provide information, especially about previous school or child-care experiences or language use in the home. Parents can also help teachers understand if shyness is a personality trait or represents real fear of the new situation. Language differences can exaggerate insecurities; but young children's natural curiosity and interest in language should, in time, contribute to socialization.

Supportive Environments in the Preschool and Kindergarten

A classroom environment that supports the language growth of all its students is the best environment in which to learn a standard dialect or second language. Both activities and people provide scaffolds for language learning. Interesting activities give children a context from which to draw information. They see what is going on and what is being used; they hear labels, names, and descriptions. They listen for extended conversations and verbal formulas that draw the activities together. They begin to learn English while English is being used purposefully and naturally. Studies of preschoolers have repeatedly affirmed that peer teaching begins almost immediately and is a powerful tool.[10] It develops from children's mutual desires to communicate. Much like babies and toddlers, second language learners often manipulate situations so to obtain information about language from their peers. They ask for names of things, repeat utterances, and initiate conversations as they explore the sounds and structures of their target language.

The routines of the classroom also provide scaffolding. Second language learners can perceive the structure of the classroom, understand and participate in many activities, and grasp intuitively the communicative nature of many interactions. Discussions, storytime, movement to centers, snack and lunch times are observable, understandable events within the day. Children must first learn what the routines involve and then listen for the key words or phrases they can understand and perhaps begin to use. The relative predictability of these routines becomes the scaffold. Visual scaffolding from classroom labels, charts, and decorations gives children and teachers something specific to talk about and contributes to vocabulary growth.

Routines such as taking dictated chart stories (language experience) and storytime are especially valuable. Teachers may be able to take dictation in children's first language in addition to English. Dictated stories can be made more meaningful with pictures or cartoons drawn over significant nouns or verbs. As teachers transcribe dictation, they use children's names, and children realize that their names are being used in a nonthreatening situation. Feeling part of the class, they also match peers' names and faces, and other children get practice hearing and saying what may seem to be difficult, foreign names.

As mentioned before, books with predictable story lines and repetitive language and situations are excellent for storytime. Children can identify the connection between teacher and student verbalization and the illustrations in the book. Predictable refrains and repetitive sentence patterns encourage second language learners to join in. Again, the material and the situation provide the scaffolding. (See Appendix 1.)

Modeling, expansion, and elaboration, natural procedures for encouraging first language acquisition, work equally well for second language learners. Teachers model standard grammar, varied sentence structures, and interesting word choices for all children; and with second language learners, teachers may want to point, gesture, or emphasize sentence patterns such as "This is a _____, but this is _____." This should be done within the context of normal conversation or instruction about other topics, not as a drill exercise. Unless the children themselves initiate a copied response ("Thisisa_____."), they should not be made to "Say it after me." Classmates, too, provide models for their peers, as do books. Elaboration takes utterances even further. Children say something, and teachers expand the utterance structurally and add new information as well. Information may be syntactic or semantic, that is, elaborated sentence structure or new vocabulary with which to discuss the topic. Teachers may elaborate informal conversations or structure small group sessions to discuss pictures or objects. These should be purposeful and relevant; it is best to talk about things that can be manipulated or exciting pictures that are full of recognizable action.

Teachers use elaboration when they discuss activities such as block building and painting with children. Other activities such as cooking, puppets, art work, or dramatization offer contexts on which teachers may comment and from which children can draw language. If English speakers are participants in group activities, they will probably have provided a verbal accompaniment to the project and will contribute to teachers' discussions. Allen (1986) wrote of activities that provide "not only a spectrum of language opportunities but also nudge children to use language in a variety of ways" (p. 62). *Nudging* is not the same as demanding use of the target language and in no way carries judgment.

INSTRUCTION IN EARLY PRIMARY GRADES

The instructional value of teachers who speak the children's language cannot be overestimated. They provide links with home, often share children's cultural background, become role models, and can communicate easily with parents. Unfortunately, except where bilingual programs are common, teacher/child language matches may be rare. I once worked with a man from a Spanish/Chinese background who spoke both languages fluently. Children in our school spoke BE. Every year he tried to transfer to a school where his skills and cultural backgrounds would be more valuable. He may still be trying!

When children who do not speak SAE enter the early primary grades, the tasks they confront extend beyond oral language to acquisition of literacy. Unlike bilingual classrooms, where teachers use the home language to teach basic skills and later encourage transfer of skills to English, teachers in English-dominant classes must find ways to teach proficient speakers while extending the skills of nonstandard speakers and children of limited English proficiency. For all children, they must preserve self-concepts, build academic self-esteem, and teach basic skills in content areas. Modeling, scaffolding, expansion, and peer teaching all contribute to children's success, as do meaningful, social interactions requiring the use of the target language. For practical purposes, the following section will discuss dialect speakers and second language learners separately.

Speakers of Nonstandard Dialects

Children who speak nonstandard dialects usually sound different, and teachers must be very careful not to confuse assessments of children's phonology and sentence structure with determination of academic potential. While accepting children's nonstandard dialect, teachers work to expand children's verbal skills to include standard English. Teachers model standard forms and encourage their use through low-key and context-dependent training rather than with specific grammar drills.

There seems to be no causal relationship between mastery of SAE and success in learning to read.[11] With support and appropriate instruction, nonstandard speakers can read standard English with ease. In addition to basal reader series, children's literature (much of which sensitively represents minority lifestyles) and language experience dictation can be relevant and stimulating beginning instructional material (See Chapters 11 and 12). Nonstandard speakers must be allowed to use their own dialects as they read orally. When presented with standard written English, they take in the information and translate it to their own oral register. Oral reading, then, represents dialect and deviates from actual text. Deviations that do not change meaning can be thought of as "miscues" rather than errors: They indicate that readers have comprehended the text at a deep level and have produced a surface rendering that is accurate in meaning but inaccurate in wording or sound. Comprehension is the ultimate goal.

Nonstandard speakers should be encouraged to write extensively and to depend on their own sense of grammar and phonology for sentence structure and spelling. Writing lets them manipulate nonstandard and standard language, test their ideas about differences, and eventually compare a concrete representation of their own language against what they are encountering in texts written in SAE. From this active construction will come increased awareness of differences and attention to SAE in speech and reading.

Second Language Learners

Children who do not speak English and who have not learned to read and write in their own language need to be surrounded by print and by people reading and writing. Teachers who have some familiarity with children's own language can communicate directly to them (as I used French with my Haitian students) and can make classrooms somewhat bilingual. Signs and charts can be written in two languages, language-experience dictation can be transcribed in children's first language, and teachers can translate all or parts of storybooks as they read. Immersing children in situations that stimulate oral language use and model reading and writing skills is preferable to drill and practice activities that foster rote memorization of often meaningless patterns of language. Immersion is *not* preferable to the kind of emotional and intellectual support that comes from hearing and using one's own language for learning, so teachers should always try to enlist the help of volunteers, even older children, who can spend time conversing with nonnative speakers and encouraging the use of English.

In early childhood classes, second language learners can sit in on beginning literacy instruction and participate by looking at pictures in books, following along in print, listening to reading, and, as skills increase, answering teachers' questions. Children who can understand peers' oral reading can probably answer some comprehension questions, and even a physical response such as nodding yes to the question "Did you like the story?" represents real participation and makes children feel competent. From this kind of involvement children learn expected behavior for instructional groups, listening skills in general, attention to English (reading, discussion, questioning, and responding), English vocabulary, and varied question and statement patterns. Like any beginning language learner, they take what they can from the interaction, add it to what they know, and increase their skills.

What distinguishes this involvement from "sink or swim" immersion programs is that teachers accept the level of participation children seem capable of achieving. Children who willingly read a bit and answer questions orally are not necessarily ready to do independent, follow-up work at their desks. Requiring independent work discredits how much children *have* actually learned and causes unnecessary frustration. They might, however, be able to retell the story or to draw about it.

Learning the "language of school" is part of the task facing these children as they learn to read and write. Concepts such as letters, sounds, words, and sentences may be new to children who do not come from literate home environments, but they can often master the concepts before they gain control of the language needed to *talk* about them. It is more important that children participate in meaningful literacy activities than that they learn this specialized vocabulary; it is more important that they learn to speak, read, and write the words they encounter in conversation and in their books than the words used to talk about reading skills.

Equally, children do not need correct spelling and complete control of grammar to begin to write. Children who are allowed to take risks with language use, who know that they will not be punished for mistakes, construct their own rules as they use language. This is as true of second language learners as it is of native speakers. Recognizing that beginning efforts will be ungrammatical and reflect code-switching, teachers should encourage second language learners to participate as soon as possible in classroom writing activities. They will benefit more from "real" writing than from sentence and grammar drills. Collaboration with an English-dominant partner can provide informal instruction and language scaffolding as well.[12]

MULTICULTURAL EDUCATION

Multicultural education encourages students to develop positive attitudes toward all cultures, presents accurate representations of diverse peoples without stereotyping, and teaches students to detect and eliminate subtle forms of bias. It stresses equality and helps students avoid sexist behavior and stereotyping. To be truly effective, multicultural education must represent a philosophy or approach to a curriculum and not be merely adjunct activities brought out at appropriate times. The best approach with young learners is using multiethnic/multicultural material whenever possible to teach the basic skills. The most obvious example of this approach is using stories about different groups as part or the core of a beginning reading program. Social studies also provide excellent opportunities to extend children's knowledge about the world as a whole, to study their own and others' backgrounds, and to raise their social consciousness. Books about strong, active women in different professions can be introduced, as can books that develop children's awareness of handicapping conditions. Properly presented with appropriate material, even highly egocentric preschoolers can benefit from these activities.

In addition to benefiting from the vicarious experiences that books provide, children can actively participate in many multicultural activities. In early childhood classes, a good place to start is with the children's individual families. Children discover that there are different kinds of families: two-parent and one-parent families; nuclear and extended families; and even families with no parents, when children live with relatives. From there, specific customs within families can be noted and traced, perhaps, to cultural differences. Cooking ethnic foods is a favorite activity, and parents often volunteer to help. Pictures of native costumes and countries from which children have come provide a focus for discussion, and music, folk dances, and games can be introduced as well. Learning centers or bulletin boards that spotlight one particular culture can be developed, and relevant fiction and nonfiction books can be displayed.

To be effective, activities must extend well beyond studying the cultures represented by classmates. From that familiar base, teachers must present information about and activities concerning *other* groups as well, if children are, in fact, going to begin to expand their views of the world beyond their own families and neighborhoods. Teachers might provide information on Puerto Rico, read about famous Puerto Ricans, cook Puerto Rican foods, and present appropriate songs, stories, and dances. In a truly multicultural approach, teachers might next introduce Mexico *even if* there were no Mexican children in the class and draw children's attention to similarities and differences between the cultures. Alternatively, teachers might introduce Chinese cultures, not because there were Chinese children in the class but because there was a Chinese community in the same city. It would not, however, make sense to introduce next the study of, say, Scandinavia to a class of young Puerto Rican children unless some logical thread of common interest could be demonstrated. Later in the school year, after studying familiar or immediately relevant cultures, Scandinavia could be appropriate. By then, children would have a broader sense of the world geographically and culturally, so that fair-skinned children living in the far north would seem more real.

As teachers introduce different cultures, they would try to find unifying activities or themes to provide continuity. Cooking activities are always good, especially if they can demonstrate some commonality. Indochinese eat rice; so, too, do Hispanics and other groups; rice is a grain, and spaghetti and other pasta products are made from grains. Tortillas are a form of bread; children might make or taste Chinese dumplings, French bread, German brown bread, matzohs, or Indian chapatis. Uses for corn or beans in different cuisines can also be studied. In selecting foods to cook, teachers must remember how picky young children can be. Folk tales or children's games can also be unifying themes.

Teachers' own biases can easily creep into multicultural education, as can those of children's parents. Teachers must analyze their own feelings and not slant information to present stereotypes or cliches. They must also be prepared to defend the validity of multicultural study and to discuss in length their objectives for its use. Finally, teachers need to anticipate possible negative reactions children might have. For example, attitudes toward animals differ across cultures, and children may find some distressingly counter to Americans' fondness for pets. Patient explanations bring children to accept and generally appreciate cultural differences.

SUMMARY

The realities of recent immigration patterns mean that classes anywhere in the United States may include children who do not speak English. Dialect differences among children also present specific instructional challenges for teachers. Early childhood teachers who understand language development and who structure their classrooms to provide meaningful opportunities to use oral language help children expand their language skills to include mastery of a second language or SAE and understanding of the all-important language of school. Oral language mastery is the base upon which literacy skills grow—no matter whether children's mastery is of SAE, a dialect, or a language other than English. Strategies for helping nonstandard speakers master literacy skills are included throughout this book. These strategies should be part of every teacher's set of skills, no matter where he will eventually teach. They are based on principles of language development and curriculum planning that apply in any situation.

Also included throughout the book are strategies for integrating multicultural education into early childhood curricula. Multicultural education affirms individuals' differing backgrounds and opens all children to the awareness of differences and similarities among different ethnic groups. Children learn information about different groups and about the world and also learn to be more tolerant of differences within their own class environment. Children's literature is often a starting point for multicultural activities, and Appendix 1 includes many fiction and nonfiction books with multicultural themes.

REVIEW QUESTIONS

1. Be sure that you can define these terms:
   bilingual education
   Black English
   dialect
   multicultural education
   second language learner
2. Think about the responsibilities faced by teachers of immigrant children. What specific accommodations must teachers make to provide a sound emotional environment for young children whose families have fled civil wars and other political instability?

3. List as many ways as possible for early childhood teachers to provide second language learners with meaningful opportunities to use English in routine classroom interactions. How do these opportunities motivate mastery of English?
4. Visit several early childhood bilingual classes (daycare, kindergarten, and early primary grades). Observe different approaches to curriculum and language use. Contrast your observations.
5. Find several of the multicultural books listed in Appendix 1 and read them to young children. How do the children respond? Tape-record their discussions of the books and analyze their responses for accuracy of interpretation of the concepts presented in the book.
6. Read about a holiday that is unfamiliar to you, for example, Chinese New Year, Mexican Independence Day (16 September), or Passover. Find appropriate children's books and plan a unit of study that could be used in an early childhood class. Include cooking, music, art, and literature activities. If possible, try the unit in a classroom.
7. Correctness of children's oral production in early childhood classes is less important than their having a supportive environment in which to practice and test their second language or new oral registers. Errors, however, may alarm some people who do not understand the nature of language development. How would you explain the oral language errors young children make as they move toward mastery of SAE?

NOTES

1. West, B. E. (1983). The new arrivals from Southeast Asia: Getting to know them. *Childhood Education, 60,* 84–89.
2. West, *op. cit.*
3. Labov, W. (1970). *The study of nonstandard English.* Urbana, IL: National Council of Teachers of English.
4. Cullinan, E. B. (Ed.). (1974). *Black dialects and reading.* Urbana, IL: National Council of Teachers of English.
5. Fryburg, E. L. (1974). Black English: A descriptive guide for the teacher. In B. E. Cullinan (Ed.) *Black dialects and reading* (pp. 190–196). Urbana, IL: National Council of Teachers of English.
6. Garcia, E. (1980). Language switching in bilingual children: A national perspective. In E. Garcia & M. S. Vargas (Eds.) *The Mexican-American child: Language, cognitive and social development.* Tucson: University of Arizona Press.
7. Schmidt-Mackey, I. (1977). Language structures of the bilingual family. In W. F. Mackey, & T. Anderson (Eds.) *Bilingualism in early childhood* (pp. 132–146). Rowley, MA: Newbury House.
8. *Time Magazine, 126* (1), July 8, 1985. Growth of a nation, pp. 31–35; Final destination, pp. 36–39; For learning on ethnic pride, pp. 80–81.

9. El Paso Independent School District. (1984). *Bilingual Immersion Program Handbooks*. El Paso: El Paso ISD.

10. Genishi, C., & Dyson, A. H. (1984). *Language assessment in the early years*. Norwood, NJ: Ablex.

11. Cullinan, *op. cit.*

12. Edelsky, C. (1986). *Writing in a bilingual program: Habia una vez*. Norwood, NJ: Ablex.

5

Knowing and Applying Research on Literacy Development

T he rest of this book discusses the way children gain the basic foundation of literacy. While teacher behaviors will be presented, the major emphasis is on what children learn themselves and how teachers can encourage their students to refine their literacy skills. Today's children are surrounded by written communication, even if their own parents do not read or write much themselves. Children's need to communicate, their curiosity, and their skills for making sense of their world drive them to form and test hypotheses about literacy. By observing print in the environment, asking questions about it, and piecing together a basic understanding of how print functions, children gain considerable knowledge about literacy skills long before they encounter formal reading or writing instruction.

The key term here is *developmental learning*. Children seem to pursue information about literacy as a natural "next step" after learning oral language. Adults support the process of reading and writing with models and answers to children's questions. A brief look at the history of reading research and instruction during this century will place the developmental approach in perspective. The conclusion of the chapter describes how the research should be implemented.

TWO THEORIES

The history of reading instruction is a story of twos: two theoretical points of view, two approaches to instruction, and, recently, two distinct literacy behaviors brought together. The theories or points of view became most pronounced around 1925[1] and represented opposing attitudes about reading instruction that are still voiced today.[2] One theory maintained that children gain reading skills by repeated practice of sequential skills through lessons *carefully planned and structured by adults*. By 1925, complete basal reader series or instructional packages were widely used, and teachers had both manuals to follow and material to structure practice on a wide range of reading objectives. These basal reader series sequenced skills, introduced limited vocabulary in each book and featured silent and oral reading with skills work in workbooks or dittoed worksheets. The basal approach still dominates elementary classrooms because it is organized and easy to use.[3] The emphasis in this approach is on teaching skills.

The second theory maintained that the *search for meaning* dominates reading and that children should be taught with meaningful material.[4] Reading with understanding begins with the child's own knowledge base and is strengthened by using things that interest the child, that she is curious about, and that she already knows. As in oral language acquisition, children are curious about communication and seek meaning from literacy contexts. An "experience approach" was recommended in which children dictate stories for teacher transcription and read these for meaning. However, "[having] pupils use stories of their own composition based upon firsthand experiences as beginning reading material was, indeed, a radical departure [from traditional instructional approaches]. This practice was not widely accepted till later, but progress had been made in evolving the idea" (Smith, 1965, p. 94). The idea was that even beginning reading should be a *quest for meaning*.

TWO INSTRUCTIONAL APPROACHES

Two approaches to the teaching of reading have dominated the past century: the **sight-** or **whole-word approach** and **phonics** instruction. The sight-word approach starts with the visual representation of whole words so that children develop a "sight vocabulary" that enables them to read simple material almost from the beginning. Essentially, children memorize words from which they generalize letter-sound correspondences. Gradually, their skills for independent "word attack" increase and they can figure out unfamiliar words.

Phonics instruction has stressed the importance of children's learning letter-sound correspondences to "sound out" words as they begin to read. Although usually considered inappropriate, some phonics programs recommend that first graders learn sounds in isolation from words, so that they make automatic connections between letters and their sounds. Often, no sight words are introduced until most sounds have been mastered. The resulting problem is obvious: Many words in English do not neatly fall within common phonics rules and cannot readily be sounded out. Motivation can lag before children's usable storehouse of phonics rules is large enough to allow them to read interesting stories.

Some phonics programs do include some irregular sight words, while others have personified the sounds as distinct characters, used singing, introduced typing, or provided games for reinforcement.[5] Still others coded symbols to represent the letter-sound relationships. For example, i/t/a introduces a 44-character alphabet, and "Words in Color" uses colors to code vowels, consonants, and digraphs. With these, coded material is gradually removed as children make a transition to regular print. Research on coded symbol-sound systems has indicated some success, but use continues to be limited, most often because of the expense involved in special materials.

Both sight-word and phonics approaches emphasize commercial materials, which, used by the teacher who follows directions in a manual or guidebook, comprise the bulk of what children use to strengthen their reading.

TWO PROCESSES: WHICH COMES FIRST?

Writing and reading make up the final set of two. The relationship between writing and reading has recently drawn much attention from researchers, who stress that the two behaviors must be considered part of a total developmental continuum. Children learn first to communicate with gestures, then with oral language, and finally with print. Combining reading and writing instructionally in early childhood acknowledges this continuum and capitalizes on children's early explorations of literacy.

The integration of reading and writing, along with emphasis on listening and speaking skills, is sometimes referred to as the **whole language approach** to literacy acquisition. The idea stresses that all language processes are related and mutually reinforcing and builds on children's curiosity about communication systems and their need to make sense of the world around them. The approach recognizes that, by the time children enter school, many have gathered extensive data about print and that they are motivated to refine and extend new concepts. The premises of the whole language approach—that children learn much about literacy on their own and are motivated to master **literate behavior**—underlie the discussions in this book.

ALTERING VIEWS OF CHILDREN'S LEARNING: CURRENT RESEARCH

Researchers reevaluating the traditional view of the way children master literacy have focused on what children discover about language and how they develop and test language rules. To use the insights this research provides, we must remember children's innate interest in and inclination toward oral language. From infancy, they want to communicate; within their own time frames, they learn to use oral language, progressing toward mastery of the grammatical and semantic structures of their language community. Progress is marked by mistakes reflecting hypotheses about language use and attempts to refine initial, tentative rules about grammar. Children's intense intellectual efforts to learn to communicate verbally are part of the natural process of growing through the early childhood years. Literacy skills in normal children are developmental, driven by curiosity, and very similar to growth of oral language and listening skills. This concept of developmental growth is the core of all instructional implications that can be drawn from this work.

Research Studies and Methods

Common to most of the recent research is a technique that has been called *kidwatching*.[6] **Kidwatching** is observing children to see how they learn, especially in rich environments where they are encouraged to investigate objects and ideas. Researchers also study the actual products—scribbles, drawings, stories—children make during experimentations with print. Kidwatching requires re-

---

A YEAR OF KIDWATCHING: DAVID

David entered my combined first- and second-grade classroom at the beginning of my fifth year of teaching. I had had his older brother the previous year and knew and respected the family. The brother had been a model student, well behaved, motivated, very creative, and self-confident. David, the mother told me, was not the same and, in fact, was virtually opposite to his sibling except in their shared high intelligence and sense of belonging to a warm, supportive family. The first thing I noticed about David, besides his booming voice and wiry movements, was that many of the other children who had been in kindergarten with him were either afraid or in awe of David's outrageous behavior. David seemed to recognize the power he had and probably was determined to gain control of our classroom as soon as possible.

David and I battled too much the first few weeks of school for me to watch him extensively. He tried to terrorize the children through noise and aggression, and I fought back the dreaded words "Why can't you be like your brother?" The best way to keep him under control was to keep him close to me, and he became my shadow. David held my hand, David sat next to me, David even stayed in and ate lunch with me from time to time. Rather than resenting this attention, the other children seemed to realize that they were being protected. David especially liked to be near me during storytime so that he could see the pictures and print close up.

David refused to do much of the independent classroom work, so he stayed close by during all small-group instruction. My rationale was that he would learn through repeated exposure to the material and that he would not be on the loose to bother other children. As I finally was able to begin to watch this fascinating child, I noticed his intense interest in whatever I and the children said and did. Because the class had both first- and second-grade children, David was bombarded with instruction, but he followed along with all the lessons, contributed to story dictation, even began to volunteer answers to questions. The twinkle in his eye as I handed him a book to "look at" was heartening. He was clearly more interested in "real" reading instruction than in the readiness work I did with the children who had been in kindergarten with him.

spect for the intellectual efforts children bring to their self-motivated investigation of reading and writing. Researchers often have to infer or make educated guesses about the reasons a child performed a specific act, made a specific statement, or asked specific questions. By observing many children, often over long periods of time, researchers identify patterns of behavior that substantiate their inferences. Of course, confident teachers do this all the time. The case study summarizes a year of my own kidwatching.

Important Findings

Several important findings have emerged from current research. First, most pre-schoolers form general conceptualizations about the purpose and nature of

---

After about a month, David began to write notes for me. He "delivered" his first note by crumpling it into a ball and hurling it, baseball like, onto my desk. I can't remember what the note said, and I didn't keep that first effort. But I do remember being amazed at the clarity of what he wrote. David had used "invented spelling," a powerful behavior common to young children, and while the spelling was not correct, it did approximate the letter-sound correspondences of traditional English. Clearly, David *was* learning and was trying to show me his progress. I was impressed and vowed to watch his literacy behaviors more closely.

David obliged my interest by writing profusely. He continued to sit close to me through all reading and language arts instruction, participating when he wished and doing an increasing amount of independent seatwork, silent reading, and writing. Throughout the year, he loudly maintained that he couldn't read, but frequently he curled up in the library corner just looking at books. On the test at year's end, he scored considerably above grade level in reading.

My management of this child was untraditional and stemmed from a desire not to spend my time scolding and disciplining him. I still wish I had been able to incorporate him more successfully into the overall classroom activities but feel that he did gain in two ways. First, he learned to read and to write well. Secondly, he left first grade feeling good about himself as a written-language user, confident that he had academic skills that were as good as anyone else's. That success strengthened his self-concept enough that he seemed more willing to accommodate himself to the requirements of his second grade. (I left the school that year, sad that I would not be able to follow him further.)

David taught me a tremendous number of things, not the least of which was the value of looking very closely at the child's behaviors. He reinforced an idea that was already emerging in my mind—that the environment rather than direct instruction will often "teach" children literacy skills. He also shared his progression in invented spelling with me, almost as though *he* wanted to tutor me to be more interested in this common early childhood behavior. By watching David and by studying the work he did for me, I discovered new dimensions of children's learning strategies and did, in fact, alter my approaches to literacy instruction.

print. They realize that writing and drawing are different behaviors, that marks called "letters" are used to communicate information, and that certain principles underlie letter formation of letter-sound correspondences. Children gain substantial insight into literacy long before they themselves can read or write.

Secondly, children develop a way of **placeholding** meaning in their early writing and reading. Just as babbling and early speech had held the place of conventional speech, scribbles, letter-like shapes, random strings of letters, and early attempts at spelling placehold children's written messages until they have mastered conventional spelling. Children's oral renditions of stories represent reading placeholding. This behavior is reading-like in that children visually track the lines of print, turn pages appropriately, and tie their oral production closely to the story sense indicated by the pictures in the book.

The third finding is that the quantity and quality of **literacy events** to which children are exposed strongly influence their acquisition of literacy skills. Literacy events are planned or spontaneous situations in which children attend to some aspect of literacy or participate in some event that requires reading or writing. Initiated by adults or children, literacy events strengthen children's conceptualization of literate behaviors.[7] Figure 5.1 lists the kinds of activities that can be classified as literacy events.

The fourth "finding" is really a warning, one which has direct implications on curriculum: "Reading is not deciphering; writing is not copying; and progress in literacy does not come about through advances in deciphering and copying" (Ferreiro and Teberosky, 1982, p. 272). Deciphering is translating a graphic image to a verbal message without necessarily making sense of what was stated or implied—that is, reading without meaning. Copying is manually reproducing a graphic image, again with little or no regard for meaning. Progress in literacy is movement toward greater competency in using both reading and writing as a means to gain and convey meaningful information.

Because forms of copying and deciphering have been the core of much early childhood reading and language instruction for many years, it is logical to assume that at least some educators have trusted them to promote literacy. Too much emphasis on deciphering or sounding out encourages children to believe that reading involves no more than making the correct oral response for each printed word they see. Beginning handwriting instruction can produce incorrect ideas if it stresses accuracy in copying letter forms rather than writing for communication.

The final "finding" comes from analysis of past research on child language acquisition and growth. Children progress at their own pace through specific developmental sequences, as they form, test, and refine their ideas about the world. Testing ideas about producing and reading print is part of this process. Throughout their progress, children reach crucial periods called "zones of proximal development" (Vygotsky, 1962). These periods represent the "discrepancy between a child's actual mental age and the level he reaches in solving problems

Parents involve children in **literacy events** when they:

- ☐ suggest that the children write a letter to send to a grandparent
- ☐ encourage children to prepare and take their own grocery list to the supermarket
- ☐ ask children to find a specific book in the bookcase (children will use the cover as a whole to recognize the book)
- ☐ allow children to follow along in a recipe or instruction sheet as the parent does something
- ☐ point out what a street or traffic sign says
- ☐ ask a child to "read" a familiar sign or label.

Teachers encourage **literacy events** when they:

- ☐ ask child what a street sign says during a neighborhood walk
- ☐ provide appropriate printed material for children's learning centers, for example, travel brochures to consult in a travel agency center
- ☐ ask children to "read along" on a parent letter and add their own comments
- ☐ encourage children to pick out favorite books by "reading" the covers
- ☐ ask children to read their beginning writing efforts and discuss the contents enthusiastically
- ☐ listen to children retelling stories that have been read in class.

Children initiate **literacy events** when they:

- ☐ ask what a sign or label says
- ☐ point out that a word "begins like my name"
- ☐ ask an adult to "read" a scribbled message
- ☐ ask an adult to transcribe a story on a painting or drawing
- ☐ scribble within the lines on junk mail or other forms as a kind of "writing"
- ☐ experiment with reading or writing behaviors and ask for confirmation of what they are doing.

FIGURE 5.1
Examples of literacy events.

with assistance." Vygotsky, who proposed this concept, stated, *"What the child can do in cooperation today, he can do alone tomorrow"* (pp. 103–104, italics added). Children's questions attest to their search for "cooperation" today so that they can "solve problems alone" tomorrow.

We can think of the zone of proximal development as the **appropriate teaching point.** In practical terms, the zone of proximal development means that teachers must be sensitive to what children have mastered and must provide opportunities to help children build upon and expand that mastery. This concept *does not mean* that children should constantly be given work that is just a bit too hard for them; instead, it encourages teachers to recognize each child's inherent motivation and to provide appropriate, challenging opportunities for individuals to use their emerging literacy skills.

Liberation to Teach

These research findings should strike a chord of liberation in the hearts and minds of creative, caring teachers. Accepting that most children are interested in literacy and have formed ideas about reading and writing prior to school entry, teachers need not lock themselves and their students into predetermined curricula that may be appropriate for only a few children in each class. Instead, teachers can build on children's inclination to form hypotheses about literacy behaviors, test them through their own experimentations, and use these ideas as the base for refining reading and writing skills. Children realize a lot about the way written language functions, but the amount will vary from child to child. Teachers must assess how much each child knows and teach to that knowledge base, if instruction is to be meaningful. Kidwatching helps here. Teachers need to trust that the real impetus for literacy learning lies in children's interests in and needs to communicate in an "adult" fashion; impetus does not lie in methodological considerations like basal reader series, workbooks, or ditto masters. Early childhood teachers who respond to children's needs and interests and help them test and refine their ideas about literacy contribute to children's natural progression in positive, supportive ways.

IMPLEMENTING THE RESEARCH

Much of the recent research has looked at literacy development within home environments in which parents share reading and writing with children, provide reading and writing materials, and encourage their children's emerging skills. Children learning about literacy by interacting with their environment are often said to be learning in a "natural" way. See Appendix 2 for a discussion of the ways parents can support young children's literacy growth. Early childhood classrooms can approximate the ideal supportive home environment when teachers structure a literate environment in which experiences with language, reading, and writing activities are offered throughout the day, not just at times of formal instruction. Many theorists use the term *whole language* for the instructional approach that stimulates a good home literate environment and builds on children's knowledge of communication skills. Creating a literate environment is a rewarding task for early childhood teachers, one that takes thoughtfulness and commitment to supporting children's individual progress toward literacy. Consider the following essay, which an undergraduate wrote about a hypothetical literate kindergarten environment as part of a final exam.[8]

AN ESSAY

Once upon a time, there was a brand new teacher for the kindergarten. He had just finished school and was ready to try some new ideas about working with children. His classroom had two neatly done bulletin boards up on the wall. One was entitled "All Words Are Made of . . ." and had letters with velcro backs on a felt board so that children could spell words on the board. The other board was "Numbers Are . . ." In the play area, cartons containing specific items were stacked and labeled in the corner. As far as labeling goes, the objects in the room were all labeled. Labels with students' names were even neatly taped to the desks. The reading area was a circle. An easel stood next to the teacher's chair for the big books and other instructional charts the teacher had prepared. Plus, there were three shelves of books for the students to enjoy by themselves or with the teacher. Everything in the classroom could motivate the children to tell stories, from the blocks in the play area to the picture books in the class library. . . .

This new teacher was aware that children know that the spoken word is a useful form of communication and that children need to know writing and reading are important extensions of communications. . . . The novice dreams of the wonderful involvement in the reading group. He will begin with the books he has carefully selected for his classroom—wordless picture books, picture books, caption books, and big books, all of which can stimulate writing. . . .

The teacher is prepared to take children's dictation, to help them write their own books, and to have each child begin a "word bank" of personal sight words. When children dictate a story, the teacher will write it down on a big tablet. The teacher will use the children's investigative abilities by asking, "I don't know how to spell that word, do you think you can find it in your word bank for me?" After the story has been written, the students will color pictures to illustrate it. All of this writing is done so the children will realize the importance of the written words. . . . After each art project, the students will be encouraged to write a message. Even if the story doesn't look like traditional script, it will be ok, and the children will be asked to read what they have written.

Thinking back to his field experiences, this teacher remembered that children seemed to enjoy learning if it was a game. He determined to let the children play with language as much as possible so that they would explore and find out about reading and writing themselves. He also remembered how valuable talk was to young children and decided to encourage peer teaching and conversations as much as possible. He wanted his classroom to be full of language—and not just his own.

All of a sudden, the first bell of the first day of his first class rang. Brought back to the real world by the loud noise, the new teacher opened the door and greeted his 15 new students with a smile and "Good morning."

Setting Up a Literate Environment: Physical Concerns

Teachers use their theories of the way children learn to make decisions about how their classrooms are structured. The student quoted above clearly believes

Permanent—functional

    Colors
    Numbers
    Days of Week
    Months of the Year
    Alphabet (at eye level)
    Calendar

Permanent—informal (to be changed as appropriate)

    Classroom Rules
    Children's Birthdays
    Holidays
    "Hooray! I Lost a Tooth" (on which children record each tooth they lose)
    Calendar
    "Messages" to Parents
    Language Experience Stories
    Names of Centers
        Number of children allowed
        Rules/procedures for behavior in centers
        Procedures for using equipment, if appropriate

Topical

    "Count Down to Vacation" (on which they cross out school days)
    Our Favorite Books
    Our Favorite Authors

FIGURE 5.2
Charts and labels for the literate environment. Labels and charts become part of the environmental print and gradually enter children's sight vocabularies for reading and writing. All charts should be displayed where children can easily see them, as close to eye level as possible. All writing should be clear and dark, large enough for children to read easily.

that young children are curious about literacy and need continuing encounters with print to reinforce the realization that written language is meaningful. He would agree with Don Holdaway, who recommends making the classroom a "total environment alive with print, displaying all its functions, from things as simple as signs and labels right through to literature" (1979, p. 71).

    Teachers usually want their classrooms to be attractive, cheerful places; however, creating a literate environment takes much more than commercial classroom decorations, which are often pictorial and present little, if any, writing. A classroom "alive with print" is full of words, many of which are charts and lists of words and phrases. (See Figure 5.2 for suggestions.) Signs and

Charts and graphs

> Foot, Hand Sizes
> Heights and Weights
> People in Our Families
> Favorite Foods
> Favorite Colors
> Pets in Our Homes

Instructional (depending on grade)

> Seasonal or Topical Words for Use in Creative Writing
> > Fall, winter, spring, summer words
> > Holiday words
> > Spooky words
> Synonyms
> Antonyms
> Vocabulary Lists for Units of Study
> Editing Marks (for revising children's writing)
> Description of Good Writing
> Comprehension Strategies

Labels

> Furniture
> Centers
> Bulletin Boards
> Cubbies
> Traffic Signs (for example, SLOW to control traffic flow near cubbies)

FIGURE 5.2
continued

labels, as well as a large calendar, are also essential. These items represent classroom environmental print, and children soon recognize the words by sight.

Along with books, a literate environment has magazines, junk mail, brochures, and pamphlets for browsing, "reading," and investigating the many ways in which print can be organized visually. Pencils, crayons, and pens along with plastic, cloth, sandpaper, and wooden letters allow children to explore letter and word formation and try out beginning spelling skills.

Absolutely essential, even in preschool, is a library with many books within easy reach, comfortable chairs for sitting, and rugs and pillows for sprawling. The library should have a prominent place in the classroom and be attractive and inviting. The books need not all be new, crisp-backed, hard-covered copies of children's classics; paperbacks are fine, even those that have been ripped apart, laminated, and rebound, or those held together with staples and tape. Favorite books should be available at all times; others may be changed periodically. Appendix 1 suggests a basic classroom library. The "big books" mentioned in the student's essay are teacher-made versions of children's favorites. (See Chapters 11 and 12.)

Teachers in a literate environment will, of course, read to children, and they should also provide listening stations or centers where children can listen to a tape and follow along in a storybook. Commercial book-and-tape sets are available, and teachers can make their own tapes of children's favorites. Children benefit from the repetition of a read-along story, whether they are merely gaining familiarity with book handling or building their sight-word vocabularies. A truly literate environment welcomes children's writing as equal to teachers' or commercial print and affirms children's emerging sense of themselves as users of written language. Writing may be children's scribbles, letter-like forms, or notes and stories written in invented spelling. Children's art work should also be displayed, and children should be encouraged to write or dictate some annotation about their pictures.

The overall purpose of abundant print is to reinforce children's understanding that print communicates meaning. By demonstrating that reading and writing are purposeful tasks and by allowing children to engage in these tasks at their own rates, teachers help children refine and strengthen their emerging literacy skills.

Literate Environment: Interpersonal Components

No matter how full of books and print their environment, young learners need contact with other literacy users. In her discussion of literate home environments, one researcher (Leichter, 1984) stated that "the child's literacy opportunities are conditioned by moment-to-moment interpersonal interaction with parents, siblings, and others in the household with respect to informal correction, explanations, and other feedback for the child's experiments with literacy" (p. 40). As children ask questions, make statements, and test hunches, those around them respond with correction, elaboration, assistance, and encouragement directed specifically toward clarification of concepts about reading and writing. This behavior within a family continues the scaffolding or feedback provided as children begin to use oral language.

Achieving similar interpersonal interaction with children in early childhood classes is in no way easy; there are so many children and so much to do. As stated before, teachers rarely just converse with children; instead they ask questions and lecture. To create a literate environment, teachers must find time to talk about literacy with children. By talking about reading and writing behaviors and about printed material, children expand their vocabularies to include words such as *read, write, word, story,* and so forth, the school-related terminology and concepts needed, if they are to act on their belief that they can learn to read and write. Additionally, these experiences allow young learners to "gain ownership of strategies of [reading] comprehension and composition similar to those they have used in oral language, making allowances for the different constraints of written language forms and functions. They become more intuitively aware of the transactions among the reader, the writer, and the written text" (Goodman, 1984, p. 103).

Good early childhood teaching methods build on what children know. Teachers recognize that a "highly structured instructional system that focuses on mastery of one rule of skill before another loses sight of the complexity of learning written language. It oversimplifies what children really do learn and focuses some insecure children on insignificant and often erroneous principles about learning" (Goodman, 1984, p. 109). To illustrate, consider two first graders, the first a girl mentioned by Harste, Woodward, and Burke (1984, pp. 183, 184). A written-language user since age 3, she was to make a Thanksgiving "book" by copying and illustrating "When they got to America they found corn and saw unfriendly Indians." The stated objective of such a task was to use "writing" (actually copying) to support reading by having children attend to print. The child perceived the objective as neat handwriting: "Because of the lined school paper [she] tried to be extra careful . . . concentrating on letter forms she got worse rather than better [and produced] a carefully done maze of crowded letters and words." At home, the same day, she drew a snowman in a pilgrim's hat and wrote: "THE POGROMS HOD A LONG WOTH AND BOLT SNOW MON AND WON WAS A POGRAM MAN SNOW MON THEE END." [The pilgrims had a long winter and built snowmen and one was a pilgrim snowman. The end.]

The child's writing a story at home affirmed that she had things to write about and the skills needed to express herself. Had her teacher wanted to structure the assignment to take full advantage of the first graders' emerging literacy skills, she would have invited the children to write an original sentence or two for their Thanksgiving books. This would have been a structured literacy event, in that the teacher and children could have discussed what they might write and draw and how the book might be bound together at completion. As children wrote and drew, the teacher could have circulated among them for individual conferences. She might have rewritten the children's sentences in conventional spelling or transcribed dictation from children who did not choose to write themselves. When children had finished, they might have been asked to read their stories and could have shown drawings to each other for yet another valuable sharing of literacy efforts. These were the very behaviors of another first-grade teacher, one of whose students wrote: "The May Flower salud and salud in to thay land it. sum indyns hulpt the pelgrems the men owse sher food. they pray to god they Love itsh uchu" [The Mayflower sailed and sailed until they landed. Some Indians helped the Pilgrims. The men always shared food. They pray to God. They love each other.] This writer's first language was

Spanish, and he was only beginning to communicate fluently in English. His teacher had demonstrated that she valued her students' ideas, and they wrote confidently.

Structuring Literacy Events

Teachers can strengthen the interpersonal component of their early childhood literacy environment through three key behaviors: **integration, exploitation,** and **demonstration.**

Integration refers to an attitude and a pattern of classroom organization. Attitudinally, it means that teachers view language learning as the core of the curriculum from which other content areas are enriched. Literacy and oral language learning work together as a "whole language" approach. Traditional early childhood methods have underestimated children's emerging literacy skills.

Organizationally, integration means that teachers tie the curriculum together, with the mastery of reading and writing skills as a unifying thread. Planned literacy events flow easily from an integrated curriculum, and children exercise their emerging skills in purposeful activities for mastery of content information. Essentially, children try out the literacy behaviors they will need for on-going success in all school subjects. The pilgrim stories demonstrate integration with social studies work; science units can provide similar opportunities. Work on dinosaurs, for example, should extend beyond picture cards, teacher-led discussions, and dittoed worksheets to include browsing through reference books, making experience charts, and writing individual compositions about drawings and paintings.

Exploitation refers to teachers' constant watchfulness for opportunities to use reading and writing, to talk about literacy, and to encourage children to exercise their own skills. Often it may seem efficient to ignore these moments and simply give children specific information, incomplete answers, or alternative assignments. Of course, no teacher can be expected to be as attentive and responsive as an individual parent interacting with one curious child; but sadly, many valuable, teachable moments are lost because of time constraints and the demands of large classes.

In the science unit mentioned above, a teacher would use exploitation by telling children, "Look in the book to see how to draw a stegosaurus. Why don't you write a sentence or two under your picture; maybe tell what dinosaurs used to eat. Look at how long the name *Tyrannosaurus rex* is; it takes a long time to say it and lots of letters to write it. Did you notice how many dinosaur names end in *-saurus*? Let's see if we can find out what that means. Ask a friend to help you look up how big a brontosaurus actually was. . . ." Some of these interactions require the teacher's attention, others are merely passing comments to arouse thinking, and still others suggest that the children themselves exercise their emerging skills. All would help children grow in independence, confidence, and ability to use reading and writing for self-directed information gathering and learning.

Demonstrations are experiences that give children insight into the way literacy functions and how they themselves must function as literate people.[9] Children essentially "demonstrate" to themselves how reading and writing are done, how print is organized, and how they must organize their own behaviors to gain information from print. Literacy events provide demonstrations for young learners, but even more is needed. Instruction and reinforcement activities must allow children to practice, experiment, test, and refine skills. Children must solve linguistic problems and work through the puzzle of how literacy functions. Through mere copying, matching, coloring, or circling words and filling in workbook pages, children do not stretch the boundaries of what they know and refine their skills. Instead, such activities can ultimately become boring and confusing.

MAKING THE LITERATE ENVIRONMENT WORK: PRESCHOOL AND KINDERGARTEN

A classroom alive with print and a teacher committed to children's natural acquisition of literacy skills—these are a start. Making a positive, supportive environment work for young children takes skill, planning, and willingness to move beyond traditional curricular approaches. Making it work also takes patience, for children will progress at individual speeds and with personal needs. Teachers in preschool centers often miss opportunities to integrate, demonstrate, or exploit opportunities for literacy events. Highlights of an ordinary day in a preschool follow and are accompanied by suggestions for capitalizing on children's emerging literacy.

Arrival. When children arrive, they sign in in the attendance book and put their belongings in a cubbyhole marked with their own names. Children are encouraged to select a book for browsing while waiting for circle time.

Circle time. The teacher displays a chart containing the pledge to the flag and points to each word as children recite; a teacher-made calendar is also displayed, and words for the month and day of the week, yesterday and tomorrow are discussed. A chart tablet is again used for visual reinforcement as children learn a new song. The teacher knows that the children cannot read these texts but wants them to become familiar with print directionality and sight words and with the idea of having a visual equivalent to what they say.

Center time. Centers are labeled with signs, occupancy quotas, and rules. The class includes a literacy center where the teacher helps children write a caption book entitled "A Book About Me." The top of the first page reads "This is a picture of me . . ."; at the bottom is written, "My name is ____." The teacher reads each page to the children and shows them where to write and draw. Children in the art center are encouraged to write on their work or at least to dictate a sentence to be transcribed. The library center is used for quiet browsing and listening to tapes of stories. The housekeeping center includes ample writing materials so that children can take phone messages, write letters, pay bills, and make shopping lists. An assistant teacher and several children make pudding for a snack. The teacher begins asking children to "read" the package label, which they do as "pudding," "Jello," and "chocolate." They follow a recipe, written on a chart tablet, that uses words, pictures of cups and measuring spoons, and an actual pudding package; it displays a "What-you-need" and "What-you-do" format familiar to the children.

Free Time. Browsing through books, playing with junk mail, working in the literacy center (for example, with a typewriter) are all encouraged during free time. Children may request transcription of stories developed as part of dramatic or block play or art work.

Storytime. Storytime includes a new story and an old, favorite, predictable book that has been rewritten as a big book. The teacher points to the words in the big book, and children read along with parts they know by heart. The teacher calls on individuals to read specific parts, and the children read with confidence, sometimes not reading the text exactly but always keeping to the main ideas. During the new story, the teacher asks for responses to simple questions and discusses the book after reading.

Letters Home. Mimeographed letters about a trip are to be sent home, but children are given time to "write" their own messages at the bottom of the letter. Parents, accustomed to this process, will spend a few minutes reading the whole letter with their children and discussing plans for the outing.

Throughout the day in this preschool, children see print being used and even participate in producing written messages. Their efforts are respected and welcomed, and they begin to get the feel of using reading and writing purposefully. These strategies could be used as effectively in kindergarten classrooms.

MAKING IT WORK: EARLY PRIMARY

Early primary classes should also offer many, varied literacy events. Reading, writing, and talking are encouraged throughout the entire day and supplement the direct instruction through which children refine what they know and are introduced to new, useful skills. What follows is an overview of literacy events and instruction during an ordinary day in an early primary class, which, for the sake of illustration, is a second grade. The classroom has library, media, and literacy centers and is attractively decorated with commercial and teacher-made charts. The library center has many books and is decorated with children's "reviews" of favorites. The media center also has charts about the books recorded on tape and has language arts games with recorded instructions. Also stored in the media center is the class computer, which is used for word processing as well as for its educational software. Hung on the wall of the literacy center are strips of vocabulary words that the children have brainstormed—fall words, scary words, words that mean run, descriptive words, and so forth. Samples of children's writing are also displayed, as are charts of punctuation, grammar rules, and story ideas. A container holds folders for each child's writing. Other areas of the room also are full of print; for example, signs in the science area tell about the classroom pets and latest experiments, and maps and charts adorn the social studies bulletin board. A large language experience tablet is also visible. Much of the work around the room has stories attached, and there is a record of children's cooking experiences as well. Within this literate environment, literacy events are an integral part of the daily routine. Specific techniques mentioned in this description will be discussed in detail in the following chapters.

Children arrive. The children hang up their coats and take their places at their desks, talking softly. The teacher completes clerical tasks, including collecting money for the children's book club. She tries to comment on each child's choice ("Remember when I read that story to you; I'm glad you are buying it") to reinforce their enthusiasm for independent reading. The first activity will be a morning discussion and writing. On the board is the beginning of a journal entry "Today is Wednesday, October 30. We have an assembly this afternoon." Volunteers read each sentence, and the teacher asks for guesses about the assembly. After hearing a few, she tells the children that they have 10 minutes to write in their journals. Some children bend over their work immediately; others seem to be planning mentally; some begin by drawing.

Reading Instruction and Independent Work. After 10 minutes, the teacher calls the class to attention and announces which reading group will meet with her first. Other groups of children are referred to alternate independent work. Two groups have math review worksheets, which they will follow with independent self-selected reading. Three children are reminded that it is their turn to work on the computer. They will finish editing stories they have written and saved on disk; they know that they will have extra time to finish their math or reading later. Another group is assigned silent reading and questions to prepare before meeting with the teacher. All children understand that they can browse through books, draw, or write when they have finished their work.

The teacher begins the first reading group with a few questions. These are weak readers who need extensive support to maintain progress. Next, they look at a language experience chart dictated at their last meeting, as she points out and questions them about punctuation. This "skill lesson" with student-generated material is followed by discussion of the questions the students prepared in writing the preceding day. The questions target critical reading skills as well as main ideas and details. The children read the questions, suggest answers, and then, with teacher guidance, go back to find the answers in their stories. Finding the answers reinforces the concept that reading should be meaningful and models the processes needed for higher levels of reading. Next, the teacher says, "Let's read the story for fun. Who wants to start?" The teacher asks a few questions during the reading but emphasizes reading for fun. She tolerates misreadings when children seem to understand the text and lets children figure out unfamiliar words on their own, but provides words when children are floundering. The children seem not to notice her soft-voiced prompts because they are working so hard to sustain meaning. They clearly enjoy reading. When they finish, each child then is given a math assignment and sent off to work independently.

After working with another group, the teacher circulates among those children finishing up their work and working on independent activities. Those who need help receive it individually, and she engages others in quiet personal conversations.

Transition.   After 1 1/2 hours of work, the children take a brief break and have a snack. After the snack, it is time for in-class music. The children cluster around the teacher, who sits next to a chart holder with *Our Big Book of Songs*. She opens the book to a Halloween song, which the children sing enthusiastically. The next page has the lyrics of "Over the River and Through the Woods" written on it in large block printing. She asks who knows the song, and a few hands are raised. She tells them that this is an old song and asks for volunteers to read the words. The words "the horse knows the way to carry the sleigh" confuse some children and generate a brief discussion. Only after reading the lyrics is the recorded melody played for singing.

Checking Homework.   After music, the children get out their homework notebooks. The assignment had been to write a descriptive paragraph. Several children read their work for group comment, and the class is then given about five minutes to look over their papers before turning them in.

Composition.   Immediately after checking homework, the teacher presents a brief language arts lesson on using quotation marks. She has prepared an overhead transparency of a brief story with unpunctuated dialogue. She reads the story aloud to emphasize the dialogue. After explaining the rules for quotation marks, she has the children read the story silently and suggest where to punctuate it. The children then receive a ditto of a similar unpunctuated story, which the teacher also reads with appropriate emphasis to demonstrate where dialogue occurs. The children must finish this skill exercise by filling in needed punctuation before turning to independent work in their composition notebooks or to revising previous efforts. One child takes her place at the computer and loads the story she has been editing. She has a "hard" copy of the story on which she has indicated changes she wants to make. The teacher meets quietly with a small group of children, who have prepared work to discuss with each other. After that, she calls several children to her desk for individual conferences about their writing.

Assembly. The normal routine is interrupted by the assembly, a Halloween play presented by a local theater troupe. When the children return, their energy is channeled into drawing pictures of the presentation as thank-you notes to be sent to the actors.

Reading Time. Near the close of the day, the children gather around the teacher for a story time. Today's choice is a Halloween book, and the teacher presents it by title, author, and illustrator. She states that the illustrations merit extra attention because they are especially spooky in places. As she reads, she asks questions about the plot development, use of language, and effectiveness of the illustrations. In addition to encouraging enjoyment, she is modeling reading skills.

Homework and dismissal. Another descriptive paragraph is assigned for homework, with the special directive that the work should be related to Halloween in some way. The teacher reviews the scary words that had been brainstormed previously and asks for some suggestions about scary plots. There are 10 minutes before dismissal, but the extra time is usually allowed for language arts work. After stating that "synonyms are words that mean nearly the same," she says, "Who can give me a synonym for cold?" She calls on one child who raised his hand; and when he says, "Icy," he is allowed to get his coat. The children look forward to this kind of "drill" and dismissal is accomplished without the tussles and arguments so common with young children.

  In both classes, children use all their language skills and instruction clearly demonstrates a whole language approach to literacy acquisition.

SUMMARY

Recent research has supported some old ideas about how young children learn and has affirmed what many parents and early childhood teachers have long known: An environment rich in print and opportunities to use print motivate children to experiment with literacy. Children perceive reading and writing as new ways to communicate, different from oral language and definitely worth exploring. They observe environmental print, take advantage of literacy events, and play at reading and writing. They get the feel of literacy as part of their natural development. Preschool caregivers and early childhood teachers can play important roles in children's acquisition of beginning literacy. Classrooms must be structured to allow children to explore literate behaviors, to play at writing and reading, those two very grown-up behaviors. Teachers must share literacy with children, by reading to them, letting them see adults read and write, and by using reading and writing as part of daily routines. By allowing children these explorations, teachers are not "teaching" reading and writing but are allowing children to use their whole set of language skills to make discoveries that will help them refine their skills and take full advantage of later instruction.

REVIEW QUESTIONS

1. Be sure that you can define each of these terms:
   appropriate teaching point
   demonstration
   exploitation
   integration
   kidwatching
   literacy events
   literate environment
   phonics
   placeholding (you need to expand your definition to include literacy
     behaviors)
   sight words
   whole language approach
2. Develop a detailed definition of *kidwatching.* List the behaviors you think an adult should have to be a genuine kidwatcher. After you have done so, compare your definition and list with those of a peer. Revise your ideas as needed.
3. Read the quotation from Ferreiro and Teberosky on p. 72 again, and restate their ideas in your own words. Suggest instructional implications of this idea.
4. Make a list of questions you would ask the beginning teacher whose essay is included on p. 75. You can develop them from the point of view of a parent in his class or a co-teacher. Try to imagine how *he* would answer your questions.
5. Make a list of all the opportunities you can think of to integrate, exploit, and demonstrate literacy in both the home and the school environments.
6. Visit an early childhood class. Observe and interview the teachers; determine whether they base their decisions on kidwatching. If they do not, what criteria are they using? How well do these criteria work?
7. What kinds of charts and environmental print do you see in the early childhood class? What suggestions would you make to improve them?
8. Criticize the classroom's library areas and writing centers. Are they inviting? Do they have enough supplies? Do children use them?

9. What do the teachers in each classroom do to help children refine their literacy skills? What more could they do? List behaviors you would like to use yourself.

NOTES

1. Smith, N. B. (1965). *American reading instruction.* Newark, DE: International Reading Association.
2. Smith, F. (1979). Conflicting approaches to reading research and instruction. In L. B. Resnick & P. A. Weaver (Eds.) *Theory and practice of early reading, Vol. 2* (pp. 31–43). Hillsdale, NJ: Lawrence Erlbaum.
3. Durkin, D. (1984). Is there a match between what elementary teachers do and what basal manuals recommend? *The Reading Teacher, 37,* 734–745.
4. Smith, N. B., *op. cit.*
5. Aukermann, R. C. (1984). *Approaches to beginning reading* (2nd ed.). New York: John Wiley & Sons.
6. Goodman, Y. M. (1985). Kidwatching: Observing children in the classroom. In A. Jaggar & M. Smith-Burke (Eds.) *Observing the language learner* (pp. 9–17). Newark, DE: International Reading Association.
7. Harste, J., Woodward, V. A., & Burke, C. L. (1984). *Language stories and literacy lessons.* Portmouth, NH: Heinemann Educational Books.
8. Ward, R. (1985). Final exam, ECED 3455. Excerpted and used by permission.
9. Harste, Woodward, & Burke, *op. cit.*

6

Handwriting: A Tool for Communication

Very young children notice print in the environment and observe people around them writing. Curious about what they see, they attempt to understand print by experimenting with writing tools and the whole process of making marks on paper. They see writing as a social activity and want to participate. Marcia Baghban (1984) kept a three-year, comprehensive diary of her daughter Giti's oral language, reading, and writing development. Giti observed her parents writing but was not specifically taught to write herself. Baghban's record of Giti's writing growth is summarized here to illustrate this aspect of child development.

Giti Baghban saw her parents write frequently in their professional roles (her mother as a graduate student, her father as a professor) and as part of routine household tasks. Curious about their activities, Giti "made a connection between the movement of the pen and the traces on paper and [once] she was assured that these effects could be repeated, she fell in love with the production . . . she was determined to write" (pp. 89–90). By 17 months, she began to scribble on sheets of paper, and by 19 months, she began to control the amount of print on each page. She progressed to dots, circles, and wavy lines. At 21 months, she discovered 4th class mail and began to write on whatever her parents gave her. By 23 months, she would write for 10 minutes; by 24 months, she babbled over her work as if reading a story. Soon she made an important realization. "The day she looked at the *KMart* logo on a card, pointing to the *m* and saying, 'Onalds,' she attempted *m* in her writing. After completing a row of peaks, she began another row and said 'Marce,' associating *m* with [her mother's first] name as well" (pp. 52, 54). Having received a puzzle with her name for her second birthday, Giti soon began to practice *G*'s in isolation.

Dictation began at 27 months. Giti asked her parents to write names of family members and favorite places, which she studied carefully. She also began to spell her name orally—*iti*—and to singsong *baba*, probably in response to the frequent requests for spelling of her name and the family name. Giti also continued to write, especially on junk mail and catalogues, "always on the side that had lines which needed to be completed. Rather than writing on the written language, she started to aim for the spaces between the lines for her own writing" (p. 60). By 29 months, her dictation sessions could last 30 minutes and were followed by her intoning and practicing the words herself. G seemed to be her favorite letter, and she frequently wrote *Giti* and *Grandma*. She also liked to write *McDonalds*. At 30 months, she approximated her name independently.

Giti's letter forms became more sprawled and looser, closer to drawing. She began to say "I draw" at 31 months and could distinguish her drawings from her writings by 32 months. She began to play school (where the subject was writing) but was beginning to take more interest in others outside of the home. At home, she wrote letters and put them in envelopes, which she "mailed" by taping them to her door. She could fill in forms neatly, sticking to the allowed spaces. Her writing ran from right to left, top to bottom across a page until her 34th month, when her orientation became left to right. At that point, she also learned to underline.

Giti's writing looked like scribbling but represented genuine attempts to communicate through print. Her parents and others supported her efforts and talked to her during and about her writing. Was Giti Baghban advanced, gifted, precocious? Not necessarily. Research has indicated that given a paper and pencil, average children will scribble spontaneously by 18 months—and will do so earlier if given some demonstration (as Giti was) of how to write. Emilia Ferreiro and Ana Teberosky (1982) observed lower-class children in Mexico City progressing through an ordered developmental sequence in their awareness and use of print. Lacking pencils and pens, they wrote with pieces of brick and sticks.

Just as mastery of oral language seems internally motivated and inherently motivating to young children, literacy skills seem to hold an intrinsic fascination. They explore their environment to discover how this alternate communication system functions and progress from random scribbling to "invention" of letter forms and close approximations of the graphic images they have observed.[1] Their efforts are **placeholders of meaning** until they master conventional letter formation.

WHAT CHILDREN DISCOVER ABOUT PRINT PRODUCTION

Giti Baghban had books around her, her own and her parents'.[1] Not all children are so fortunate; indeed, one researcher reminds us of "middle-class homes where print is noticeably absent and of working class homes littered with papers and books."[2] Still, examples of written communication literally bombard children. This kind of writing has been called "environmental print," and it teases young children, even those who do not have books, into wondering how writing functions and what purpose it serves. From encounters with environmental print, books, and other examples of writing, most young children realize the social interaction and communicative nature of print and form ideas about how writing works. Marie Clay (1976) has classified the realizations children make about print into several distinct, observable principles.

Intentionality

Children first realize that just as gestures, babbling, and beginning speech were placeholders for communication, these mysterious squiggly marks are intentional placeholders of some other kind of meaning. Understanding **intentionality** of written language is the first step, an important foundation, in children's ultimate understanding of literacy.

Unaware of the mechanics of reading (including letter-sound correspondences), children try to make sense of graphic images around them.[3] Think about examples of environmental print that children see in their homes, in their own neighborhoods, and in their communities as a whole. Most children can read at least some product labels and signs such as KMart, McDonalds, and Burger King. Many can read Krogers, Safeway, or some other supermarket name, even if they identify the sign simply as *Supermarket* or *Food Store*. Children may be attending to the entire environment (parking lot, location, etc.) rather than merely to the sign; but they consider themselves to be reading. Next, think back to the previous chapter. The need for labels and other examples of environmental print should be even more obvious now.

We can see other examples of children's understanding of intentionality as they explain their drawings. Often children will point to one mass of scribbles as a picture and to another mass as the "name of the picture." Some will use only pens and pencils for writing and crayons or markers for drawing. First efforts at "letters" to relatives and friends also seem identical to drawings, except to their young writers. Gradually, the "writing" scribbles approximate real letters.

The word that carries the most meaning—and does so intentionally—is the child's name. Often a child begins to "sign" drawings long before he has moved beyond scribbling. There is some evidence that the shape of the first letter of a child's name (circular, linear) will influence the kinds of letters he first produces. Figure 6.1 shows a "sign-in sheet" for 3-, 4-, and 5-year-olds at a daycare center. As part of the routine, these children wrote their names daily when they arrived at their center.

Recurring Principle

From observation of environmental print, children learn that writing is achieved by using relatively few strokes of the pen or pencil and that these strokes are

SIGN IN/SIGN OUT

Child's Name	Parent's Signature	Time In	Time Out	
Valerie				↓*VALERIE*
LEAH				L ₹ A H
Christine				Ch ꜰ i s₊ i ꔵ ᴇ
Victor				VIC₊OR
Lucas				L U.CA ꜱ
Elizabeth				E l i Z a ᑲ6Eʰ
Virginia				V i ꜰC i h i a
Jennifer				⊳∿ ꜱⵔ D O b꒐
michael				MI< hll ꜱ
Anita				A N I ₊ A
uzo				(₄) ꓔ O
Christal				CᴏD ꜰ⌐l
Nicholas				⊖ Lᴊ I ∧
Von				ꝑᴀ
Jeremy				

FIGURE 6.1
Each morning as they arrived at their daycare center, 3-, 4-, and 5-year-old children signed in. This was part of their daily routine. Notice the variety in signatures. (From LBJ Day Care Center, El Paso, TX. Used with permission.)

used over and over to accomplish all written communication. This is aptly named the **recurring principle.** These strokes can be classified as vertical, horizontal, diagonal, curved, and open or closed circles, often called "circles and sticks."

Generative Principle

In order to vary what they write, children also must discover the **generative principle,** that is, that writing is produced by relatively few letter elements used in infinitely varied ways. The generative principle motivates practice: Children produce long strings of letters and pseudo-letters that actually begin to look like conventional writing. Gradually, they apply the principle to words and create a distinct pattern of marks for one word and different patterns for other words until they have "written" a list, letter, or story, which they can "read" quite successfully. This writing does not reflect letter-sound correspondences, but is more than random scribbling or drawing. To demonstrate the recurring principle, children first "generate" pairs of letters or pseudo-letters or use these shapes for decorative purposes on drawings. As skills increase, children even write repeated words or phrases with great enjoyment and attention. This practice is spontaneous and not the same as assignments to write spelling or reading words 10 times each. As children actually demonstrate the recurring principle, they are investigating how letters are formed, how their hands feel as they write, and how they can vary the basic pattern of each letter or word without loss of meaning. Figure 6.2 shows examples of the generative and recurring principles.

Flexibility Principle

Through experimentation with letter formation, children learn the **flexibility principle,** that is, that the strokes used to form letters can be varied only within certain limits if real letters are to result. Clay (1976) explained: "Left to experiment with letter forms children will create a variety of new symbols by repositioning or decorating the standard forms. In this way they explore the limits within which each letter may vary and still retain its identity. Many 'errors' in children's early writing must be regarded as indicators of such flexibility" (p. 43). Wider observations of print, spontaneous practice, feedback from those with whom they share their writing, and actual instruction give children control of letter formation.

Directionality

Children discover that there seems to be some order or **directional principle** at work when letters are placed on a sign, box, or page. Achieving complete understanding of all that directionality implies takes children a long time because the principle is a complex one and because environmental clues can be misleading.

How letters face is the first important aspect of directionality. Circles and sticks used to form the letters in the alphabet must face in specific ways if the letters are to be correct. There are slight but very significant differences in the orientation of the strokes needed for *b, d, p, q,* and at times *g;* depending on penmanship style, the same can be true for *m* and *w, n,* and *u.* As children learn letter-sound associations, they may confuse and reverse letters, although the specific instructional strategies discussed later in this chapter can be helpful.

Children must also learn that print traditionally begins at the upper left corner, moves from left to right in a line, makes a downward left turn, and moves again from left to right in a parallel line. Signs and other writings that move vertically, in circles, or in waves can be confusing. The child whose letters march from left to right across the bottom of the page understands directionality

Sample 1. Child drew lines to make paper look more "school-like."

Sample 2. This writer is still discovering how letters are oriented on the paper. She also used decorations.

Sample 3. The smiling star was used for decoration in this example of self-initiated exploration.

FIGURE 6.2
As children discover the principles of letter formation, they "play" with what they are learning through what becomes self-initiated practice. Notice the repetition in these samples as children manipulate the few "circles and sticks" of the writing system.

more than the child who scatters words all over; but neither is as advanced as the child who tries to write horizontal lines of print but spreads them diagonally left to right across his paper. This last child knows what to do but is impeded by immature visual-motor coordination. Gradually, visual-motor coordination improves and correct directionality becomes a habit. Even so, according to Clay (1979): "When a child with some experience in writing happens to start at the right top of the page in error, the pressure of his sequencing habits seems to make him reverse the whole pattern of directional movement. This means that he not only begins in the wrong place but he also carries out most of the other directional principles in relation to that false start. It is as if the whole movement schema has been flipped over or reversed" (pp. 24, 25).

Sign Concept

Children who know that writing conveys meaning and who are internalizing the principles that govern letter formation must also recognize the major distinction between drawing and writing. A direct relationship exists between drawing and the objects that a drawing represents. Children who understand the concept *dogs* will draw something that vaguely resembles a dog, even though personal experiences will somewhat determine how that dog actually looks. The graphic images known as words are both arbitrary and fixed. The combination of letters *d - o - g* stands for dog and could be written as a label on a picture of either a beagle or a great Dane; these letters are a *sign* that says *dog* to anyone who can read English. Children must realize that the graphic image—the squiggles on paper—hold no visible relationship to the object, person, or concept they stand for, but that they are predetermined, fixed, and unchangeable. The only changes that can be made in the *d - o - g* combination of letters, if the word is to remain *dog,* are those that can be made because of the flexibility principle, as illustrated by Dog, dog, or DOG. Children's first efforts at composition are often labels of their drawings or a combination of words and pictures. This behavior demonstrates that the **sign concept** makes sense to them. Figure 6.3 shows combinations of words and signs that express children's ideas.

HANDWRITING PRACTICE AND GROWTH

For this chapter, *handwriting* is defined as the task of forming letters on paper. Handwriting may be practiced for its own sake, as in Figure 6.2, or may be the means by which children record their efforts at composition for others to see. Word processors, as discussed in Chapter 14, give young writers a second means of composing.

Handwriting (or penmanship) instruction has long been a standard part of the early childhood curriculum. Traditional belief has held that children must be taught how to place their papers on their desks, hold their pencils, and position the letters carefully on large-lined paper. Instruction supposedly should com-

FIGURE 6.3

Young writers discover that words and pictures are different but still use "signs" to convey their messages. In Sample 1, the child used a backwards 2 for *to*; Sample 2 shows a heart standing for *love*; and Sample 3 incorporates a sticker into the message "I won."

mence only when children have achieved an appropriate level of maturity, adequate eye-hand coordination, and the small-muscle motor control to hold a pencil correctly. Yet, many preschoolers and certainly most kindergarteners have developed ideas about how letter formation and print communicate as communication. You may also remember Emilia Ferreiro's point (1982): "Writing [meaning composition] is not copying, and progress in literacy does not come from advances in deciphering and copying" (p. 272). Another researcher, Lev Vygotsky (1962), suggested that the main difficulty in children's mastery of writing is "the abstract quality of written language . . . not the underdevelopment of small muscles or any other mechanical obstacle" (p. 99). Neither statement means that handwriting instruction should be eliminated entirely from early childhood classrooms; for, as Baghban asserted about beginning writing, children need a model so that their handwriting will gradually conform to a standard, comprehensible code.

The total act of learning to form and remember (and later to read) the letters of the alphabet is a monumental task for young learners, and teachers' role is to make the task manageable without undermining children's natural inclination to communicate in this new mode. The question facing teachers who value children's emerging literacy skills is not as simple as "Should handwriting be taught?" Researchers have shown that handwriting skills can improve without direct instruction when children are given ample opportunities to copy letters and words and are motivated to do so.[5] To depend, however, on purely internal motivation from all children and to eliminate handwriting instruction entirely on the assumption that "they'll learn it anyway" is foolhardy. A truly literate environment provides opportunities for appropriate instruction and practice through purposeful communication tasks.

In planning handwriting work for early childhood classes, the first step is identifying what children already know about letter formation. The goal is to refine children's knowledge and to expand their skills to include more letter forms, better legibility, and greater efficiency. Legibility will come with increased small-muscle control, practice, and motivation. Playing with manipulatives and puzzles strengthens the small muscles that control a pencil, as do drawing, painting, and working with different-sized writing tools. Sandpaper and plastic letters are excellent manipulatives because children also become familiar with the shapes of letters and may even use the manipulatives to form words. Shaping pipe cleaners into letters is helpful, and children also benefit from "writing" in or with modeling clay and drawing or writing in finger paint, shaving cream, pudding, or whipped cream.

As children form shapes with these media and see that some shapes look like letters, they are attending to the **distinctive features** of the letters. This is the flexibility principle in action: Children make connections that will help them remember what makes each letter distinct. "Oh, look at the L I made," a child manipulating pipe cleaners might say, only to be corrected by her friend, who flips the pipe cleaner over and says in a most superior way, "You made a *T*. The *T* has a bar all the way across the top; the *L* has a little bar at the bottom, and it points toward the right." The child who has been corrected replies, "Oh," but has learned some useful information about the distinctive features of upper case *L* and *T*. This information is needed for both handwriting and reading. Letting such experimentation take place is a vital part of the preschool and kindergarten literacy curriculum.

Learning More About Letter Formation

Many children will practice handwriting skills spontaneously. Fascinated by what they discover about print, they often "take stock" by making lists. Clay (1976) called this the *inventory principle*. Children first list letters or numbers, then letter combinations, words, and eventually phrases and sentences. They may copy examples of classroom environmental print, and eventually structure inventories to pose challenges and suggest tasks. A child might write "I can write the ABCs" and then write the letters; another might write "Do you know my friends?" and then list them. Writing "Numbers I can write" or "Words I know" are common variations. Figure 6.4 shows a sample inventory.

Generative Principle (Again)

As children practice handwriting, they again apply the *generative principle* to explore the various ways in which readable letters can be formed. Once children are more aware of the distinctive features of the letters, they can vary height and width to make tall, short, fat, and skinny letters and add curls, hearts, and/or other designs to their letters or stories. Children also explore punctuation by dotting *i*'s and *j*'s elaborately and by inserting periods and commas throughout their text. Such experimentation indicates that children are confident enough about their skills and curious enough about print that they will stretch the traditional boundaries of "proper" print. Figure 6.5 shows how several children experimented with their names.

Motivating Practice

Early childhood classrooms should provide many opportunities for spontaneous handwriting practice. An ample supply of tools should be available, including thick *and* thin pencils, ball point pens, magic markers, crayons, and chalk. Children may need instruction in keeping pencil sharpeners from consuming their pencils and erasers from ripping their papers, and teachers should stress that handwriting work is "just for practice." At all times, teachers themselves should remember that writing small, writing large, writing with magic marker all over huge sheets of brown paper will strengthen the eye and hand muscles needed for legible handwriting. Size can be adjusted through general instruc-

ABCDEFG#IJKLMNOPQR
STUVXYZ
TAMMYS
MOMMY

Sample 1.

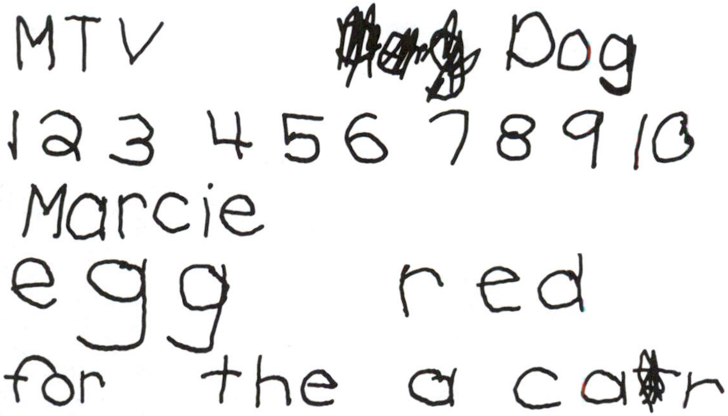

MTV
123 456 78910
Marcie
egg red
for the a catr

Sample 2.

The moon
It's big
it's pretty

it's fat

it's fall

it's in sgace-

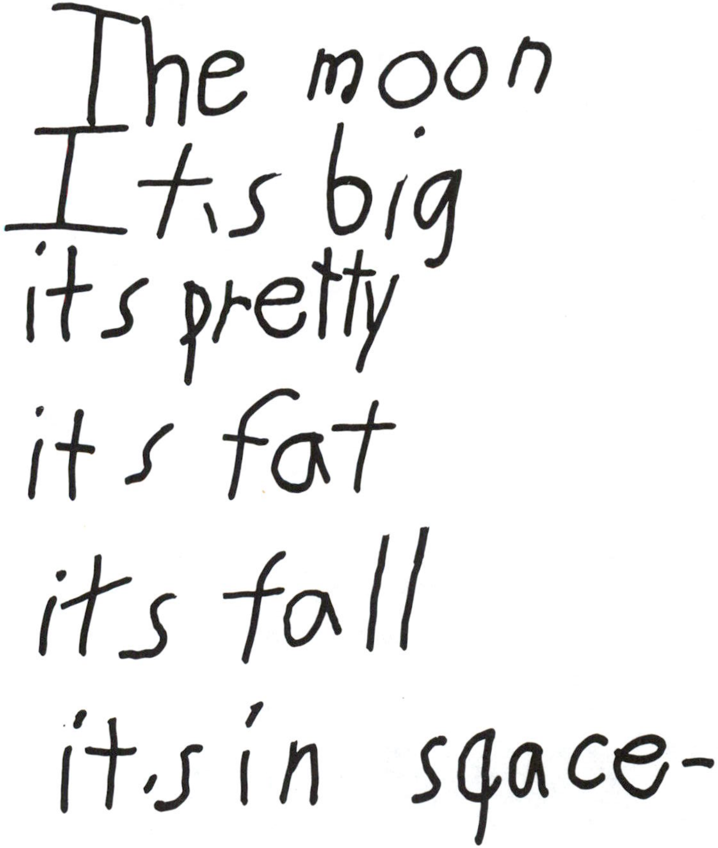

Sample 3.

FIGURE 6.4

Self-initiated inventories of numbers, letters, words, and sentences are valuable learning experiences for young language learners.

Albert

Pearl

Pearl

David

Crystal

FIGURE 6.5

Children who feel confident about their writing will often experiment. Albert added what he referred to as periods to his name for decoration. Pearl wrote her name in English and Spanish (Perla) and added decoration. The same child wrote a multicolored version of her name and became so involved that she used a *B* instead of an *R*. David (from the case study in Chapter 5) showed his emotions in a signature on a drawing. Crystal also used periods to decorate her name.

tion and should not be criticized as "wrong." As they write more, children will themselves often discover and correct handwriting "flaws."

A "literacy center," "office center," or "post office" invites children to practice their emerging skill in free-time activities or for communication with each other or the teacher. A notepad in the housekeeping center can be for grocery lists or telephone messages; children can illustrate and write menus and travel brochures; and they can write receipts, bills, and personal checks. Junk mail is valuable, too, for giving children practice in attending to lines in filling out order forms and questionnaires. Junk mail also demonstrates the various ways in which print can be arranged. These activities extend opportunities for handwriting practice and reinforce children's awareness that handwriting is an important tool for written communication.

FORMAL HANDWRITING PRACTICE

Formal handwriting instruction should not be used in preschool and should be introduced in kindergarten very carefully. Children will benefit from this work only when they can see its purpose and can place *their* learning in the context of *their own* communication needs. When kindergarteners show an interest in communicating in writing, they are indicating that they will be receptive to carefully paced, thoughtful help in refining their handwriting skills. If they cannot see the value of this school work in terms of their own needs, the practice may seem tedious and pointless.

Handwriting practice should take many forms and should be as free as possible from the judgment of "neat" or "not neat." Tracing activities are superior to those that require children to connect dots to form letters. When children trace a fully formed letter, they attend to a full visual image and its spatial constraints. They can concentrate on how the letter actually looks rather than how it *should* look. As teachers introduce tracing activities, they should read the message the children will trace and should discuss both spatial orientation and formation of individual letters. By talking about the way individual letters are made and how they are similar to and different from each other, teachers help children see and remember the distinctive features that characterize each letter. Discussing letter orientation in relationship to the top, bottom, and sides of a paper furthers this awareness.

Teachers can easily make sheets of words, phrases, sentences, even short stories for children to trace. These sheets should be colorful, neatly written, and perhaps accompanied by appropriate pictures. Shortened versions of class language experience stories recopied from a chart tablet can make excellent, motivating tracing sheets. As children work with a familiar story or trace individual words or phrases that accompany a picture clue, their sight vocabularies grow as well. Tracing sheets can easily be laminated for continued use with water-based magic markers.

Eventually in their school careers, children will be expected to be able to copy from the board or from seatwork. Copying is difficult work. Children must look at the image to be copied, segment a piece of it to be written, look away from the model, reproduce the model from either a mental image or a tactile "memory trace" of the model (how it feels to form the letter), check on the accuracy of what has been written, look up again, find the end boundary of what has just been copied, and begin the segmenting process again. If that sounds like a complex visual, motor, and memory activity, imagine how it seems to a young child. Teachers must recognize this complexity. Children can copy from their tracing sheets, from charts placed close to their desks or tables, and from the board. Practice copying from near, middle, and far ranges develops children's flexibility in exercising this complex task.

Ideally, children should aim for accuracy, speed, and neatness in copying. It is unreasonable, however, to expect all three desirable characteristics at first, and teachers should reward what children actually do. Suppose children are to copy the "morning message" from the board into their notebooks. As the teacher checks the work, she notices that one child has copied the entire message messily but *accurately* for the very first time, another has achieved a new level of *neatness* but did not get the last few words written before the board was erased, and a third child finally managed to copy the message *to the end* but happened to leave out a word or two. The accuracy, the legibility, and the speed of these three children all represent progress; praise for what each child has accomplished will give these young learners a distinct message: "Your teacher knows that this is a tough job! You are doing great!"

A final essential point about handwriting practice and instruction is brevity. Instruction and formal practice sessions should be kept very short because the *real* growth in handwriting skills will come from the frequent, purposeful writing as part of other schoolwork. As they write in the meaningful contexts of reading, composition, and other content areas, children recognize the need to develop speed, accuracy, and legibility so that they can more efficiently communicate their ideas.

ACHIEVING COMPETENCE

Legible handwriting should be the goal, but some children may never be able to achieve perfectly slanted, perfectly formed, perfectly spaced handwriting. If they produce legible writing in a reasonable amount of time and look upon handwriting as a tool to convey their thoughts, these children have accomplished a lot.

Children need to realize that there are actually three modes of handwriting. The first, **fast handwriting,** is used for scratching down ideas in drafting a story or scribbling off a note to a friend or even taking tests. As long as fast writing can be read, it has served its purpose and ought not to be criticized for messiness. The second mode is **regular handwriting.** It is accomplished at a regular, efficient pace and is the kind of writing children should use for most of their school work. In achieving regular writing, children may sacrifice some of the speed of fast writing to produce neater, better-formed letters. The final form of writing, **best handwriting,** is produced slowly and carefully, usually when children are going to "publish" their work for others to read.

Realizing that each mode serves a distinct purpose, children can adapt their writing behaviors to specific tasks. Also realizing that they will not be graded on fast writing or criticized for less-than-perfect regular writing, children work toward a balance of speed, efficiency, and perfect letter formation and continue to view handwriting as a communication tool.

HELPING WITH MEMORY LOAD

In addition to the manual tasks required in handwriting, children must exercise their memories in two ways. First, they must remember the basic conventions of page arrangement and layout. Teachers can help make left-to-right and top-to-bottom progression second nature to young writers by providing mnemonic devices to help children remember what they are to do. If children generally write seated at their desks or tables, a strip of masking tape across the top and down the left side can remind them how to orient their writing. Tracing sheets should have some mark such as a star in the upper left corner to remind children how to position their work. Teachers can make similar marks on papers given to children for handwriting practice or any activity requiring independent writing. Reminders such as "Make the star point toward the window" help children even more.

Second, children must remember the graphic image of letters and the motoric process needed to reproduce each image. They must engage in a kind of graphic thinking and must do so quickly before the connected memory traces slip out of their short-term memories. Teachers can present mnemonic devices here, too, and help children think up their own ways to remember how to form letters. While presenting individual letters for practice or helping children refine spontaneous writing, teachers should verbalize the distinctive features of letters that seem to cause problems or confusions. Distinctive features are those specific characteristics that children attend to as they begin to discriminate individual letters in reading. Think, for example, about the letters *b, d, g, p,* and *q.* All have "circles" and "sticks" or "tails" in similar enough combinations that the letters can be easily confused. Descriptions like "above the line" or "under the line" are not nearly so good as "toward the ceiling, floor, or window." Counting the "humps" on *m* and *w* and talking about whether the humps point up or down give children something concrete to remember when they attempt to make the letters on their own.

Remembering how to recognize and construct two forms of 26 letters is an enormous task, and any memory aid children can learn or develop to assist themselves will make handwriting easier. Making letter formation as easy and as close to automatic as possible frees children for the complex task of creative writing. The two behaviors then can be mutually supporting and reinforcing as children more confidently move toward literacy.

SUMMARY

Adults accept that children are strongly motivated to develop oral language skills. Research indicates that many children are equally motivated to master other modes of communication, including print. The first stage in their learning to use print is experimentation with handwriting. At first, children scribble, but gradually, the scribbling becomes a placeholder for actual print. By studying and figuring out models in the environment, children learn the basic strokes of manuscript print and experiment with actual letter formation.

To be effective, handwriting instruction must take into account what children already know about letter formation and about print as a means of communication. Handwriting "practice" should go on all day in a literate environment with children writing, drawing, using manipulatives, and otherwise strengthening their eye and hand muscles. Because it does not seem to matter what kind of pencils or paper children use, actual instruction should focus on helping children perform school-related writing tasks (such as copying) more quickly, more legibly, and more precisely. Children should never lose sight of handwriting as a tool for communication, a vehicle for getting their ideas across to others. While children should strive to develop legible handwriting, perfectly formed letters and neatness for its own sake (rather than as a courtesy for those who will read what one writes) are not valid objectives for handwriting instruction.

REVIEW QUESTIONS

1. Be sure you can define each of these terms:
   best handwriting
   directional principle
   distinctive features
   fast handwriting
   flexibility principle
   generative principle
   intentionality
   placeholder of meaning (this is another update of your definition)
   recurring principle
   regular handwriting
   sign concept
2. Collect samples of young children's writing and drawing. What do the children know about the principles discussed in this chapter?

3. Spend time with preschoolers (who have had no instruction in handwriting). Ask them to write something for you and ask them to talk about what they are doing. How much do they know about handwriting? Do any of them seem reluctant to talk to you? Observe children writing on their own. Do they seem to do more when no adult is around?

4. Think back to the last chapter and its discussion of "situations to exploit" for literacy learning. Make a list of situations in preschool, kindergarten, and first-grade classes where children could practice handwriting in ways that are meaningful yet fun.

5. Think about the writing tools and paper you would like to have in a "writing center" for preschool, kindergarten, or early primary classes. Make a list. Anticipate objections to your idea of having a writing center (children are too young, children need formal practice, etc.) and write a justification for a writing center for the particular age group you select.

NOTES

1. Clay, M. (1976). *What did I write?* Portsmouth, NH: Heinemann Educational Books.

2. Taylor, D. (1983). *Family literacy.* Portsmouth, NH: Heinemann Educational Books.

3. Harste, J. C., Woodward, V. A., & Burke, C. L. (1984). *Language stories and literary lessons.* Portsmouth, NH: Heinemann Educational Books.

4. Donaghue, M. R. (1985). *The child and the English language arts* (4th Ed.). Dubuque, IA: William C. Brown.

7

Spelling: Invented and Beyond

hildren discover letter formation by observing environmental print and people using writing to communicate. They experiment with manuscript and cursive writing and play at communicating in print. Convinced that they are writing, children string together letters and pseudo-letters and confidently read their messages to themselves and interested adults. Initially, children have only a limited understanding of the concept of words as distinct units of both speech and writing. They write messages together with no separations between words; yet, they often maintain that they have used "lots of letters" for long messages, while shorter strings are used for messages that sound shorter when uttered. These behaviors strengthen the muscles that control writing tools, increase eye-hand coordination, build awareness of left-to-right orientation and letter discrimination, and reinforce children's awareness that print is a valid form of communication.

Beginning writers have not understood that standard spelling reflects a correspondence between letters and the sounds of oral language. These sounds—or **phonemes**—are represented by specific letters, and consistency in letter-sound matching allows readers to interpret the messages presented in printed text. Early writing efforts represent the first stage in children's discovery of composition; they demonstrate the use of the deviant or prephonemic stage in what is commonly called **invented spelling.**[1]

Understanding the importance of invented spelling helps early childhood teachers appreciate what young children are trying to do as they move from experimentation with speech and letter formation finally to composition. Like early speech and pseudo-letters, invented spelling is an example of children's efforts at placeholding meaning. Writing with invented spelling, children attempt to communicate in real texts with real messages by manipulating what they know about letter formation, letter-phoneme correspondences, sentence structure, and word meaning. They do this naturally, without the inhibitions of

1. Children see environmental print and realize that these symbols communicate meaning.
2. They observe people around them writing and realize that writing is a form of communication.
3. They experiment with letter formation and discover that they, too, can produce printed symbols.
4. Gradually, they generalize information about the sound characteristics of letters, using, for example, the letters of their name and of familiar environmental print.
5. They pay close attention to media such as "Sesame Street," books or records that teach letter-sound correspondences, and comments about spelling from adults or siblings; they delight in playing with rhymes and initial consonant substitution; gradually the number of letter-sound generalizations they know increases.
6. Having become aware of letter-sound correspondences, children move through a series of stages in invented spelling that will lead them to closer approximation of correct spelling.
7. Formal instruction supplements what children have discovered and increases their understanding of spelling and writing conventions.
8. Writing practice, instruction, and knowledge of the irregularities of the spelling system make children sensitive to what can and cannot be correct; they learn strategies for spelling unfamiliar words and correcting errors.

FIGURE 7.1
Origin of invented spelling.

older children and adults more conscious of the formalities of composition. Invented spelling develops from incidental learning and the reasoning process outlined in Figure 7.1.

DO NAT DSTRB: GYNS AT WRK

Glenda Bissex (1980) studied her son Paul with the same intensity Marcia Baghban extended toward her daughter Giti. Bissex's interest was literacy, and her book *Gnys at Wrk* chronicles Paul's growth from ages 5 to 11. The title comes from a note Paul taped on his door, DO NAT DSTRB GYNS AT WRK. Bissex captures the importance of invented spelling in children's literacy learning:

> Five-year-old Paul was in the house. I was outside on the deck reading. After he had tried unsatisfactorily to talk with me, he decided to get my attention a new way—to break through print with print. Selecting the rubber letter stamps he needed from his set, Paul printed and delivered this message: RUDF (Are you deaf?!) Of course, I put down my book (p. 3).

Paul lived in a literate environment, but his "family had given him no instruction in letter sounds or letter formation, though letter names were frequently referred to . . . he wrote his own name (which no one remembers teaching him); [and] he formed letters and enjoyed writing them" (p.4). Within that environment, Paul's discovery of invented spelling was part of his normal development.

Paul's growth was not just a middle-class phenomenon. Bissex's detailed study complements and is supported by the works of Emilia Ferreiro and Ana Teberosky (1979, 1982). These researchers, studying middle-class and lower-class children in Mexico City, found developmental sequences similar to those of Paul Bissex. They maintained that children exposed to print will attempt to make sense out of what they see to gain "ownership" of literacy skills. Ferreiro and Teberosky (1982) stated that educators should not view children's "literacy development as the acquisition of a set of marks" (p. 172). Instead, they must recognize that "[children] pose deep questions to themselves. Their problems are not solved when they succeed in meaningfully identifying a letter or string of letters, because they try to understand not only the elements or the results but also, and above all, the very nature of the system."

Not all children would label themselves a *gyns* as they experiment with invented spelling, but all children should be given the opportunity to progress through this important learning sequence. There is strong indication that all children explore invented spelling on their own and even stronger proof that children in early childhood programs encouraging creative writing will use invented spelling naturally and confidently. Children in a bilingual, whole language program in a southwestern city began writing in Spanish and progressed smoothly to English composition with dependence upon their ability to "invent" spelling in both languages. They also moved with relative ease to monolingual English instruction.[2] Indeed, many researchers believe that children who have not had opportunities to play with invented spelling and beginning writing will not benefit from traditional spelling instruction.[3]

The Beginnings of Invented Spelling

The first stage, as mentioned above, is often called **deviant spelling**—random letters and pseudo-letters, strung together to convey a message. Because deviant spelling can be read only by the child who has written it, it is easy to overlook the importance of this stage in emerging literacy. Chapter 6, on the development of letter formation, presented examples of children's deviant spelling.

As children use deviant spelling, they progress from knowing "for sure" that they are actually writing "real" words to realizing that there is more to writing than they at first thought. This knowledge—that there must be some match between the letters they write and the phonemes they hear as they utter words—leads them to the next stage in invented spelling.

The second stage has been called *prephonetic* or **early phonemic spelling.** This spelling shows a primitive awareness of alphabetic principles with one-, two-, or three-letter strings to represent phonemes children hear in words they are trying to spell. Sometimes children stop after writing one or two phonemes of a word; they may use only those to placehold the entire word or may fill in the rest with a random string of letters. It is easy to understand the sparseness of the beginning spellers' output when we think about the total mental effort they must expend. Figure 7.2 illustrates how invented spelling is another form of placeholding and shows what beginning spellers must do.

The third stage is called *phonetic* or **letter-name spelling.** It demonstrates an "almost perfect match between letters and phonemes" (Gentry, 1981, p. 379), because children consciously break each word into its phonemes and try to match letters on the basis of the similarity between the phonemes they hear and the names of the letters. Many letter-name spellers are still prereaders in that they can read their own writing but can read at best only a few sight words in standard spelling. When they spell, children select primarily those consonants with a stable and predictable letter-name match or those that regularly represent only one phoneme. If they use vowels at all, they will primarily use long vowels, which "say their name."[4] Examples of this stage include: *mstr* (monster), *pla* (play), *dfrint* (different), *nz* or *ns* (nice), and *bln* (balloon). Children gradually master other consonants, as illustrated by *ylo* (yellow), *coct* (cooked), *wus, wuz,* or *wos* (was), *Srlit* (Charlotte), *ostric* (ostrich), and *spnh* (spinach). Control of vowels comes more slowly and is marked by inventions such as *mentis* (minutes), *acras* (across), *dinusooer* (dinosaur), and *fayvurit* (favorite). References at the end of the chapter suggest additional sources of information about the sequence of invented spelling. Figure 7.3 contrasts examples of prephonemic and letter-name spelling that accompanied drawings collected on the same day in a kindergarten class.

At this stage, children may not actually have conceptualized the process of "spelling"; rather, they think of their behaviors as part of a dynamic process called "writing." Bissex (1980) reported "Paul himself described what he was doing as 'writing' rather than 'spelling' . . . had his main interest been in spelling *words*, he would have written word lists; what he wrote, however, were *messages*" (p. 35). This concept of spelling and writing as a continuous, interrelated skill is positive and productive for young writers, for according to Harste, Woodward, and Burke (1984) "the perception that when one writes one must spell correctly appears to be the single biggest constraint which 5- and 6-year-old children see as the reason why they can't engage in the process" (p. 131).

Progress in Invented Spelling

Literacy progresses through frequent opportunities for purposeful writing, in observations of people writing, and through incidental and direct instruction. As children confirm the stability of some letters and discover irregularities of English spelling, they put the pieces of the spelling system together and use

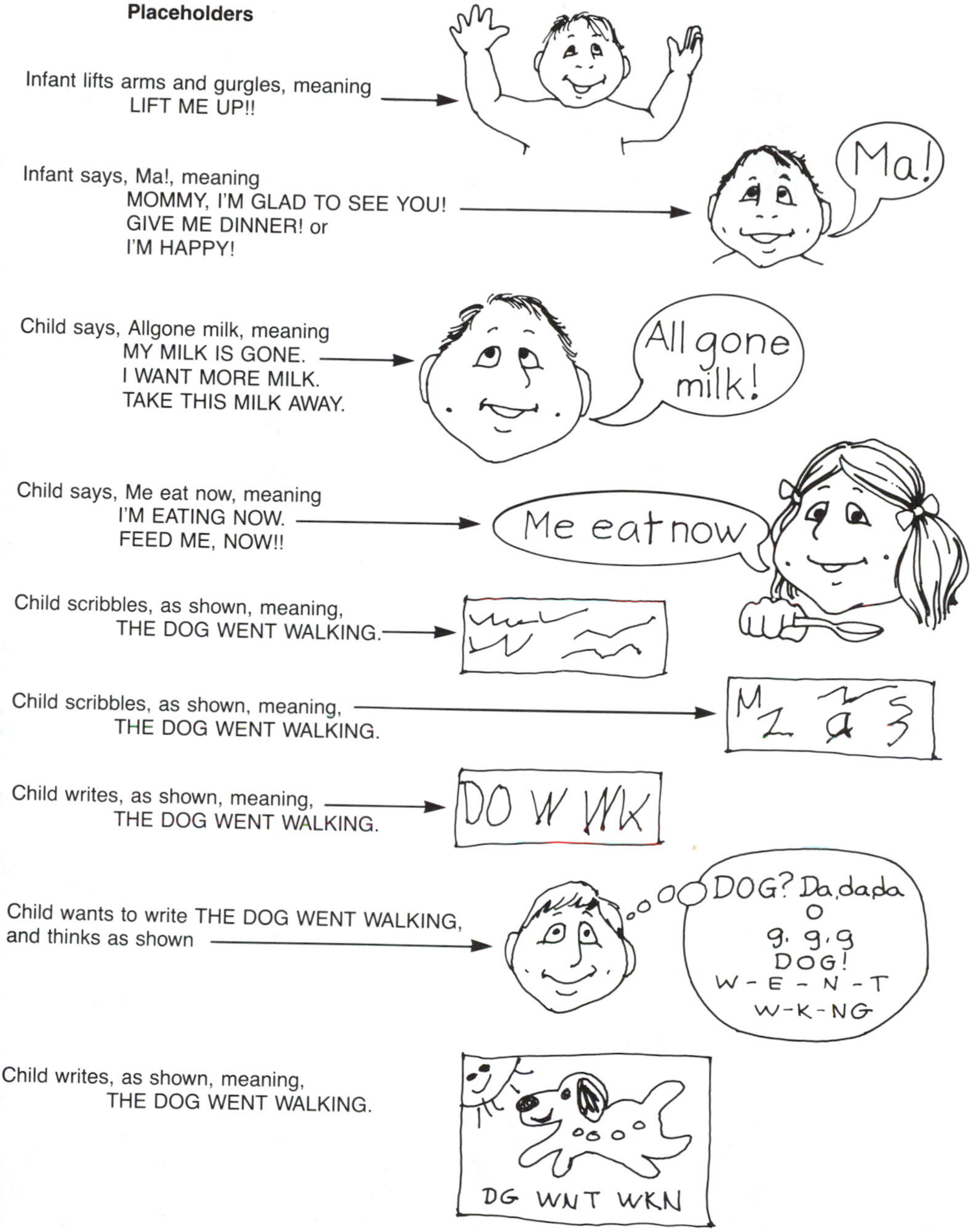

Placeholders
Infant lifts arms and gurgles, meaning LIFT ME UP!!
Infant says, Ma!, meaning MOMMY, I'M GLAD TO SEE YOU! GIVE ME DINNER! or I'M HAPPY!
Ma!
Child says, Allgone milk, meaning MY MILK IS GONE. I WANT MORE MILK. TAKE THIS MILK AWAY.
All gone milk!
Child says, Me eat now, meaning I'M EATING NOW. FEED ME, NOW!!
Me eat now
Child scribbles, as shown, meaning, THE DOG WENT WALKING.
Child scribbles, as shown, meaning, THE DOG WENT WALKING.
Child writes, as shown, meaning, THE DOG WENT WALKING.
DO W WK
Child wants to write THE DOG WENT WALKING, and thinks as shown
DOG? Da,dada
O
g. g. g
DOG!
W - E - N - T
W - K - NG
Child writes, as shown, meaning, THE DOG WENT WALKING.
DG WNT WKN

FIGURE 7.2
Beginning spelling is another form of "placeholding." This figure reviews how children have placeheld their communications prior to their learning to spell and indicates the steps children must take to come up with their efforts at invented spelling. Placeholders, whether verbal, gestural, or written, are dependent on context for interpretation.

ILabfR

1. I learned about fire.

i BWZ. mTb

2. I broke the window with my table
   (per instructions given at fire station).

If9A9At
AFSF

3. I finally got out of the fire station.

I L RND'HOWTO
POSÕOP DrP
and PoL

4. I learned how to stop, drop, and roll.

I L R ND Hot
STOPROP an
RO W

5. I learned how to stop, drop, and roll.

6. You better stop, drop, and roll.

I lic to lrn a bдot flyr
the fyr is dag ras

7. I like to learn about fire
   The fire is dangerous.

8. I learned how to get out safely.

FIGURE 7.3
After a visit to a fire station, kindergarteners drew and wrote about what they had learned. Part of the demonstration had been how to "stop, drop, and roll" in case of a fire at home. Children in this class had been writing for several months. Notice the variety of expression and invented spelling. (Used by permission of Carolyn Kidder.)

their writing to externalize what they are learning. Their spelling enters the **transitional** stage.

Transitional spelling looks like standard English because it contains vowels, including digraphs and diphthongs, consonant blends, and inflected endings. Efforts written in transitional spelling may also contain many conventional spellings that result from children's memory of sight words or accurate application of emerging spelling skills. Nonconventional spellings in this stage reflect young writers' attempts to make sense out of the spelling system. Remember the previous discussions of overgeneralizations of oral syntax (for example, *runned, swimmed, one children,* and so forth) and how these "errors" indicate that children are actively constructing or "inventing" an understanding of the grammar they hear around them. Invented spelling reflects the same kind of active involvement in constructing meaning, and transitional spelling clearly demonstrates a developmental stage similar to that of the oral language of preschoolers. Look closely at the stories presented in Figure 7.4 to see what these young writers were thinking about spelling, punctuation, and the mechanics of composition.

Correct or Conventional Spelling

"Correct spelling," the final stage, demonstrates nearly correct spellings in most spontaneous and assigned writing activities. It is perhaps more appropriate to think of this stage as "conventional" spelling because invented spellings are usually "correct," that is, developmentally accurate, when young writers produce them. Some children achieve conventional spelling on their own; others approximate correct spelling but children "don't discover rules in a vacuum. Specific information *does* need to be supplied" (Sowers, 1981, p. 44–45). Good spelling instruction in the whole language approach recognizes the continuum of communication skills and stresses the connection between oral language, composition, and reading. Spelling is viewed as a skill to be mastered in order to make one's writing more efficient and effective and builds upon what children have discovered for themselves about writing. Specific strategies will be discussed later in this chapter.

Timing

Children's progress through invented spelling does not follow a precise timetable: It is developmental and dependent on environmental input, opportunities to hypothesize and experiment, individual interest in language, and encouragement and acceptance of what is attempted. Awareness of letter-phoneme correspondences seems to evolve over time, as children use what they are discovering. Bissex (1980) reported these changes in her son's spelling of the word *directions:* DRAKTHENS (5 years, 7 months), DRAKSHINS (5 years, 8 months), DIREKSHONS (7 years, 5 months), DIRECTOINS or DIRECTIONS (8 years, 1 month), and finally DIRECTIONS (8 years, 7 months). She commented, "That particular word, or any word, could have been corrected earlier but might have stood as an isolated item to be memorized. When Paul finally mastered *directions,* he wrote lists of what he titled 'hard words,' including many ending

1. I god to Magick Landing [amusement park]. I went on the ship. It tikld my tumy.
2. This rboot will empte The trash and fixe icecreme. What it does is clene. Your bed and does your home wrce to and sonmtims it dro you a Pigshr.
3. My naybor plantid my fayvurit tree. It is a red maypel. Its name is sweet maypel. Sweetmaypel is about 20 feet.
4. Ones Apon a time. There where three kings Papa kind momo kind and baby king. Oneday they wint to the zoo and they was a lat of animls. And they buyd six tiggers and six lions.
5. Ones upon a time there were two care Bear's thay lived in a land cald ca-realot there names were Love a lot and Wish bear. They love peple.
6. I was rideing my cusins bike and my cusin was on it to. In our stret there was a ramp. One day we tryd to jump it I fell down so did my cousin. I had to go to the hospetl.
7. There was a spidre and her nam was Srlit [Charlotte] the Spidre. Srlit was alon and then two bugs cam and one ov the bugs sid my nam is riche and the avr bug sid my nam is Jonne so they wint in hr web and thet is the End. [Added on other side of paper: The ril nam wer buges.]
8. Once upon a time this broom bilong to a wich. Wen the wich sas acbrcdra it will come to her. Sutenly she ment to say abracdra and the broom went to her. A man kame and nock on the door and he told her are you the wicet wich of the west? Yes i am the wicet wich fo the west. The end.
9. Once uponatime a old inventor was lonly. so he desided to make a robot that talked, and did all the things he sed it did things nice. and likes chasing the cat, and it wus medl.
10. I wash taht I had a Computer Be cus Computers are fun. Thay hlp you like scool.

ANALYSIS

Look back at the samples to note the varied uses of punctuation and capitalization. The writer of sample 2 probably decided to continue his sentence after writing the period after *clene*. The writer of sample 9 probably added a comma whenever she stopped to think what to say next. Sample 7 is a classic run-on, except for the additional comment written on the back. Some children were clearly aware that punctuation and capitalization are used in written communication, but they were not exactly sure where the marks are needed. Random use of both capitals and periods is evident throughout the samples. Look also at what children were trying to do. Samples 4, 6, and 7 show logical sequence; samples 7 and 8 use dialogue.

Now think about the spelling displayed in these samples. Children over-generalized vowel rules or selected the wrong letter for a vowel sound in these cases (sample numbers appear in parentheses):

FIGURE 7.4
Samples of children's use of transitional spelling

clene (2), feat (3), stret (6)—long vowel digraph

ment (8)—short vowel digraph

naybor, fayvurit, maypel (3)—overgeneralization of -*ay* for long *a* sound; overdependence of "sounding out" to spell *favorite* and *maple*.

nam, alon, cam, wer (7)—no silent *e* at end of words

wus, sed, ses (several sentences), bilong (8), peple (5), wint (4), be cus (10)—words written as said by writer

cusin (6), dro (2), pigshr (2)—no vowel diphthong

Children had difficulty with word endings in these cases:

god [goed], buyd (4)—incorrect past tense of verbs

tikld [tickled] (1), plantid (3), cald (5), rideing, tryd (6)—incorrect formation of inflected, past tense

fixe (2)—added silent *e*

empte (1), riche, Jonne (7)—*e* used to represent "empty," "Richie," and "Jonny"

medl, animls—*e* omitted; contrast with *maypel* in (3)

Children had difficulty with consonants, consonant blends, and consonant digraphs in these cases:

tumy (1)—did not double *m*

Magick (1), wrce [work] (2), wicet (8)—misuse of *ck*

pigshr [picture] (2)—wrote word as it probably sounded to him; heard *g* for *c* in middle of word; *sh* is logical for sound made by *ture*

wich, wen, nock, kame (8)—lack of familiarity with *tch* blend, *wh* digraph, and silent *k* in these words; *k* on *came* was probably careless error because the writer did know *went* and *will come*; writer was second language learner just beginning to write in English

Srlit [Charlotte] (7), scool (10)—misuse of *sh* and *sch*; writer of *Srlit* probably concentrated on *r*-controlled sound of *Char-*

Samples 2 and 10 show errors in letter placement that probably resulted from carelessness or inattention rather than poor spelling: roboot for *robot* and taht for *that*. Other words in these samples indicate their writers' strong grasp of transitional spelling. Sample 7 is interesting because of the back-of-the-paper addition: "The ril nam wer buges." The child wanted to write "The real names were bugs" and in trying indicated that he knew to use the plural form of the verb *to be* even if he omitted the inflected ending (along with the silent *e*) on *names*. He also attempted an incorrect form of the inflected *s* ending, as he added *es* to *bug*. The child who wrote this retelling of a favorite book was the David mentioned in the case study in Chapter 5.

FIGURE 7.4
continued

with -*tion*. His spelling reflects the learning of a principle, not merely a word" (p. 88).

Even within supportive, literate classrooms, children will progress at different rates. Henderson (1985) has given a rough outline of spelling development that actually begins with children aged 1 to 4 years who are experimenting with writing while still unaware of letter-sound correspondences. Invented spellers are children aged 4 to 6 years who begin to attend to letter-sound matches and to discover spelling principles. Competent spellers, aged 5 to 8 years, bring reading instruction to bear on their words and make constant progress toward conventional spelling.

GROWTH IN SPELLING COMPETENCY

Researchers have suggested practical guidelines for helping children move toward mastery.[5] The first should sound familiar by now: Children learn to spell most efficiently when surrounded by print in *literate classroom environment*. Environmental print plays a major role in helping children initially "invent" spelling and carefully selected classroom print becomes children's beginning dictionaries. Books and other printed matter serve as models for correct spelling.

The second suggestion is to encourage *active involvement in language*. Word play and spelling games encourage children to manipulate sounds and letters to spell new words, guess at nonsense spellings, and verbalize (or write) the spellings of sight words. Competitive spelling bees favor children who can memorize lists of words and should, therefore, be avoided.

Children should be encouraged to continue to form hypotheses about spelling. Teachers may ask children to suggest spellings for Language Experience Approach (LEA) stories or other teacher written activities or for special words (for example, *gigundo, humongous monster*) so long as no criticism is implied for wrong guesses. Asking children to "check the word" on classroom charts also involves these children in thinking about words.

Creative writing is the most productive involvement with language. "Good spellers," one researcher wrote (Gentry, 1981) "are those who from the beginning form a spelling consciousness through purposeful writing" (p. 380). This "consciousness" enables writers to evaluate their work, recognize nonconventional spellings, and have numerous strategies available for changing an incorrect word. Children moving beyond transitional spelling continue to need both structured and spontaneous writing opportunities. As their sight vocabularies and word attack skills increase, they become more efficient at spelling new words and recognizing and correcting their own errors.

The third suggestion is *deemphasis of standard spelling*. This is easy advice for kindergarten or first-grade teachers to follow, but second- or third-grade teachers may shudder at the thought. Deemphasizing standard spelling encourages children to write. "Spell it the best you can, we can always correct the spelling later" gives children freedom to experiment in writing, take risks, use their imaginations, and refine their skills. Through writing, they refine (and speed up) their ability to break words into component sounds and to match those sounds with letters. They learn to look at their spelling and match it visually with their memory of how the word "should look." They develop a spelling consciousness.

Additionally, nonconventional spelling gives teachers a reflection of children's knowledge about letter-phoneme correspondence and irregularities in the spelling system. Viewing nonconventional spelling diagnostically, teachers should attempt to find an underlying system or pattern in spelling errors rather than counting the total number of misspellings. Nonconventional spelling may mean any of the following:

1. Children hear phonemes incorrectly because of speech problems, hearing loss, or temporary hearing difficulty (colds, allergies, etc.). Difficulties may correct themselves in time or respond to speech therapy; alternatively, children may need to learn compensatory skills. The child with a hearing difficulty, for example, may need to learn to depend more on visual memory than on letter-phoneme correspondences in learning to spell.

2. Children are matching phonemes and letters according to their own pronunciation, which is influenced by regional dialects, second language learning, or speech difficulties. Awareness of what they are doing helps children monitor their spelling.

3. Children have not learned certain concepts, such as silent letters (*lam* for *lamb*, *rench* for *wrench*), consonant digraphs (*fone* for *phone*), double consonants (*swiming, leanned*), or dropping terminal-*y* (*pennyies, ponys*), and so forth. Children may still be uncertain about vowels, especially digraphs and diphthongs. Finding an underlying error pattern to these errors allows teachers to focus instruction. "Let's look at these words," a teacher might say; "they are all wrong because of *just one thing:* you didn't use the right letter combinations for the /ow/ sound. Let's talk about it. Here are some words with the /ow/ sound . . . "

4. Children have mislearned some common sight words or do not know or have not mastered certain irregular words. Again, direct instruction can help, along with this reminder: "Some words just have to be memorized. Put a picture of the word in your mind to help you."

The idea of looking at spelling diagnostically implies that each child in a class may need an individual prescription to remedy his or her spelling difficulties. In all probability, this will not be the case, for patterns of errors will clump together to allow for whole class, small group, and individual instruction.

A well-planned, logical instructional program, with adjustments made for individual help, is the final suggestion for helping children learn to spell. Bissex

(1980) made an important point about teaching spelling: "[Instruction] may be useful or crucial at only some stages . . . youngsters have a sense of how they learn and [should] be allowed and encouraged to take more control of their own learning. The teacher's function would then include more helping children listen to themselves and less the entire burden of diagnosing the needs of every student" (p. 114). Children will differ, she stated, and teachers should be sensitive to whether students are experimenting or are seeking focused help and direction. She added, "Development of spelling ability may not rest on any particular sequence [of instruction] but on an ever-changing concept of spelling that increasingly approaches the actual nature of [the conventional spelling system]."

SPELLING INSTRUCTION

A strong, responsive, and flexible instructional program should: (a) limit daily study time but encourage ample practice; (b) recognize differences in spelling difficulty; and (c) use modeling and other instructional strategies. A good program should be based on awareness of language patterns, mechanics, and structure, and aim to strengthen children's vocabularies and store of sight words which they can spell independently.

Instructional Time

In 1895, Joseph Meyer Rice, one of the first spelling researchers,[6] stated that no more than 15 minutes should be spent on spelling instruction but stressed that practice should be required on a daily basis. Rice's 15-minute guide is a good "rule of thumb" for today's teachers. In those 15 minutes, teachers might play a word game, introduce and discuss new words, point out the spelling of words on a new classroom chart, hold an informal, noncompetitive spelling bee, or present a combined vocabulary and spelling lesson.

Structured workbook and ditto activities should be viewed with caution. Commercial materials are based on linguistic principles but do not necessarily reflect what children have actually learned through their own invented spelling. Bissex (1980) wrote about her son's experiences with a first-grade spelling workbook: "In first grade he . . . received explicit workbook instruction in spelling patterns. Most of the patterns Paul already used correctly in his spontaneous writing . . . [So], he learned little about spelling from this workbook. A more advanced one that included polysyllabic and Latinate words could have provided richer material for him" (pp. 62–63). When writing and reading are integrated for instruction and practice, children spend more than 15 minutes using spelling skills. This practice makes previous instruction more concrete, for children can continue their growth by both "[generalizing] spelling patterns and principles from an unstructured set of correctly spelled words and accumulating learned words" (Bissex, 1980, p. 62).

Whether or not to present lists for spelling tests is a thorny issue for early childhood teachers because prepared spelling lists may be irrelevant, inappropriate, too easy, or too hard. Lists of words tailored to children's interests or needs can be useful, however, and tests themselves can be beneficial as long as grades on tests are not the sole assessment of spelling achievement. Presenting a list on Monday, discussing its linguistic and semantic characteristics, "playing" with it through oral and written activities, and finally testing on Friday can supplement and help structure children's ongoing acquisition of spelling skills through independent writing. The following sections discuss categories of words that can generate spelling lists, and Figure 7.5 presents sample lists.

Rice also recommended beginning spelling instruction with common, easy nouns, words children use in their everyday speech. Children often begin to write these words themselves, dictate them in LEA stories, and encounter them in children's literature. While many of these words do not present direct letter-phoneme matches, they do form a good basic spelling vocabulary. Grouping them by theme, such as numbers or color words, demonstrates the usefulness of mastering these words. Again refer to Figure 7.5.

Difficult Words

Rice encouraged teachers to recognize the obvious: Some words are more difficult because they violate letter-phoneme correspondences, come from other languages, or have "trick" parts such as unexpected double consonants. Many of these words, unlike *directions*, which Paul Bissex found difficult, do not fit into spelling patterns and must be memorized. These are words frequently termed "spelling demons," although a former second grader gave them another name:

> Jenny sought logic and rules in everything she did and could not
> understand the illogic of English spelling. She pestered me so much for
> explanations about irregularities that finally I merely said, "Life is hard,
> Jenny; some words just have to be memorized." That statement dented her
> concept of order somewhat but generated her category of words—the "Life
> Is Hard" words.

Difficult words need instruction, probably beginning at second grade. Work on difficult words should become "word study," and children learn to control the irregularities of the spelling system. Teachers should select groups of "difficult words" carefully and present them to children in as motivating a way as possible. As these words are introduced, teachers explain possible difficulties (irregularities, tricks, and so forth) to increase children's "spelling consciousness." Teachers grade spelling tests of these words less demandingly than they would another list. Spelling half of the "demon list" right might be more of an accomplishment for a second grader than an 80% on an easier test.

Color words

- [ ] basic color words
- [ ] unusual color words (beige, aqua, fuschia, etc.)

Category words

- [ ] names of the seasons
- [ ] names of the months
- [ ] names of days of week
- [ ] articles of clothing
- [ ] subjects taught in school
- [ ] animal names
- [ ] names of foods
- [ ] names of monsters (let children recommend these)

Number words

- [ ] first and second decade numbers for functional use
- [ ] higher numbers for interest and word study; this also assists in understanding place value.

Names of holidays
Names of children in class ·
Words related to holidays

- [ ] Halloween: spooky, ghost, costume, etc.
- [ ] Christmas: tree, Santa Claus, present, etc.
- [ ] Thanksgiving: turkey, Indian, Pilgrim, etc.

FIGURE 7.5
Specialized spelling lists are motivating and fun. These are only a sample of the kinds of lists that can be generated for use in early childhood classes.

Awareness of Language

As children discover oral language, they trip over features such as irregular past tenses and inverted word order for negative sentences. As they learn to read and spell, they encounter even more irregularities such as double consonants, prefixes or suffixes, homophones, contractions, or possessives. These spelling changes are not always evident in speech and may be confusing. Misspellings such as an all inclusive *theirryre* for *their, they're,* or *there* show that children have remembered that there is *something special* about these words but they are not sure what the irregularity is. Specific instruction on these mechanical and grammatical aspects of language, along with attention to their spelling peculiarities, helps children remember when to use and how to form such words.

English spelling may seem totally irregular, as it did to Jenny, but there are

SPELLING: INVENTED AND BEYOND

Synonyms

☐ many words for *run*, etc.
☐ many words for *pretty*, etc.

Content area words

☐ words related to units in science or social studies
☐ words related to math, e.g., *plus, minus, add*, etc.
☐ compound words

Difficult words

☐ irregular past tenses or plurals
☐ word with silent letters
☐ words with irregular vowel patterns
☐ plurals with *-ies*, etc.
☐ polysyllabic words
☐ latinate words

Words with specific morphemic structures

☐ root words and words with prefixes
☐ root words and words with suffixes

Homonyms (homophones)

☐ words that sound alike but are spelled differently

FIGURE 7.5
continued

many consistencies and predictable aspects that children can learn and use.[7]
Teaching children structural analysis (also called morphemic analysis) is a traditional part of beginning reading instruction that belongs in spelling as well. When Bissex (1980) stated that Paul finally learned the underlying *-tion* principle and could spell "direction" and other *-tion* words, she meant that he discovered and could apply a morphemic principle. Learning how prefixes, suffixes, and root words are manipulated gives children insight into how English works. Consider these words as examples: *like, likely, dislike, unlikely, likelihood*. When learning "word parts" is presented only in reading instruction, children may not realize that they, too, can create new words by juggling prefixes, suffixes, and roots. As they create, accept, giggle over, and possibly discard "new" words such as *undeliciousness* or *stupidiosity*, they are increasing both their sensitivity to language and their spelling skills.

Modeling

Modeling can be part of "specific instruction" to spelling. Modeling externalizes the problem-solving strategies that accompany the cognitive act of spelling. Teachers should demonstrate the "self-talk" children must learn to use as they attempt to spell unfamiliar words. Gradually, children adopt the same approach. The following is a good example of what a teacher might say: "Now this word *found* that I have to spell. What are the sounds in *found*? fff-ow-nd. Yes, *found*. I know the beginning sound, *f*. Now what letters make the *ow* sound? Do I know any other words like *found*—sound, round, etc.? *Ow* has the *ou* sound also—in words like *cow, now,* etc. I will write the word as *fownd* and also *found* and see which one looks better" (Russell, 1984, p. 69).

Varied Instructional Strategies

Rice recognized that spelling involves visual, auditory, and tactile-kinesthetic channels, and he strongly advocated teaching spelling through various instructional modes. Too frequently, children are told to "study" their spelling but are not told that their studying should include attending to the individual letters and to the total word, saying letters and word to themselves, and writing or tracing the word as well. Failing to understand what they are supposed to do, children merely look at their words and puzzle at not remembering them. Just writing spelling words can be counterproductive if children do not know to look closely at the words and say them softly as they write to set the visual image in their mind. A second misuse of writing is shown in Figure 7.6, an exercise in which children wrote each word three times and illustrated it. Drawing *is* a good way to reinforce spelling, but the child whose paper is shown did not focus on words as individual units. Writing by itself, is not very valuable; composing sentences using spelling words is more beneficial.

Spelling should be practiced orally, too, although visual learners may need to write possible spellings at the same time. Words should also be presented in a variety of print styles so that children are fully aware of the visual image they must remember. As children learn to write in cursive, they should see their spelling words written in two distinct forms. Evaluating spelling in cursive can be tricky: Is the word misspelled or are the letters misformed? Children should be allowed to write in either manuscript or cursive, and an oral check ("Spell this word for me out loud, please") can always determine what a child knows.

Vocabulary and Sight Words

Activities to build vocabularies and sight words benefit spelling skills as well. Lists of interesting vocabulary choices should be posted in the classroom as part of the environmental print; children can refer to them as they write and gradually become able to spell the words on their own. Words presented for vocabulary growth may or may not be included as actual spelling words; possible lists are presented in Figure 7.5.

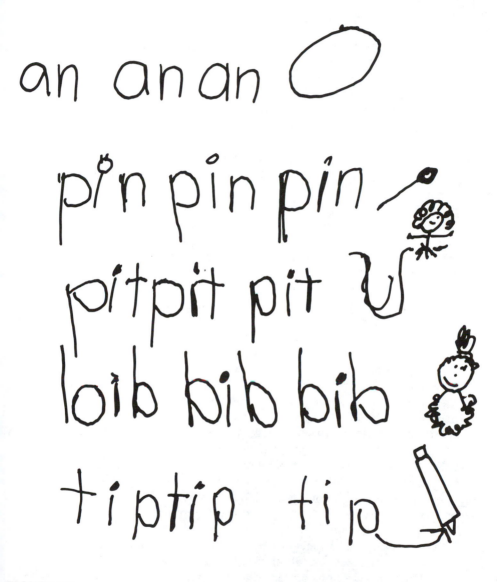

FIGURE 7.6

This child's task was to write each spelling word three times and draw a picture. Because the child did not leave space between the individual words, he could not adequately "study" his words to learn them. Writing spelling words will be beneficial *only* if children attend to the distinctive features of each word. One has to wonder about the picture for the spelling word *an*!

Vocabulary lists or informational charts as classroom environmental print increase children's reading sight words and their supply of words that can be spelled automatically. Teachers might add a word or two from environmental print to each spelling test to encourage children to look at environmental print closely enough so that when a word is included unexpectedly, they can pull a mental picture of the word from memory and attempt to spell it. This essentially convinces children that they *can* spell whatever they want, that they have the cognitive strategies to spell new words with confidence. Children should, of course, not be marked off for misspelling an unexpected word.

Memory Aids and Spelling Strategies

The goal of spelling instruction should be to help children become the best possible spellers they can be, and for some children, becoming good spellers may necessitate learning some valuable "tricks." These tricks include **memory aids** and sheer memorization, recognition of personal "demons," use of the dictionary, and **subvocalization.** Children may also need to be reassured that the hypothesizing that has been central to their invented spelling is a valid strategy for continued spelling growth.

Many children, especially those who have not been encouraged in their invented spelling, may think that they must memorize every word that they will ever use and that there are no specific strategies for spelling unfamiliar words. This misconception takes its toll in creative writing. Instruction should give children insight into spelling as a cognitive activity, and mnemonic aids like *"i before e except after c, except when sounded as a as in neighbor or weigh"* serve as flags to alert children to spelling irregularities.

Creative writing reveals patterns of errors that can lead to developing individualized memory aids. Children who have trouble with the long *a* sound will be careful with words such as *wait, late, weight, hey,* and *day.* They attend more closely to the visual image of these words when encountered in print, and try to remember the various letter combinations that make the phoneme; they then try out and analyze possible spellings when they want to spell a word with a long *a* sound. Knowing about potential difficulties in little words helps them attempt polysyllabic words that include the same sound. Specific words can also be personal "demons" for young writers, and as they gain sensitivity to these words—"Oh, look, I spelled *from* like *form* again, I have to change the *r*"— they realize that misspellings can always be corrected.

If children speak a nonstandard dialect or are learning English as a second language, they should be helped to recognize how their oral production and correct spelling may differ. For instruction, the "most efficient materials are those which allow children to relate written English to the spoken English they already command. . . . Dictations by children and later stories written by the children are logical. . . . The children's own words then are available for numerous word study activities, including the examination of spelling patterns" (Stever, 1980, p. 50). The message is clear: Let children dictate and let them write.

Learning to use the dictionary is also important, and the excuse that "I don't know how to spell it, so how can I look it up?" should never be accepted. Children who have been forming hypotheses by "spelling it as it sounds" can easily apply the same process to dictionary sleuthing by thinking of the many *possible* ways a word might be spelled. Group modeling is a good way of teaching children to do this: The teacher selects a difficult or irregular word and together the group generates and discusses possible spellings. The correct spelling can then be found in the dictionary. Demonstrating the process shows children what they should do individually and helps them realize what they do know about spelling.

The drawback to introducing the dictionary early in children's school years is often the dictionary itself. School dictionaries, especially for young children, are often limited. Investing in a few high quality, current children's dictionaries is worthwhile. Picture dictionaries, often with words arranged by categories, are fine for very young children because they introduce the concept of a "book of words" but should be followed quickly by real beginning dictionaries with words arranged alphabetically. Some children may simply browse through a good dictionary, looking for words, studying pictures, charts, and diagrams; familiarity with this resource is invaluable.

Subvocalizing is the final aid that children must learn to use. Inventive spellers vocalize what they want to spell, but older children need to quiet their voice to a whisper to use this valuable auditory aid in spelling unfamiliar words. Children who view spelling as memorization may be especially reluctant to subvocalize, as are children who have not realized the connection between sounding words out in reading and in spelling. Teachers must acknowledge that subvocalizing is part of the spelling process for many words and that it is not, as one child told me, "cheating—you know, you are supposed to be able to spell the word from your memory." Some children will need scrap paper so that they can write down the results of their subvocalizing to compare the various possible spellings for unfamiliar words.

SUMMARY

Think about your own spelling behaviors. How many "tricks" do you use? How many of these tricks did you figure out as you mastered the cognitive processes of spelling? How many did teachers actually tell you to use? It makes sense to *tell* children as much as possible so that they can "get a feel" for spelling as a dynamic and masterable task as they refine what they have discovered through invented spelling and move on confidently toward continued spelling growth.

Teaching spelling as a mysterious, memorization process, on the other hand, violates what children have learned about manipulating letters and sounds, penalizes nonstandard speakers, and frustrates young writers. Teachers should encourage children to build on what they know about oral and written communication as they master spelling skills.

REVIEW QUESTIONS

1. Be sure you can define each of these terms:
   deviant spelling
   early phonemic spelling
   invented spelling
   letter-name spelling
   memory aids
   phoneme
   subvocalization
   transitional stage spelling
2. Study the sample spelling lists presented in Figure 7.5 and make suggestions to expand it.
3. Discuss Rice's claim that instruction should begin with words that are easy to spell in terms of your own experiences. Do you agree or disagree with him?
4. What attitude should teachers adopt toward spelling errors? How can a poor attitude discourage young learners?
5. In what ways can instruction in developing and using memory aids in spelling be more beneficial than having children merely memorize lists of words?
6. Even though there has been extensive research on invented spelling, many people do not know or understand about it. Write a letter that you might send to parents at the beginning of the year to explain and justify your reasons for encouraging children to use invented spelling.
7. Find and examine some early childhood (grades 1–3) commercial spelling programs. Compare them against Rice's criteria for good instruction. How do they rate?

NOTES

1. Gentry, R. C. (1981). Learning to spell developmentally. *The Reading Teacher, 34,* 378–381.
2. Edelsky, C. (1986). *Writing in a bilingual program: Habia una vez.* Norwood, NJ: Ablex.
3. Russell, D. (1984). Teacher assistance for children learning how to learn spelling. In W. McVitty (Ed.). *Children and Learning* (pp. 65–71). Rozelle, New South Wales: Primary English Teaching Association.
4. Temple, C. A., Nathan, R. J., & Burris, N. A. (1982). *The beginnings of writing.* Boston: Allyn & Bacon.

5. Gentry, J. R., & Henderson, E. H. (1978). Three steps to teach beginning readers to spell. *The Reading Teacher, 31,* 632–637. See also: Beers, C. S., & Beers, J. W. (1981). Three assumptions about learning to spell. *Language Arts, 58,* 573–580.

6. Venezky, R. L. (1980). Spelling instruction and spelling reform. In U. Frith (Ed.). *Cognitive processes in learning to spell* (pp. 9–30). New York: Academic Press.

7. Chomsky, C. (1971). Write first, read later. *Childhood Education, 47,* 296–299.

8

The Beginnings of Composition

This chapter discusses the very beginnings of composition—the way awareness of letter formation and invented spelling merge in children's first attempts at creative writing. Samples presented throughout this chapter show the natural emergence of composition skills in prekindergarten, kindergarten, and first-grade classrooms. Reports from two graduate students will introduce the topic. These reports chronicle their writers' own experiences with children's beginning writing.

The first report was written as part of an end-term project by a student who was herself only beginning to discover the potential of children's writing.[1] The second report resulted from a longer period of teacher experimentation. Notice the ideas this kindergarten teacher tried and rejected.

Both classrooms were exciting places. The first report is from a teacher in a half-day, public preschool for Spanish-speaking children from low-economic families. The second describes a full-day public kindergarten in an upper-middle-class neighborhood in the same city. In both situations, the teachers recognized that writing should be an integral part of the early childhood curriculum and supported children's emerging literacy. Both teachers were kidwatchers, whose skilled observations guided their interactions with their students.

REPORT NO. 1

Many children bring beginning skills and an awareness about reading and writing to preschool. The extent of these skills is affected by factors the teachers often cannot control, but two factors a teacher can control are the quantity and quality of literary events offered in the classroom. Every time learners use language, they are learning language, learning through language, and learning more about language. My contention has been that children use literate language for learning, and they learn through literate language. Once a week we make a class book. The children are given a topic, draw something related to the topic, and bring their drawings to me to write what they tell me about the picture. Drawing is one way to provide a meaningful opportunity to use literate language and increases their understanding of the way oral and written language interrelate to represent meaning. The children in my classroom know their drawings represent ideas or things. For about the first three books the children orally "labeled" their drawings. At the beginning all I wrote were labels. Then I began restating the "labels" in complete sentences and writing them down that way. Soon, when the children described their drawings, they talked more in complete sentences.

The purpose of giving each drawing a caption has been twofold. First, we increase the child's vocabulary by taking his ideas and adding more words. Second, we show the child that writing is another form of symbolism for his ideas. Although drawing maintains a relationship of similarity to the object or occurrence it refers to, writing does not. Writing is a system with its own rules.

Gradually, the children began to "write" more freely, and it became obvious that all the children were drawing something related to the theme presented, sometimes even in the form of pictures rather than individual items to be labeled. It became safe to say that the descriptions of their drawings began to take on a "story-like" quality. Writing has varied from some added punctuation marks, others grouped letter-like symbols written together for words or phrases. None of the children said he didn't know how to write.

The children clearly began to feel comfortable with "writing." One important factor in the transition was the use of writing instruments. Crayons had always been used for drawing and writing. Now markers and pencils were placed at the tables for the children to use. They have been a major motivational factor.

Classbooks have opened up a whole new world of literature for the children. These books have become treasures that they want to share with others. Writing is indeed one area where I noted much progress. . . .

REPORT NO. 2

Last year was the first year I asked my students to write their own sentences using words from the sight word list. . . . About the middle of this year, I noticed some of my more advanced students writing on their own. I showed these pictures to another teacher and learned that the writing was a valuable learning experience for the children. I started to give the students papers and encouraged them to write. Some of the children claimed they simply could not do it. Little by little, they saw the other children doing their own writing and tried it themselves. It took constant reassurance before these children began to feel secure.

About this time, I read my first literature on invented spelling. I began to experiment with formats with which my children would be comfortable. I found they loved colored pens on white paper. They also liked to draw pictures with their stories. I found that they wanted to read their stories to me as soon as they finished. This presented a problem when the whole class wrote at once. Some of the less mature students forgot what they had written before they could read it back to me. If I were able to write down what they had written, in normal spelling, before they forgot, I could tell them if they then later forgot. I eventually began to have the children write in small groups on a rotating basis.

The form the children most often used was a picture with the story on the same page. The more advanced students started with the story, then the picture. Soon, all the class was using this method. . . . Once, a child wrote a whole series of disjoined sight words and told me a sentence that neither made sense nor followed the sight words. I asked him what his picture was about. He told me. I then asked him to write it while I watched. He started to sound out and write his words. He was very nervous! After he finished, I read his sentence back to him, pointing to each word as I read. He was amazed that I could *read* his writing. He was thrilled when *he* saw *he* could read *his* writing. Here was a child that was "far below grade level" having his first major success in the game of reading, writing, and spelling. I truly felt like a teacher.

My only regret is not starting sooner. Next year I will start at the beginning of the year. . . .[2]

BEGINNING EFFORTS AT COMPOSITION

As children discover the basic principles of letter formation, they begin to write. These first efforts may be nearly illegible, may be in pseudo-manuscript or in pseudo-cursive, and will show the deviant stage of invented spelling with no letter-sound correspondence. Just as beginning speech is context-dependent, beginning writing cannot be understood without help from the young writers. You just have to be there—to talk to the children about any drawing they have done and to ask what they have written. While some beginning writers claim that they do not know what they have written and others read their message confidently, all have realized the differences between writing and drawing—that writing is placed linearly on a page, that there is variety to the forms of individual letters, and that writing consists of multiple-unit displays of several letter-like forms.[3] Beginning efforts are often single-word labels placed near the drawing they represent.

Labels to Captions

Preschool and kindergarten teachers encourage children to write on their drawings by offering to transcribe messages into standard language. Teachers should always read the transcription back to the young artist-author and should never express judgment about children's work. They can, however, question and shape children's behavior. For example, children may begin to write *on* their drawings before they realize that they are supposed to write *about* them. If what children want transcribed seems to have no relationship to the drawing, teachers should question further by saying, "OK, but do you want me to write something *about* your picture? Tell me *about* what you have drawn." Gradually, children will realize what is expected and will usually then begin to request **labels** for the various parts of their art work. This understanding—that they are supposed to be able to write and to talk about their pictures—falls within the category of behaviors known as pragmatics, discussed in Chapter 3. It is part of the social use of language within a school setting.

Teachers also can expand labels to captions verbally by restating and writing, "This is a ____." Children soon learn this longer statement and dictate **captions** themselves. Teachers should ask for additional information about children's pictures to model the process of "writing" longer and longer messages but must always be sensitive to children's level of interest and motivation. Requesting too much information too quickly can take the pleasure away from beginning writers; dictated stories lengthen on their own as children gain understanding about producing texts. Figure 8.1 shows these beginning efforts.

Text Production and the Language Experience Approach

As they write and dictate, children are actually producing texts, while teachers do the manual work. The process of children dictating while teachers transcribe is usually called the language experience approach (LEA). Its most common application is in beginning reading, but its importance in beginning writing should not be overlooked.

In traditional language experience sessions, teachers merely transcribe and then read back what the children say. Extending LEA to transcribing what children have written demonstrates the one-to-one correspondence between oral and written language. This concept is vital for beginning writing and reading but is often not clear to young learners. "When asked to point out words, a child may indicate letters or whole lines of text. Since words are actually separated by spaces greater than those between letters, the information on the page *should be fairly easy to distinguish once the child has the concept of a graphic word*. The fact that words are units of speech and also units in a printed text and as such correspond is obviously a basic concept to get across early in the game" (Gibson & Levin, 1975, p. 242, italics added). Teacher transcription of children's print reinforces the concept of a graphic word, distinct from oral language.

Language experience chart stories also help children understand text production. In these LEA sessions, teachers elicit ideas from children about a shared experience (a trip, for example) or a stimulus question or topic (families,

Sample 1. Child wrote in deviant spelling and dictated label.

Sample 2. Child labelled parts of his picture: "VOLCANO FIRED" and "VOLCANIC ACTION."

Sample 3. Child wrote her own labels on pictures of her friends. She also wrote "SCHOOL IS OVER. I LIKE SCHOOL."

FIGURE 8.1

The beginning of writing is labeling. Children may request that teachers label parts of their drawings or may use deviant spelling to label parts themselves. Gradually, labels expand to captions.

the neighborhood). As children dictate, the teacher writes and records ideas and constructs a story to be shared. Often teachers record exactly what children say, quoting directly and using each child's name. While this does present a *form* of text production, the result is often boring. Transcribing exactly what each child says is not necessary, especially if teachers wish to use LEA sessions to model text production as a dynamic process involving decisions about word choice and sentence structure. Thus, after the trip to the zoo, teacher/student interaction might begin like this:

Teacher:	Let's write a chart story about our trip. What shall we call our story?
Tommy:	Our Trip to the Zoo.
Teacher:	Any other suggestions? No? Ok, that's our title. [She writes the title at the top of the chart.] Who has something to say first?
Mary:	We went to the zoo.
Teacher:	Great. Look what I am going to write. [She writes: "We went to the Zoo."] What did we see first?
Rachel:	We saw elephants.
Teacher:	That's right. We saw elephants. Anyone want to add something?
Mike:	They were big, big elephants.
John:	They had big, floppy ears.
Susie:	They were huge.
Manny:	They were my favorite.
Teacher:	Very good. Look what I am going to write. [She writes: "We saw the elephants first." She draws a quick sketch of an elephant and continues to write: "They were . . ."; she stops and looks at the children and asks:] What word shall I use? *Big* or *huge?*
Children:	Use *huge,* it means bigger than big.
Teacher:	OK [she continues to write: "They were huge and had big floppy ears. Manny said they were his favorite."] Who else liked them best? Oh you did, Paul? Watch what I can do. [The teacher uses an arrow and inserts the words *and Paul* in over Manny's name, crosses out *his* and writes *their;* the revised sentence reads: "Manny and Paul said they were their favorite," pointing to each word with her finger.]

Dynamic transcription of LEA stories demonstrates many aspects of text production. It shows children that writers plan, make choices about words and sentence structure, even change words and add further ideas. Additions of pictures to the LEA story lets children know that they, too, can use pictures to placehold words they cannot spell. The actual LEA chart story is less important in this method than the lessons children learn about producing texts. As they watch the teacher integrate oral statements into a text, they are also seeing their unstated ideas woven into the total story. Who said what doesn't matter as the story itself unfolds. Even children as young as 3 or 4 years will benefit from this approach, for what they see confirms and expands their own ideas about writing.

Gradually, depending on the age and abilities of their classes, teachers can add more complex conventions to LEA transcriptions. Asking for suggestions for descriptive words, for example, provides indirect instruction on adjective use and precise vocabulary choice. The differentiation above between *big* and *huge* could have been expanded to include choices such as *large, enormous, gigantic,* and *humongous*. Deliberate use of quotations in the transcription can introduce quotation marks to young writers. Asking children in the transitional stage of invented spelling to "help" with a difficult word or suggesting that "We can look that word up in the dictionary" also demonstrates the dynamic aspect of text production. As children manipulate language in LEA sessions and observe their teachers fine tuning their ideas for transcription, they both confirm their hypotheses about writing and learn new ideas. It is not uncommon for children to experiment with a convention included in an LEA story in their own writing. To quote Vygotsky again, "What children can do in cooperation today, they can do alone tomorrow." Harste, Woodward, and Burke (1984, p. 192) more specifically remind teachers that "children's latest language discoveries are always more fun to think about than those which [they] already think [they] have sorted out."

MAKING PROGRESS IN COMPOSITION

Allowed to draw, encouraged to write, and reassured that invented spelling and experimentation are fine, children in preschool, kindergarten, and early primary grades make progress in composition. When children are allowed to write, other language-related activities in early childhood classes become integrated and mutually supportive. Learning standard spelling and legible handwriting is viewed as means to communicate more efficiently in writing; reading is valued because it represents sharing ideas with other authors. Practice in all language skills reinforces mastery of the others. This is the nature of whole language instruction.

Drawing

Drawing serves as a "warm up" or prewriting activity for some children.[4] As children draw, they think about the story they want to tell and organize their ideas accordingly. Writing in deviant spelling affirms their intent to tell a story, but they may well elaborate on their basic story when they dictate to a teacher. Children using more advanced levels of invented spelling will show consistent relationships between picture and writing, although they, too, may elaborate in dictation.

Drawing can also help children remember what they want to write about. As they draw, they think about the pictorial and verbal representations of their story. Because the process of invented spelling can take a long time, children may forget some of the things they wanted to convey in print. Pictorial representations jog memories about content and help children stay on task. In similar fashion, drawing may sometimes replace writing, as when children draw a picture instead of writing a difficult word. When children begin to write extensively, some may simply give up writing and finish their story by "drawing the end."

Whether children write or draw first or go back and forth between the two, drawing can motivate more elaborate stories. A child draws something and writes a single sentence. Looking back at the drawing, he decides to add something else, which requires an additional sentence. The drawing and story together become more complex. Drawing can also help children organize the format or conventions of writing. Small pieces of paper for small pictures invite only short sentences and are not perceived as difficult assignments. Several single sheets of small paper can always be stapled together to form a book for a long story. Large pieces of paper may be more intimidating in terms of drawing and writing requirements, but divided into sections they offer a handy format for telling a sequential story.

Because drawing is important, teachers should provide ample paper and a variety of writing/drawing tools. Many of the samples in this chapter were written with magic markers on the back of used computer paper. The markers themselves were motivating, and the computer paper was of a high enough quality that it did not absorb ink and "bleed." The lines of the computer paper showed faintly through to the wrong side, and some children used these as guides for letter formation. Early childhood penmanship paper with wide lines and space at the top for a picture can work well to integrate drawing and composition, but its pulpy texture is poor for magic markers, and it tends to rip easily.

Encouragement

Teachers encourage youngsters to write by suggesting that children "write something" on their papers and by showing enthusiasm for all efforts. Teacher modeling of writing and the overall literate environment of a good classroom will do the rest to move children along to produce texts themselves.

When children demonstrate that they know the connection between drawing and writing, teacher encouragement should take the form of teacher expectations. "Children in my class write a lot," a teacher might say to let children know that they are expected to write something on their drawings, to write little notes, and to communicate with others through print. As teachers express their expectations, they must be careful not to imply that all writing must be correct.

The distinctions between process, practice, and form must be made clear to youngsters so that they trust their teacher to value their efforts at strengthening new skills. One first-grade teacher who has an extensive creative writing program in her class makes sure that children (and their parents) know that "In here, we *practice* a lot!"

Direct assignments or suggestions for drawings and stories can provide encouragement, too. Guidelines for making assignments will be discussed in the next chapter, but beginners often need assignments as well. While children should be allowed to draw for its own sake, they can waste considerable time trying to think of something to draw and write about; a focused topic can help them narrow their thinking from the start. Focusing them toward a particular subject or topic (something they like to do, a class trip, favorite animals or foods) can make their effort more efficient. As they gain confidence, many children reject assigned topics in favor of their own ideas. Some children move quickly to writing about varied, often wild, topics; others move more slowly and may continue to ask, "What can I draw, what can I write?" Teachers' suggestions of a topic implies, "I know that getting started is hard but I'd really like to see your ideas about. . . ."

Invented Spelling and Experimentation

Writing can be perceived as risk-taking, as making oneself vulnerable to criticism and judgment, to being called "wrong." Yet, to advance literacy learning, writers must take risks. Harste, Woodward, and Burke (1984) commented: "Counter to current instructional folklore, recent insights into risk-taking and its relationship to literacy and literacy learning suggest that literacy programs which emphasize correct responses and attempt to eliminate error fail to best serve literacy learning. It is only when language users get themselves in trouble within what was perceived to be a moderately predictable setting that growth occurs" (p. 136).

Selecting a topic for drawing is one form of risk: What if it is silly or inappropriate? Actual composition requires even more risks as children must coordinate the following:

- ☐ what they know about letter formation
- ☐ what they know about spelling
- ☐ what they know about the conventions of print (spacing, punctuation)
- ☐ what they know about grammar and sentence structure
- ☐ what they know about vocabulary
- ☐ what they know about acceptable topics, subjects, and themes

There is a lot of room for error, so it is no wonder that 3- and 4-year-old authors, who know less about the complexities of writing, tend to be less cautious than are 5- and 6-year-olds.[5]

Teachers' overall tone of encouragement and support may not be enough to reassure cautious children or those who have been told emphatically that writing, especially spelling, must be absolutely correct. "The perception that when one writes one must spell correctly appears to be the single biggest constraint which 5- and 6-year-old children see as the reason why they can't engage in the process" (Harste, Woodward, & Burke, 1984, p. 131). In addition to encouraging practice, teachers must stress to children, "Spell it the way it sounds; do the best you can; we'll look it up later." Teachers must then accept children's writing with genuine enthusiasm and interest. Because invented spelling beyond the deviant state does follow certain logical patterns, teachers quickly learn to read at least the bulk of what their children write and can easily engage in dialogue with children about the content of their work.

Experimentations with punctuation, capitalization, sentence structure, figures of speech, and other conventions of writing must be greeted enthusiastically as well. Children learn about conventions of writing from the environment, language experience sessions, storytime, and their own reading. It seems natural to them to try these devices in their own writing. As children experiment, they show confidence in their skills and interest in language itself. Some of the best examples of young children's writing result from their attempts to master the more complex conventions of sophisticated text.

Progression of Skills: Beyond Labels and Captions

As children move beyond labels and captions, they begin to write (and dictate) sentences to accompany their art work. Because children write only single sentences at first, it might be easy to think of this stage as an extension of caption writing, yet children are actually trying to share information or tell a story by using pictures *and* writing to produce extended text. These sentences are the real beginnings of composition and will be referred to as *stories*.

A common pattern after labels and captions is the **I like . . . story** with its "I love . . ." variation. Assigned or spontaneous, these stories require few risks. The mere question "Why" is often enough to encourage expansion of the basic topic. "I like . . ." booklets can be used for more extensive writing. The simplest version has the sentence starter "I LIKE _____" on each page. Teachers can write these pages themselves or use a ditto or computer program such as Printshop to produce multiple pages for children to fill in with single words and pictures as a variation of commercial caption books. Alternatively, children can be given blank pages and the suggestion to write and draw about what they like and dislike. Figure 8.2 shows several stages of "I Like . . ." stories.

A second pattern can be called **I + [action verb] stories.** These sentences are also safe and highly personal. The thought process to develop these stories probably goes like this: "What can I draw a picture of myself doing," or "What have I done recently that I can draw," or "What do I want that I can draw

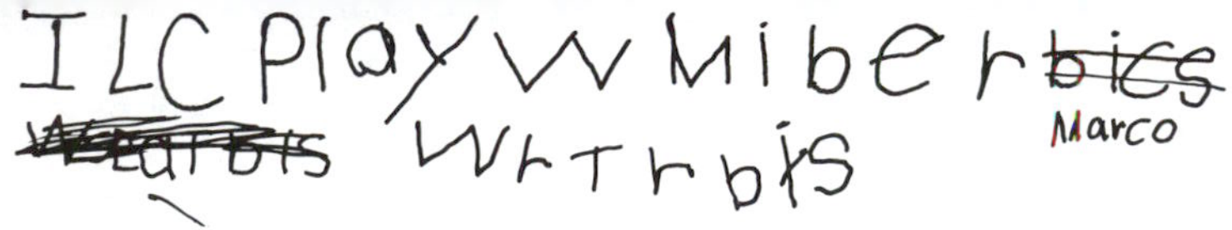

I LC PloyWMiberbies
~~Wearers~~ WRTbIS Marco

Sample 1. Child indicates what he likes to do, note correction of false start in spelling.

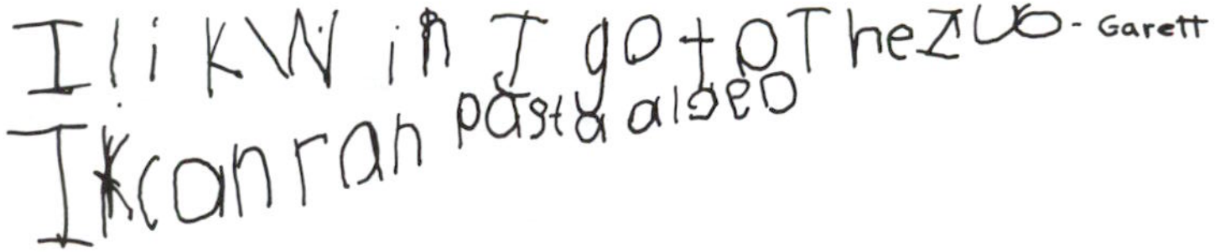

I liKW in I gotoTheZUb - Garett
IKonrah post gai8eb

Sample 2. Child indicates what he likes to do and tells something about the activity; he is still uncertain about spacing between words.

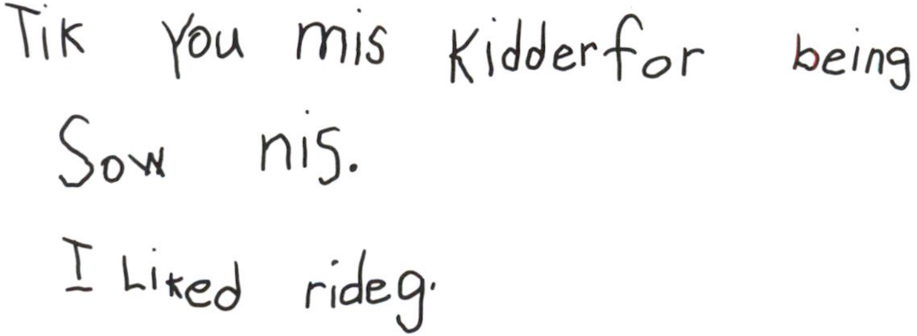

Tik You Mis Kidderfor being
Sow nis.
I Liked rideg.

Sample 3. Child thanks her kindergarten teacher for being so nice and tells her that she like(s) reading; this child leaves ample space between her words; notice the emerging spelling skills.

I Loveyou my litte red wagin
becus it is pritty!

Sample 4. The child addresses her little red wagon and attempts to explain why she loves it; she changes number in the second part of her sentence but has clearly experimented with sentence construction; note two punctuation marks.

Erin
I LiKe My Kite beekas
It hasit A pees A s t On
and it hasPritty
and My MoMMy hitegnt
ME Bot it for
and I Like it.

Sample 5. This child also states why she likes a toy, and she goes on to describe the kite and tell where she got it; notice how she corrects false starts. This is a later effort of the child who wrote Sample 4.

FIGURE 8.2

"I LIKE" stories allow children to write about things and events of special interest and significance. The basic sentence "I like _____" may be expanded with reasons and description. At times, teachers may prompt this expansion by requesting more information. These samples were collected as part of the regular writing period in a kindergarten class; transcriptions were done by the teacher.

about?" These stories begin with the first person pronoun *I* and include action verbs such as *want, wish,* or *had a dream.* Children move easily between present and past tense and eventually begin to use the first person plural (e.g., "My friend and I") as the subject. Within the safety of the "I + [action verb]" pattern, children may give current, factual information or express wishes, either real or fanciful. Children also experiment with more sophisticated language structures. They vary elements of the basic pattern to see what happens; they change the subject of their sentences; and they add extra sentences to expand their story and convey more information. Figure 8.3 shows this kind of writing.

Categories of Writing

James Britton (1970) has proposed three "function categories" or "voices" into which writing can be divided. His first category is the **expressive voice,** writing closest to oneself. "I Like" and "I + [action verb]" stories are expressive: Children write about themselves and from their own point of view with the assumption that their readers will be interested in what is written. The second category is **poetic writing.** It includes stories, plays, songs, and jokes, as well as poems, and is structured according to specific guidelines. Stories, for example, consist of a beginning, middle, and end. Within that framework, a setting, characters, problem, and resolution are all presented. Britton's third category is transactional. Directions, instructions, procedures, description, information, persuasion, advice, explanation—all these represent **transactional writing.** Children encounter much transactional writing in textbooks and other school-related activities. Even young children are capable of writing poetic and transactional prose.

As samples presented so far show, children easily figure out the expressive voice and begin to use it almost automatically. They discover basic principles of transactional and poetic writing from stories read to them, from their own reading, and from television and other media. They realize that genuine stories in the poetic voice have a particular pattern that goes from "Once upon a time" to "happily ever after." Children also realize that other "stories" serve other purposes, those of the transactional voice. Even children who have not had many stories read to them can make these distinctions from their exposure to television. For example, morning cartoons present identifiable "story lines" that differ significantly from the format of children's programs designed to convey information. A program like "Mr. Rogers' Neighborhood" has distinct breaks between "teaching" and "entertainment" segments to encourage the appropriate viewer attention.

Some children begin to experiment with transactional and poetic writing on their own; others need instruction. Movement out of expressive writing is often accompanied by experimentation with other conventions of writing such as dialogue or personification. Teachers can encourage this progress through

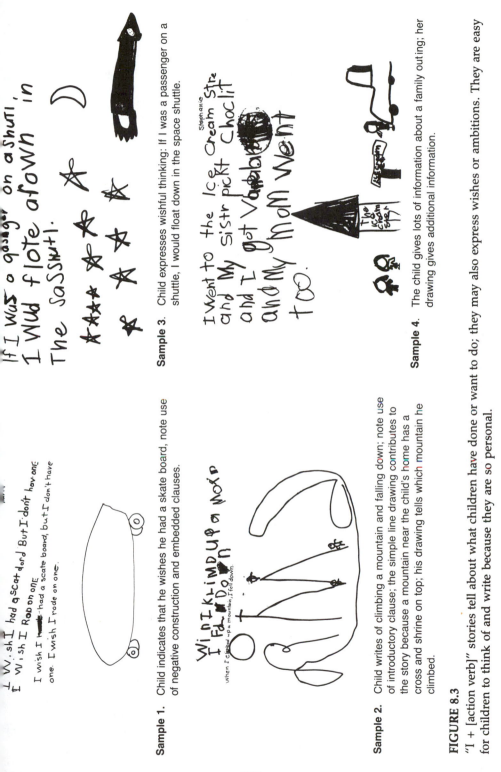

I Wish I had a scat dord But I don't have one I Wish I Rob on one

I wish I ~~had~~ had a scate board, but I don't have one. I wish I rode on one.

Sample 1. Child indicates that he wishes he had a skate board, note use of negative construction and embedded clauses.

Wi n I KLimDUP a moxd
I FaLL DOWn
When I clabar up a mountan, I fell down.

Sample 2. Child writes of climbing a mountain and falling down; note use of introductory clause; the simple line drawing contributes to the story because a mountain near the child's home has a cross and shrine on top; his drawing tells which mountain he climbed.

If I was a gassger on a shuti,
I Wud flote afown in
The SaSShti.

Sample 3. Child expresses wishful thinking: If I was a passenger on a shuttle, I would float down in the space shuttle.

I Went to the Ice Cream Str
and My sistr pickt Choclit
and I got Vanilok
and My mom Went
too.

Stephanie

Sample 4. The child gives lots of information about a family outing; her drawing gives additional information.

FIGURE 8.3

"I + [action verb]" stories tell about what children have done or want to do; they may also express wishes or ambitions. They are easy for children to think of and write because they are so personal.

children's literature. Reading an interesting, appropriate science book and talking about how well the author "gave us new information about the topic" may spur some children to write transactional prose. Discussion of "the unusual setting and interesting characters" in a storybook may initiate some poetic writing. Teachers must remember that children need to feel confident of their abilities in the expressive voice before they will willingly undertake the risk of writing in a new voice.

In reality, children's writing cannot always be categorized neatly according to Britton's scheme, especially in early childhood classes, where it is useful to think of children's writing as "transitional."[6] **Transitional writing** falls between two discrete categories as children move from expressive to poetic and from expressive to transactional writing. The "in-between" nature of transitional writing demonstrates children's reaching for mastery of new writing skills.

Playing with Ideas and Conventions

Movement out of the expressive voice is marked by experiments with ideas that parallel the linguistic play of oral language growth. When children play with ideas, they venture into fantasy, express outrageous wishes, write about supposedly taboo subjects, or attempt to shock, surprise, or even "gross out" their readers. Writing of this sort is riskier than verbal linguistic play because there is a written record of the child's thoughts. Stories may still be relatively short, but children are clearly making progress in text production.

Children also manipulate words and sentence parts in an attempt to embed clauses into sentences, string more than one idea together into compound sentences, or test ideas about grammatical rules or devices. Realizing that printed material contains punctuation, children may sprinkle periods, commas, exclamation points, and question marks throughout their stories. They may also attempt to vary sentence form by posing questions and answering them or writing in dialogue.

Often these manipulations reflect what children have heard in storybook reading or have read themselves. Their writing begins to **talk like a book.** The discussion of language experience stated that exact transcription of children's statements can mislead youngsters into thinking that all print sounds like talk, while early childhood literacy instruction should help children realize the differences between "book talk" and ordinary speech. Teachers cannot teach this difference directly, but well-prepared, enthusiastic oral reading of good children's literature provides the material from which children extract the concept themselves. When children begin a story with "Once upon a time," teachers know that the important difference between talk and text has been recognized.

Teachers' storybook reading should also make children aware that books have authors, illustrators, divisions called chapters, and specific narrative sequences. Children experiment with these concepts by calling themselves "authors" and "illustrators." To extend this experimentation, teachers can suggest that children divide large paper into several blocks or use separate pieces of paper to make a book. These separate blocks or pages help children to organize their thinking and to sequence stories. Knowing, for example, that there are four blocks to fill in with pictures and sentences tells children that they must think up four related parts for the story. If they draw and write in an inappropriate sequence, all they have to do is number the four component parts to show their order. The task, while difficult, has clear boundaries within which to function: It is risky but possible. Giving children this structured means of moving from single sentences to sequenced stories is a good example of Vygotsky's idea of helping a child solve linguistic problems today so that he can solve them alone tomorrow. Figure 8.4 illustrates children's attempts to manipulate space and ideas in early writing.

Beginnings of Narrative Fiction

Stories in Figure 8.5 represent the transitional stage between expressive and poetic writing. They are varied in theme and characters, but all show divergence from pure personal experience narration. Some show experimentation with story formats and "book language." Others show experimentations with usually "unspeakable" ideas and words that test the limits of writing: How much will teachers tolerate? How outrageous can the stories become? What words will alarm the teacher? What themes are too gruesome? Children seem to test teachers' assurance that they can "write whatever they wish." While not long, stories like these break away from the safety of personal experiences and venture into risky territory. These writers balance many variables as they played with style, language, and characters. They often use art minimally or not at all, attesting to their sense of the power of words alone to convey their stories.

Editing and Revising

Too many children do not learn that whatever is written down can be changed, crossed out, amended, or edited to include new words or ideas. In fact, they learn the opposite and never realize the learning that comes from risk-taking "mistakes." The statement "Spell it as best you can" in its most general sense may not occur to children without direct instruction. Language experience sessions in which teachers model changes may be children's first contact with this aspect of writing, and the "naturalness" of this behavior should be stressed. Allowing children to write with felt-tipped pens and magic markers has already been mentioned as a motivational device; its further purpose is to encourage editing. Because the ink cannot be erased, children *must* cross out errors and false starts, and soon they realize that writers often take their work through several drafts. The samples in Figure 8.6 show different purposes and styles of

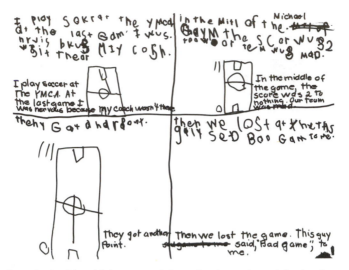

Sample 1. The child wrote and drew about a real event; having four spaces to fill rather than a whole sheet of paper made his task more manageable. Note that the drawing shows the layout of the soccer field rather than children playing the game.

Sample 2. This child drew individual "events" in his story in boxes like a comic strip; his writing was separated by dots rather than spaces; his story described the entire set of pictures; "A long time ago an old Model T just went putt, putt, putt along the road. All of a sudden a cat ran out in the road and splat the cat was gone." The child obviously enjoyed the gruesomeness of his story. Notice the HaHaHa in several blocks.

FIGURE 8.4

Young writers experiment with space and with characters as they emerge into confident writing. As this happens, they may not depend on drawing to help tell their stories.

Wen i went to sleep   I was dreming Carlos
abowt the dog in Spasce the
dog was drawing himself fling
X turn after a cat in Space. And the dog
Back and now the cat was
after the dog and the cat scard
the dog away.

Sample 3. This child wrote about a dream: When I went to sleep I was
dreaming about the dog in space. the dog was drawing
himself flying after a cat in space. And the dog got scared
and turned back and now the cat was after the dog and the
cat scared the dog away. His dreams includes made-up
characters and considerable action. Notice the arrows to
indicate which drawing is which character.

Ther was a sheap. when he went
to eat he wolud all ways
find a wolf. the shea
ran away. and the wolf wolud
get lost. Becouse the shea
p was cleaver. then he went
back to eat another wolf
found him agin! then the farmer came out and chased the
wolf away!
Carlos

Sample 4. This child began on the back of his sheet of paper by writing
a list of characters: Sheep, wolf, farmer (named Larry), Frank,
and bob. His dictation read: There was a sheep. When he
went to eat he would always find a wolf. The sheep ran away.
And the wolf would get lost because the sheep was clever.
Then he went back to eat. an d another wolf found him again.
Then the farmer came out and chased the wolf away. The list
of characters gives information that is not included in the
story, and the story itself may be a take-off on something the
child has heard or read.

FIGURE 8.4
continued

145

Sample 1. The drawing conveys the action in this story; it is full of red and black and unhappy faces. The child's text (which he read tentatively to his teacher incase she might disapprove) was: A Dog was dumb enough to go in front of the racing track.

Sample 2. This child also tested his teacher's tolerance for gruesome subjects; his story, written without drawings, read: One day a boy was playing soccer with his friends and the boy was winning. All of a sudden, the boy fell. He fell again and again and again. He cracked his head open. He died. The end. The child might have been trying to imitate a sports caster or merely shock his teacher. The writing (done without spaces between words) has a definite book-like tone that would not have been present if the child had been reporting on a real incident.

FIGURE 8.5

As children gain confidence in their ability to communicate in writing, they attempt to shock, test, or even "gross out" their readers. Experiments with gruesome subjects or taboo words should be welcomed as signs of increasing skill and sense of authorship.

W in DoL DaK DiD ThRWAA
Ca. on The pepL̓ ThSLM

Sample 3. This is a much simpler story, written with less control of spelling; it reads: When Donald Duck did throw a tray on the people, the people screamed. What is unique about the story is the characterization of Donald Duck, unless the child was reporting on something he had seen on television.

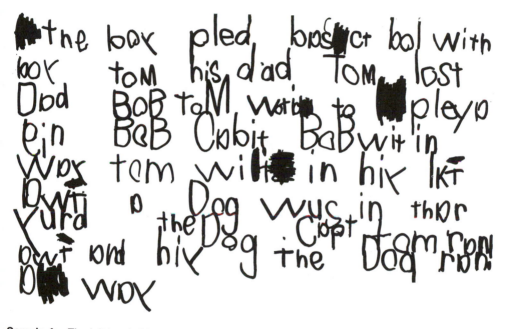

Sample 4. The left-hand side of this story lists a cast of characters. The story itself is not unique, except for the inclusion of one word. As the child read the story to his teacher, he paused and seemed to gauge whether or not to dictate what he had written; his teacher, the writer of Report No. 2, did not even flinch. The story reads: The boy played basket ball with his dad. Tom lost. Tom wanted to play again. Bob couldn't. Bob went in. When Tom went in, he looked. A dog was in their yard. The dog crapped. Tom ran out and the dog ran away. Note that the writer of this story was named neither Tom, nor Bob.

FIGURE 8.5
continued

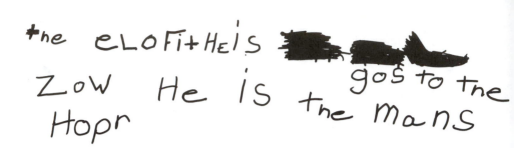

Sample 1. This child merely crosses out words she wants to change; the story reads: The elephant is going to the zoo. He is the man's helper.

Sample 2. This story has no drawing; the child had learned (through language experience) that he could add words by using arrows; his text reads: The man is cleaning the back yard and the man is playing soccer.

FIGURE 8.6

Giving children magic markers instead of pencils for their beginning writing is motivating and also encourages them to cross out errors or false starts. Letting beginning writers know that this is merely part of the writing process and is acceptable prepares them for

Sample 3. This child makes corrections by writing needed letters over the letters he has already written (as in FROG) or by crossing out.

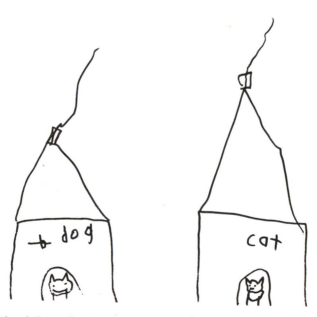

Sample 4. This story is interesting because the child corrected the text and his drawing so that they would go together; he began with The dog is in the box, changed the square box he had drawn to a house, and changed the word he used to describe the dog's location; then her changed the second part of the story as well.

FIGURE 8.6

continued

the editing and revising they will do later on longer pieces of writing. Crossing out and insertion of words with arrows during LEA models this process for young children.

TABLE 8.1
Developmental stages of beginning writing

Child's Behavior	Teacher's Behavior in Response
1. Drawing and unrelated dictation	Transcription and discussion; asks *about* drawing.
2. Drawing and related dictation	Transcription and discussion.
3. Drawing and labels	Transcription; extends label to caption (see Figure 8.1).
4. Drawing and caption	Transcription and discussion; may question to stimulate thought; suggests topics such as "What You Like."
5. "I like" stories (with or without drawing)	Transcription, if asked; questions "Why?" for expansion (see Figure 8.2).
6. "I + [action verb]" (with or without drawing)	Transcription if asked; discussion (see Figure 8.3).
7. Use of multiple first person subject (with or without drawing)	Transcription if asked; discussion (see Figure 8.3).
8. Use of third person subject	Transcription if asked; discussion (see Figure 8.3).
9. Writing with no drawing	Request for clarification if needed (see Figure 8.4).
10. Exploration of ideas, format, narrative mode	Response as needed; suggestions for change, clarification (see Figures 8.4 and 8.5).
11. Editorial changes; revisions	Response as needed (See Figure 8.6).

editing and even include one in which both text and pictures were altered as the child changed his mind about his writing.

How Much Can Teachers Expect?

Samples in this chapter were selected from children's work collected in public and private preschools, kindergartens, and first grades. They are representative of what children *can* do in a supportive, literate, early childhood classroom. The actual writing output of any one class during any one year will be influenced by many factors, including:

☐ how much writing children have done previously
☐ what children think composition involves (for example, correctness and neatness or creativity)

☐ how much prior literacy experience children have had (story reading, language experience, etc.)

☐ how verbal children are and how interested they are in language and language play

---

Sample 1. On day Bun Bun and Leafr war tacei (taking) a wak. Bun Bun Saw Brd Bode and crase carit. (Bird Buddy and Crazy Carrot).

Sample 2. On day Bun Bun had a BaeBey. She neamd hem Baebey Boney. Bun Bun got efeawon, (formula), Bae Bey Bone was qut.

Sample 3. My Cagashen (Composition) buuk
Own day when Bun Bun and Lefar was takkn a wak BunBun git qat in a trap. Lefr sed I ul help. Lefr git Bard bade and crase carts. finle tha cam weth Help. Thn tha ol wen too Bun Bun hows. thn the had denr. then tha ol went hom. To go to slep. crease carets cad not saep. he gost help from Bun Bun to hem to qaunt (count) sheep.

Sample 4. One day Bun Bun was plannting a garden ahd she asked Leafer to help. Tha planted carets and string beans and lettuse. And tha saw it gro.

Sample 5. One day wen Bun Bun and Leaker wos takn a wake. Tha kam to a plas war that havr never Ben befr. Bun Bun sed hew wl we get hom?

Sample 6. On day Bun Bun and Liefr and Bird Buddy and Crzy carrots wor tacing a walk and tha got lost. But Bun Bun sed I no the wea to liefor haws. so tha ol went to lefrs haws and tha ol went home.
the ind

Sample 7. It was thacsgeving and Bun Bun had bord Bodee and Krasee Karit and Liefr ofr for dinnr. tha had torkee and kramberee soes and pomken pei.

Sample 8. It was thacsgiving in yellow land and Torce gobol and sara sweet potatou and Bun Bun and Leefr ol had denor togegthr. But Sara sweet ptat and toke gobol got aiten up.
the ind

FIGURE 8.7

The on-going story of Bun-Bun. These stories were completed in a composition book as part of the writing work done in a first-grade classroom. Children wrote at least once every week about the characters the class had created together—Bun-Bun, a rabbit, and Leafer, a leaf. Other characters were created and introduced as needed. The samples were collected from September through November and are arranged chronologically. Note that this young author lives in New York. Her invented spelling reflects her speech patterns and differs slightly from that of the Texas children presented elsewhere in this chapter.

Many teachers who enthusiastically begin a writing program in kindergarten or first grade become disappointed. The development of writing skills takes time and energy, and progress is rarely made overnight. Teachers must be patient and supportive but also insistent that children do write as part of their regular classroom work. Table 8.1 summarizes the normal, developmental sequences of beginning writers in literate kindergarten and first-grade classes. Figure 8.7 samples one child's writing through the first half of first grade.

As children mature in spontaneous writing, teachers should help them refine their skills and reach for more sophistication. A balance of spontaneous writing, structured assignments, language experience, and direct instruction marks early childhood classrooms in which children make progress in composition.

SUMMARY

Young children can begin to compose real stories very early. Their initial efforts are often dictated messages that an adult writes to accompany a drawing or painting. Using deviant spelling, children soon write short commentaries on their work and welcome adult transcription of their ideas. Teacher support and enthusiasm spur young writers to explore conventions of writing they have heard in oral reading and to test the limits of their emerging skills. Some write elaborate stories, begin to use fiction and fantasy, and even edit their work. Language experience is a valuable means of expanding children's awareness of writing if teachers consciously use LEA sessions to model text production.

REVIEW QUESTIONS

1. Be sure you can define each of these terms:
   captions
   expressive writing
   "I + [action verb]" stories
   "I like . . ." stories
   labels
   poetic writing
   transactional writing
   transitional writing
   writing that "talks like a book"
2. Why do you think children's first efforts to combine composition and drawing are often nothing more than labels?
3. List and discuss as many uses of language experience as you can think of to demonstrate "text production" to young children. Do not limit yourself to chart stories.

4. How is drawing a "warm up" to writing for young authors? What can teachers do to encourage more writing in their classrooms?
5. In what ways is the child drawing-child dictating-teacher transcribing interaction a true literacy event?
6. Having varied kinds of paper and writing tools available motivates children to write. List as many such supplies as you can for an ideal early childhood class.
7. Visit several early childhood classes (including preschools) to assess the amount of writing going on. Is the amount adequate? What opportunities have teachers missed for children's writing?
8. Discuss children's writing with several early childhood teachers. Perhaps share with them the information in the two reports that open this chapter. What are their opinions? Do they differ from those expressed in this chapter? Are they receptive to the idea of young children writing?
9. Pretend you are the teacher in either of the classes described in the two reports. Parents do not understand what you are trying to do and maintain that their children are "too young" to write. Write a letter to the parents explaining what you want the children to do.

NOTES

1. Lopez, H. (1986). End term report, ECED 3553, University of Texas at El Paso; excerpted and used by permission.
2. Kidder, C. (1986). End term report, ECED 3553, University of Texas at El Paso; excerpted and used by permission.
3. Clay, M. (1976). *What did I write?* Portsmouth, NH: Heinemann Educational Books.
4. Myers, C. (1983). Drawing as prewriting in preschool. In M. Myers, & J. Gray (Eds.). *Theory and practice in the teaching of composition* (pp. 75–85). Urbana, IL: National Council of Teachers of English.
5. Harste, J. C., Woodward, V. A., & Burke, C. L. (1984). *Language stories and literacy lessons.* Portsmouth, NH: Heinemann Educational Books.
6. Temple, C. A., Nathan, R. G., & Burris, N. A. (1982). *The beginning of writing.* Boston: Allyn & Bacon.

9

The Process Approach to Composition

The last chapter described how children begin to compose and gave examples of ungraded, spontaneous writing that had been done as part of integrated language arts-art activities. This chapter discusses children's continued growth in writing skills in early childhood writing programs that use both frequent writing and direct instruction. Teachers need to find as many opportunities as possible for their students to write. Writing should be used as part of classroom routines, of assigned or free-time reading, of content area work, or as a free-choice activity. In their writing program, teachers need to provide balance between free and assigned writing, open-ended and structured assignments, graded and nongraded work, direct and indirect instruction, and "published" and unpublished writing. Children should write in the **expressive, transactional,** and **poetic modes** and receive both teacher and peer response.

Making a writing program work requires careful structuring, a well-conceived rationale, and close time management. Teachers often have to encourage invented spelling in their students—and to explain it to supervisors and children's parents. They need to be able to state the reason perfect handwriting is not as important as expressing good ideas and may need to justify having children write rather than doing worksheets. They also need to be willing to wait while children put together what they know about writing and what they are learning about mechanics and spelling. This process may take a long time for some children, but the wait is worthwhile. Helping children learn to write is one of the most rewarding aspects of early childhood teaching.

THE CLASSROOM IN WHICH CHILDREN WRITE

A literate classroom environment encourages children's writing. Ample writing supplies, word lists hung around the room, and bulletin board space for displaying writing encourage children to write. A positive attitude toward writing ("Children in my class write") further supports these efforts. Teachers must be willing to structure their daily routines to allow as much spontaneous and assigned writing as possible because when "children use writing in relation to what they are doing in the classroom, teachers can see how they are taking on different concepts and subject matter, what they are understanding, and how they are distilling what they are learning and making it their own" (McKenzie, 1985, p. 248).

A Writing Center

Teachers may want to set aside an area just for writing. A small classroom need not have a complete "writing center," but a localized storage place for writing materials, dictionaries, and student work folders is beneficial. The area should have various kinds of paper, notebooks, and small books for stories. Writing equipment should be in easy reach—pens, markers, crayons, pencils, clipboards, possibly a typewriter. If the classroom has a computer that is used for word processing (see Chapter 14), it can be the focal point of a writing center.

Student Folders

No matter how limited a writing center might be, all children should have folders for their work. By keeping samples of dated work, students, teachers, and parents can assess progress over time. Teachers can use the collected work for diagnostic purposes, and students can return to their old stories to revise them or find ideas to use in new works. Active and inactive folders are sometimes used, with the active folder for current stories, and the inactive folder for work that has been put aside for some reason but that might merit additional work later. Folders help children keep track of their work and encourage them to compare and combine ideas.

Writing as Part of the Daily Routines

Just as "literacy events" are part of preliteracy learning, "writing events" are important in a good writing program. Teachers need to exploit all opportunities for children to write with a real purpose. The purpose, of course, may be nothing more formal than practicing their skills.

In the morning, for example, children can be asked to "copy and compose." Teachers write a line or two ("Today is Monday. We have an assembly."), and children dictate another line to be added to the message. In time, they will compose additional lines themselves. They should be encouraged to write whatever they want, e.g., how they are feeling, what they ate for breakfast today, what they dreamed about—anything. It can be news about themselves. When children realize that they *must* write something and that work will not be graded, they will make the effort; and teachers need only check to see that something has been written.

As children gain confidence in their skills (and as they gain speed in composing), the morning writing time can be expanded for **journal** or diary writing. Children write whatever they wish and possibly illustrate their ideas; teachers should respond with brief, written comments but should not grade these efforts. The purpose is one of communication, as well as practice, and grading violates the intent of the activity. Figure 9.1 shows sample journal entries made by second graders for whom English was a second language.

"Sustained silent writing" can also be used to advantage. This approach, often called SSW, requires everyone in the class, including the teacher, to write silently for a period of time. (In its most formal school-wide use, every school employee and student writes for the same period of time.) Ten minutes of SSW is fine for an early childhood class. Children may even draw part of the time, so long as they write, too. Teachers may suggest a topic to get children started or allow self-selection. In SSW teachers, too, must write silently—no cheating, no grading papers, just writing. Efforts can be checked periodically, used for informal assessment, but must not be graded.

Copying and composing should also replace dittos as routine memory aids. Children should copy homework assignments from the board, especially when encouraged to add a thought or two of their own. They should also copy and/or compose letters and reminders to be sent home to parents. These activities, while time-consuming, demonstrate purposeful writing far better than teacher-written ditto sheets ever could. Writing to parents introduces letter-writing format. Of course, teachers need to check on the accuracy of what children copy or compose and need to stress that this activity requires both speed and accuracy.

THE PROCESS APPROACH TO WRITING

Writing researchers often refer to the **process approach** to the teaching of **writing**. The general concept of the process approach is simple and stresses that the actual process—the doing—of writing is more important than the final product. Figure 9.2 presents a model of the process approach to writing and emphasizes stages most appropriate for early childhood classes. To push children too fast toward revision, multiple drafts, and intensive peer response to writing can deflate the enthusiasm many young writers bring to beginning composition. Teachers can work toward full implementation as children write in an environment that offers support, instruction, and constructive evaluation and feedback.

Prewriting

Prewriting comes first. Prewriting is a time for discussion, generating and organizing ideas, and often teaching or reviewing skills. It is necessary so that chil-

Yesterday my mother
and I went to SAFE-
WAY [Safeway]

Today I read Story Time
and I read the story of
Little Frisky Goat.

Journal entries—Child No. 2

Feb, 8, 1985
Today I'm going to see ("V")
And then I am going to take a
bath.

Happy Friday!

Today a Mrs. came to the
cafeteria and show us how we brosh
uor teeth.

Journal entries—Child No. 1

FIGURE 9.1

These are samples of two children's journal entries. They were both in bilingual classes and had only recently begun to write in English. Notice the use of drawing as a supplement to their writing.

THE PROCESS APPROACH TO COMPOSITION

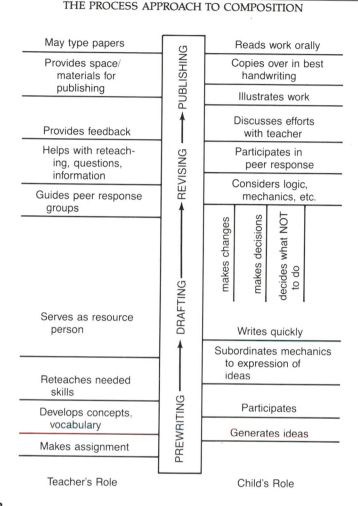

FIGURE 9.2

The process approach to composition includes many distinct steps. Both students and teachers have distinct responsibilities at each step in the approach. In early childhood classes, it is not essential that each piece of writing go through each step in the process approach, but teachers should be aware of the total process and convey a sense of the various steps to their students.

dren fully understand what decisions they have to make about their writing, what options they have, and what is expected of them. Drawing is often part of the prewriting stage, as is assignment making, which will be discussed below.

Prewriting is often used to stimulate vocabulary and organize ideas. A strategy called *mapping* works well for whole class work and can easily be learned for individual use.[1] A map is a rough outline or skeleton of what will be written, often composed only of key words and ideas. To develop a class map, teachers suggest a topic and write it in the middle of a large expanse of board space or on a big piece of butcher paper. Next, children "brainstorm" about the topic by making suggestions as to what could be included in their writing. All feasible ideas are accepted. Each separate subtopic is written on a "spoke" extending from the middle, and relevant key words are "hung" from the spokes to help writers remember their ideas when it is time to write their papers. While a map is only a guide and children may use parts of the map or add original ideas, the map does help children generate ideas and organize and remember their thoughts while writing. If mapping is done the day before children are actually going to write, teachers might wish to ditto the map for individual use. Figure 9.3 shows a possible map about a favorite topic, dinosaurs.

Drafting

Young writers need to know the concept of multiple drafts, even if many of their efforts will not be taken through several levels of **drafting.** Knowing that writers make rough drafts and "fix them up" encourages children to tinker with their

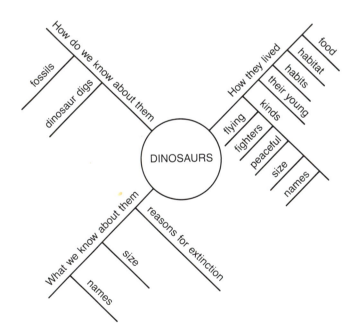

FIGURE 9.3

Mapping strategies help young writers generate and organize ideas before writing. Maps help them remember their ideas when they begin to write and see how the ideas interrelate. This map could be used for a brief report on dinosaurs. If it had been developed as a whole class activity, children could use whatever parts they wished as an outline of their individual reports.

writing, even if only to make superficial changes. Samples presented in the previous chapter were simultaneously first and final drafts in that the children knew that they would not have to copy their work over or fix the spelling. Still, many children did change words and ideas merely by crossing out what they did not want. Lucy McCormick Calkins (1981a) cited a wonderful example of this kind of writing:

> "LOOK OUT!" the six-year-old cried. "The enemy is comin' " Alex pencilled a wobbly spaceship onto the corner of his paper. "Boom! Boom! Pkeeeoow!" The first grader beside Alex glanced up in time to see giant swirls of pencil flames spread over Alex's paper. Soon Alex had destroyed his careful spaceship. Only a scribble remained.
> Now Alex writes, "The whole world was destroyed."
>
> THE HL WD WZ DSD
>
> He mutters to himself, "Destroyed. Deeee-stroyed. E. I hear an E." With his thick red pencil, Alex piles a dark E on top of the letters DSD. "Destroyed." Again he sounds the word. "Deee-stroy-tt." A *T* is added on top of Alex's already illegible smudge of letters. "There, I spelled that one good, I did," Alex announced proudly to himself. (p. 65)

Because he made changes, Alex's story is a first draft, even though undoubtedly never to be reworked.

When we encourage children to write it "the best way they can," we are asking them to draft their stories, to subordinate aspects of "correctness" to the expression of their ideas. We are making a promise that we will not grade beginning efforts but will help children learn to "fix the writing up." Many children do not believe this implied promise. Calkins has maintained (1981a): "For many children [in early primary grades], the era of exploration and spontaneity is replaced by one of deliberateness, social consciousness, and conformity. Instead of messing about with words, children practice techniques and follow rules. Instead of reinventing a new sun each time they paint, children learn to make a spiked round sun in the centre of their sky. Instead of reliving the fish on their line, children question how to convey excitement to their audience. Children no longer write only for themselves. . . . Children are concerned with product and audience. . . . [Writing] has lost its playfulness" (pp. 71–72). Convincing children that drafting provides a safe way to plan and try out ideas encourages them to continue their experimentations with writing. We encourage drafting through writing conferences, which are discussed later in the chapter.

Revising

Accepting the idea of multiple drafts means accepting the chores of **revising.** Teachers must realize that revising is much more than merely copying a paper over and that some work should not be revised. Work that exists as a single expression of feeling, true expressive writing, can stand on its own. Sometimes, too, a piece of writing has been a false start, a dull topic, an experiment with techniques the child cannot yet fully control. Such papers should be filed in a work folder, possibly an inactive one, for attention later. Coming back to the effort a month or two later, the young author may see new possibilities and use the forgotten work as a start of a new piece.

Not all children learn to revise readily. Children who build and rebuild with blocks or make adjustments in drawing and painting are more likely to revise their writing, and children most often revise stories of personal experiences and self-selected topics. Peer audiences contribute to children's revision, in that when children share their stories with peers, they tend to revise more intensely. Peer sharing and "publishing" stories will be discussed later in this chapter.

A fundamental principle is that, when a piece of writing needs revision, it is *the piece of writing,* not the writer, that is being questioned. Young writers often seem guarded against self-criticism, although they may make surface-level changes or "corrections" as discussed in the previous chapter. By the end of first grade, they realize that teachers and peers can be critics. Children may think that just as a math paper has wrong answers, so, too, can a piece of writing be "wrong." It is up to teachers to set the tone for revision, to let children know that revising a piece of writing is a natural part of the writing process. Additionally, young "writers need to learn a whole repertoire for messing up their first drafts as they change pieces, insert, take out, reorganize. When children stop erasing and instead cross out, draw lines and arrows, or change handwriting from careful printing to a functional scrawl (knowing this to be only a draft) they show awareness that draft writing is temporary, malleable, meant to be changed" (Walshe, 1981, pp. 13–14). Table 9.1 contrasts a positive and negative attitude toward revision from both teachers' and students' point of view.

Language Experience and Revision

LEA can model serious revision—the "repertoire for messing up first drafts." After mapping a topic with a small group and transcribing the story exactly as dictated, teachers lead students to discuss possible revisions. Children should be encouraged to point out grammatical errors, suggest alternative words, and ask questions about parts of the story that do not make sense. Teachers demonstrate crossing out, inserting words, and using arrows to move text around, all the while welcoming debate about the appropriateness of suggested changes. The revised story is then copied over for comparison.

The next level of using LEA is to make a ditto of the exact transcription for individual or paired revision. After children have worked on their dittoed copies, they come together to share their ideas and to decide what will work best. The story that emerges may be totally different from the original!

TABLE 9.1
Attitudes toward revising

Positive	Negative
Writing is a dynamic process best learned through frequent practice.	Children should get it right the first time.
Generating ideas and getting them down on paper is the first step toward good writing.	Beginning writers should concentrate on the mechanics of writing, including grammar, spelling, and handwriting.
Spelling and mechanics can always be corrected.	Children should get it right the first time.
Children learn through errors made by actually manipulating language.	Children should not be asked to write until they have mastered the mechanics of writing.
Ideas can always be changed; text can always be altered through deletion or addition of new words.	Children should get it right the first time.
Oral language helps in writing, whether it is writers' reading to themselves or writers and others discussing a text.	Writing should be done in silence.
Real writers always draft their work, often several times, before they are ready to publish it.	Children are not real writers.

Authentic but "neutral" stories can be used to model revision as well. A neutral story is real writing by an anonymous student author, for example, from a previous year's class. Teacher makes a ditto, large chart copy, or overhead transparency of the story to be revised. Interesting enough to catch attention and full of potential for revision, the story is presented as the writing effort of "another child, who doesn't go to this school." As the children read the story, they ask questions and suggest changes, which the teacher notes; children may also work in pairs, or on their own copies. Anything goes, as children are encouraged to make the neutral story their own. Actual rewriting may be done the same day, as homework, or the following day; but it is essential that final, revised versions be shared, enjoyed, and discussed in terms of how grammatical, stylistic, and logical problems of the original were tackled. At first, revisions will be superficial; but gradually, children will give in to their own imaginations and take control of the revising process. They realize that merely finding errors is pretty dull work. Figure 9.4 shows a "working copy" and a revision of a neutral story.

Writing Conferences

Individual student-teacher **writing conferences** can be stimuli to revision.[2] The physical setting for a conference sets tone and atmosphere. Teachers and children should work together at equal height so that teachers can make eye contact throughout the conference and give children control of the interaction. Control starts with allowing children to hold their own papers (possibly on a clipboard) and to read their stories orally. As they read, they may discover and change awkward or incorrect expressions, faulty word choice, or spelling errors.

During the conference, teachers should ask about the piece of writing, but children should be encouraged to lead the discussion as much as possible. Teacher silence and "wait time" help children formulate responses, delve back, and reorganize their original ideas. Statements like "Tell me about your writing, how's the story going?" are open-ended and nonjudgmental. Follow-up statements such as "I don't quite understand what happened—tell me what you did after you got to the zoo . . ." or "I think it is important that you *really* describe the haunted house—how big was it, what color, did it have trees around it?" point out areas in a story that need work without criticizing the writer's skill. Even comments like "Boy, that's a great story when *you* read it but I wish you would try to write just a little more neatly so that *I* can read your story, too!" emphasize the positive aspects of what a child has done and stress teacher's desire to share the writing.

Once children know the routines and expectations of writing conferences, they will be cooperative. Graves (1983) wrote, "Children will talk about their subjects. They talk when the conference setting is predictable . . . when there is a very simple structure to the conference itself. The child knows he is to speak about the [writing] topic and the process and that the teacher will help him do this. Teachers can learn to conduct conferences if they start simply. . . . [At the beginning] the teacher *puts aside* a concern for mechanics, missing information, and revising to help children get words on paper" (pp. 104–105). Through conferencing, teachers identify mechanical and stylistic problems and provide individualized immediate instruction. Sometimes, children may even request help; for example, a child might ask for the rules for punctuating dialogue. Unlike workbooks, this instruction is immediate and directly related to the student's own writing. Teachers may note difficulties and questions, and provide small or large group lessons on the particular writing skill needed by class members. In all cases, teachers encourage children to work with the draft/revising process.

Large classes seem to prohibit writing conferences, yet daily conferences are not necessary and such interactions rarely need to last more than five min-

Sample 1 text (with editorial markings):

IT ALL STARTED ONE DAY WHEN I SAW A HOLE. SO I WENT IN TO SEE WHAT WAS IN IT I SAW A SPACE SHIP SO I GOT IN IT AND THEN IT SHOT UP LIKE A ROCKET. I HAD TO SIT ON A THING DIDN'T KNOW WHAT IT WAS. ALL OF A SUDDEN IT STOPPED SO I GOT OUT OF IT.

I SAW A LOT OF DOGS ONE OF THEM CAME UP TO ME AND SAID WHO ARE YOU I SAID "ROBERT." BY THAT TIME THE SPACESHIP HAD GONE BACK.

I WISHED THAT JASON WAS HERE ALL OF A SUDDEN THE SPACESHIP WAS BACK AND MY BROTHER AND TOMMY WAS HERE. I SAID HI TO THEM AND

THEY SAID HOW DID YOU GET HERE. THE SAME WAY YOU DID. "OH WHO ARE THEY, THEY" SAID AND I SAID, I DON'T KNOW. LETS FIND OUT AND

WE COULD GO BACK TO EARTH" HE SAID "YES". BUT HOW I ASKED THE

LEADER OF US WHERE IS HE OVER THERE HE'S NAME IS PLUTO OK AND SO.

WE DID AND HE SAID ONLY ON ONE CONDITION OK WHAT. THAT YOU WILL TELL

EARTH TO KEEP ON PLAYING DISNEY OK. THE END

(handwritten annotations: "in the junk yard"; "It was big as a elgfant and as soft as a fther"; "What did the abs")

Sample 1. The child was given a ditto of this story and told to "correct and revise" it however he wished.

The Time I Met Plutons

It all started one adventurer Saturday when I saw a dark gloomy hole. I looked inside it. I saw a read with purple rocket ship. I got in and saw computers all over the place. The made me sit on the lumpiest bed I've ever seen. And then it took off. After a few minuts it stoped. I escaped and jumped off. I saw many mean PIT BULLS. One said, "Who are you kid!" I said David. I saw more gods. I wished my freind John was here. All of a sudden I was home. John was there. John said, "Who are they?" I said, "who are you?" One said, "Pluton?!" I said, "can we go back to earth?" He said yes. But how? I asked the leader. He said one one condition. "What's that" I asked. "That you tell earth to keep on playing at Western Playland."

Sample 2. Completed revision

FIGURE 9.4

Neutral stories help students learn to revise before they actually revise their own work. Sample 1 shows how a child used editorial marks and drawing to show how he would begin to revise a story; Sample 2 shows a completed revision of the same story. The writer of the second story resolved the confusing ending of the original by mentioning a local amusement park.

utes. Teachers might organize their students into two or three groups—24 children into three groups of eight each multiplied by five minutes per child gives 40 minutes per day. The whole class might be writing while individuals have conferences, or children could be occupied in independent work, silent and free-time reading, and use of centers. Good classroom management and efficient use of the conference time are the keys. Students should know that they will meet the teacher on a particular day and that if they are not ready, they forfeit their conference time for the week. Teachers should monitor folders of children who are never prepared to find causes for lack of productivity.

RESPONDING TO CHILDREN'S WRITING

Besides conferences teachers must learn to evaluate writing in ways that support rather than stifle children's growth. "Happy faces" or "Good Job!" at the top of children's papers insult young writers' efforts, and evaluations that "bleed" all over beginning writing ultimately convince children that their teachers are more concerned with how correctly and how neatly they express their ideas than with the ideas themselves.

Evaluating Writing

Holistic evaluation is a useful strategy for teachers. Basically, holistic evaluation looks at the *whole* of any piece of writing, and teachers who evaluate holistically "are not just concerned with [children] as a spelling and punctuation producing machine, but as a growing being. . . . [Teachers] discern a developmental process in children's writing, by examining its thought, emotion, moral stance, and style. This [developmental] process is not to be compared to climbing the steps of a ladder, so that one attains a stage once and for all; rather it is more like the waves breaking on a beach, advancing and retreating in particular areas. . . . Assessment is made by means of the teacher's knowledge of other work and of the child. . . . Assessment is seen essentially as a teaching not testing device" (Wilkinson et al., 1983, p. 881). Content is the variable that counts the most. If a piece of writing expresses good, interesting ideas with varied word choice and some experimentation (dialogue or a flashback, for example), even though it may have some errors, it is still considered a *better* paper than a mechanically perfect but dull, uninteresting effort. Teachers need to give children credit for what they are trying to do and to give them support as they reach for more sophisticated skills.

In holistic evaluation, writing may be compared against a scale or rubric that details the characteristics of excellent, good, and poor writing. Some scales include up to nine specific categories of writing,[3] but such detail is not necessary for beginning writing. Teachers and students need to discuss and agree on the basic elements of good writing and then look for the same characteristics in basal readers or storybooks. A teacher who had worked with children on description might select a book rich in description to read as a subtle reinforcement to the writing lesson. Together, teachers and students can develop an early childhood holistic evaluation rubric such as the one in Figure 9.5. As children internalize the rubric, they begin to evaluate their own writing and move toward revision.

Grading

A holistic evaluation rubric does not automatically translate to letter or numerical grades. Grading, however, as Graves (1983) has said "is a fact of life in all school systems." He continued, "I want grades to help, not hinder. If I must grade I make the best of a difficult situation. Children are graded on their *best papers* for the marking term. . . . Dry periods, slumps, high peaks are the pattern for writers of all abilities. We want to be remembered for our best work. The week before end of term I ask the children to choose their best work. If they wish to make the best even better at that point, they may do so" (p. 93). By term end, in classes where children write frequently and discuss their work, children should have a folder of papers from which, often with teacher help, they can select the ones to be graded. Children who do not have enough papers soon learn that when teachers say "We write in this class!", they should comply.

Frequent, regular grading that helps rather than hinders requires children to complete at least one paper per week. Second and third graders should be able to take work through at least a second draft if they write daily. Papers will be evaluated holistically and a letter grade will be assigned. An alternative to this process includes announcing that children will receive a grade on content and on one aspect of their work—punctuation, sentence variety, past-tense verbs, descriptive words—some mechanical aspect that has been taught and is now being practiced. Children focus attention on the one aspect teachers will grade, knowing that they can safely experiment in other parts of their writing. (Chapter 10 discusses teaching the specific mechanical aspect of writing.)

Responding to Writing

Teachers' comments tend to address mechanics rather than content,[4] even though comments are supposed to help children realize that content and form go together to convey the writer's ideas: Good ideas poorly expressed cannot be fully appreciated, just as perfectly written but dull papers are still dull. Commenting on *what* children are writing and *how* they are expressing themselves conveys the connection between content and form and lets children know that writing differs from subjects like math in which there are clear-cut right and wrong responses. One educator (Chenfeld, 1985) reported this example of positive responses to children's work:

> I visited a third grade lucky to have a . . . teacher blessed with a generous sprinkling of humor. "We have the most original and finest writers in this

Best Papers:

- ☐ are about interesting, unusual topics or present standard topics in an interesting way
- ☐ demonstrate some awareness of point of view, feelings of writer or others, and include intent or motivation
- ☐ are well organized with correct paragraphs, no matter how long or short papers are
- ☐ demonstrate control of sentence construction, including punctuation, pronoun referents, subject-verb agreement, and transitional words
- ☐ use a variety of sentence patterns
- ☐ use well-chosen, varied, and appropriate words
- ☐ include dialogue, figures of speech, and other devices to make writing "interesting" to audience
- ☐ are written with awareness of needs of audience
- ☐ show control of grammar and mechanics to an extent that errors are minor and do not detract from content
- ☐ are legible
- ☐ may or may not be accompanied by related art work.

Average Papers:

- ☐ present unoriginal ideas, inventories, or cliched stories
- ☐ show at best only a little intent or motivation of characters; do not show awareness of points of view
- ☐ may be repetitive
- ☐ are not well organized to present story or main points
- ☐ may include individual sentences not grouped into paragraphs
- ☐ have unelaborated sentences with few descriptions or details

FIGURE 9.5
Rubric for early childhood classes.*

class," she bragged . . . One boy held out a paper that was probably the messiest, most indecipherable I have ever seen. His teacher put her arm around him and with twinkling eyes explained, "Johnny is one of our outstanding authors, but his work is very difficult to understand. It has to be translated from the original!" Johnny grinned and proudly displayed a much cleaner, neater rewrite. Clearly signed on the bottom of his story was his name with the title, *Translator*. (p. 267)

Comments that emphasize strengths while suggesting areas that need improvement give children valid information about their writing skills. They may take the suggestions and revise a story or apply the information in their next

☐ show limited control of sentence structure by including primarily simple sentences and/or run-ons

☐ do not use transitional words or phrases

☐ lack control of grammar, mechanics, and spelling to extent that errors make comprehension difficult

☐ may have handwriting that is difficult to read

☐ may or may not have art work; may depend too much on art to convey message.

Poor papers:

☐ present generally uninteresting ideas

☐ usually lack details or description to convey message

☐ usually do not present writer's point of view or other psychological components

☐ may have "flat," unemotional writing

☐ lack organization as a means to help readers understand writing

☐ lack sense of audience

☐ may have random presentation of ideas, i.e., writing "does not make sense"

☐ lack control of sentence structure and may include fragments and/or run-ons

☐ show severe lack of control of grammar and mechanics

☐ have spelling errors which interfere with comprehension, including low levels of invented spelling

☐ have poor handwriting

☐ may or may not have art work; art work may not be related (e.g., random doodling).

*This rubric was prepared by undergraduate students who evaluated children's writing collected in first-, second-, and third-grade classes.

writing effort. Either reaction is fine, as long as children recognize that their writing does have strengths as well as weaknesses.

Peer Response Groups

Peer response to student writing[5] is a valuable tool for motivating writing growth in upper grades. If introduced carefully, the process has a useful place in second and third grade classes as well. Peer response involves small groups of children reading and responding to each others' work. Group membership may be determined by ability, by differences in ability, or by personalities. Because of the wide range of abilities among young writers, ability grouping would probably be the least frustrating arrangement in early primary grades.

The beginnings of successful **peer response groups** lie in allowing pairs of children to write together. As they collaborate on stories, they ask each other questions, criticize each other's work, and fix each other's errors. The one-on-one effort exemplifies noncompetitive interaction and cooperative thinking: Good stories come from this kind of sharing.

Three to five children of similar abilities would constitute a peer response group. To begin, teacher and group would sit as far apart from the class as possible. If an evaluation rubric has been introduced, they apply it against a neutral story, which teachers should read aloud while children follow on their own copies. As they compare story and rubric, the children ask questions about the story, identify strengths, and point out weaknesses. The goal is not to correct errors but to find and discuss places where the writing could be improved. Teachers model comments about the neutral story so that children learn the nature of substantial, helpful comments.

In the next step, individual children bring their stories to the group for comment.[6] Works presented for response may be drafts or final copies, and children should recognize that comments differ depending on the stage of development of pieces of writing. Learning to comment helpfully is the key to successful peer response. Healy (1980) categorized possible comments as useless, marginally useful, useful, and very useful. Useless and marginally useful comments may give encouragement but provide little information. Useful and very useful comments tell the writer what readers need to know to understand a story. Contrast the marginally useful comment "I thought the part about your brother throwing spinach was funny" with the very useful one "I was confused when your aunt came in. I thought you said earlier you were alone. . . ." Peer response groups depend on good critical reading skills. Variations of the basic group format will be discussed in Chapter 13 as a method to encourage and model critical reading.

For peer response to work, children must be able to see writing as an object rather than as an extension of their friends and must be able to talk about it abstractly. Introducing peer response with neutral stories and even language experience helps children move out of themselves and master a sophisticated level of decontextualized "language of school." Teachers need to introduce peer response slowly and only to children who appear ready to handle it productively. Perhaps only one peer response group can be established in the beginning of the year, with more to follow as children seem ready. Teachers also need to take an active role in modeling the process. As children become accustomed to working together in this way, teachers' involvement in the actual groups can become less.

PUBLISHING CHILDREN'S WORK

Young authors like recognition for their work, and nothing makes them feel better than to have their efforts **published.** While not all work must be published, publishing a final, finished product is an extra reward for good work.

Publishing means expanding children's audience and making work public. Published work should be as good as possible so that children can be genuinely proud; but even more important, *all* children should have opportunities to publish their work. This dual requirement causes many teachers to balk at publishing anyone's writing; they do not want to expose poor writers to the ridicule of displaying bad papers or the embarrassment of never having anything published at all. While keeping children from ridicule and embarrassment are positive teacher behaviors, there are ways around this problem.

Typing

Children's writing is usually short enough that stories can be typed quickly. Typing a batch of papers for publication can do more for young writers' morale than anything else. Typed papers look nice; differences in handwriting skills do not show, and *small* corrections can be made during typing to clarify the writer's message. Children will probably not notice the changes but will instead view the finished product holistically.

Typing also allows teachers to study their children's work individually and as a group. This analysis can lead to diagnostic insight, directions for further teaching, and appreciation for how hard children are trying to master the craft of writing.

Typed stories can go on bulletin boards, neatly mounted and displayed with pride. They can also be bound into individual class books for the library or dittoed for whole class distribution. Collections of stories and drawings make excellent gifts at holidays and demonstrate to parents and children that writing is valued.

Bulletin Boards

Displaying attractively mounted writing on a bulletin board gives children a sense of accomplishment. All authors should be displayed, and stories should be hung at eye level so that children can read each other's work. While most children will want their work hung on the board, some may be reluctant to share; if that is the case, their wishes should be respected.

Books

Making little books is one way to motivate writing and is a ready-made publishing effort. Children's first books should be simple sheets of paper, stapled together with a plain cover. (See Figure 9.6.) These are fun and do not intimidate beginning writers; if they make mistakes and want to throw a book away, they can. One sentence and drawing per page are usual for these books.

Teacher-made bound books are the next step. (Again, see Figure 9.6.) Because pages cannot be ripped out and errors are difficult to correct, bound books can be frustrating to beginners. The whole idea of *starting* with a bound

Simple Books

Materials: Paper, stapler, construction paper for cover (if desired)

Procedure: Staple several sheets of paper together between a plain cover; a long-arm stapler works well to make books that open flat.

OR: Punch holes in paper and use brads or yarn to hold the book together.

Staples

| cover | inside | inside | cover |

Staple along spine with long-arm stapler

Holes for brads or yarn

More elaborate books

Materials: Paper for pages of book and cover; stapler or sewing equipment; contact paper or laminating machine

Procedure: Cut paper to desired size.

Stack several sheets together and fold in half; staple along spine or sew; use heavy thread or sew on machine with #18 needle.

Cut two pieces of cardboard or other heavy paper for cover (see diagram).

Cover the cardboard with contact paper or laminate.

Place stapled or stitched pages in the center so that the folded spine is between the two covers.

Use rubber cement or glue to attach the end pages to the cover.

Tape end pages for decoration and sturdiness.

Clip

contact paper

cardboard cover

spine

cardboard cover

Contact paper

cardboard cover

Sew or staple along spine

Clip

FIGURE 9.6

Teacher-made books may be simple or elaborate. Teachers should present very simple, stapled books first so that children feel they can practice their skills. More elaborate books can be used to "publish" work that has been carefully written and revised. Computer software such as "Printshop" allows teachers to make uniform pages easily.

book rather than with a rough draft violates an important concept of the process approach. After children have worked through at least one rough draft of a story, teachers might suggest that efforts be transferred to a book. They might suggest that two children work on a book together so that each can check and help the other. Even more impressive than teacher-bound books are commercially made "bare books," blank pages bound together professionally. Children should be familiar with such terms as *author, illustrator,* and *chapter* from children's literature. As they make their own books, they can work in stages, first on the title page listing themselves as author, then they can fill in the rest of the book chapter by chapter. One kindergarten teacher who used commercial bare books had children complete a two-page chapter each month for the duration of the school year. The children did considerable writing all year, including composing many simple stapled books; but the bare book was a special record of their progress.

Unless children view publication of their work as the final stage in the total writing process, they will not fully appreciate themselves as authors. Publishing should not be showing off or "decorating" the classroom with children's work. It must be much more so that children understand that writing is hard work, full of decision making and effort, but work that often results in sharing of a finished product that expresses their skills and competence.

SUMMARY

Writing should be a regular part of every early childhood class. Writing gives children opportunities to express themselves and allows teachers to gain insight into what and how children are learning. Good writing habits and enthusiasm for writing are easy to instill in young children if teachers understand the "process approach" to writing and truly believe "Children in my class write." Incorporating writing opportunities into the daily routines, conducting writing conferences, evaluating writing holistically, and encouraging children to talk about their writing themselves allows teachers to find time for writing. Through frequent practice, children's skills will grow. They will still need the kinds of instruction discussed in Chapter 10, but frequent writing will give them the confidence and enthusiasm to shape their work toward more sophisticated composition skills.

REVIEW QUESTIONS

1. Be sure that you can define each of these terms:
   drafting
   expressive mode
   holistic evaluation
   journals

peer response groups
poetic mode
prewriting
process approach
"publishing"
revising
transactional mode
writing conferences

2. Why are holistic evaluation procedures appropriate for beginning writers? How do they encourage total growth?
3. Think about and list the kinds of activities that a class can be doing while the teacher conducts writing conferences with individual children.
4. Study the rubric presented in Figure 9.5. How would you present it to children? What modifications could you make to use it with kindergarteners or first graders?
5. List as many ways as you can of "publishing" children's writing.
6. Visit early childhood classrooms where children write and observe teachers' evaluation procedures. Do they encourage or inhibit writing growth?
7. What did Donald Graves mean when he said that grading should help, not hinder, writing? State this idea in your own words as though you were explaining your point of view to your supervisor.

NOTES

1. Buckley, M. H., & Boyle, O. (1983). Mapping and composing. In M. Myers & J. Gray, (Eds.). *Theory and practice in the teaching of composition* (pp. 59–66). Urbana, IL: National Council of Teachers of English.
2. Graves, D. (1978). *Balance the basics: Let them write.* New York: The Ford Foundation.
3. Tiedt, I. M., Bruemmer, S. S., Lane, S., Watanabe, K. O., & Williams, M. Y. (1983). *Teaching writing in the K–8 classroom: The time has come.* Englewood Cliffs, NJ: Prentice-Hall.
4. Searle, D., & Dillon, D. (1980). Responding to student writing: What is said and how it is said. *Language Arts, 57,* 758–761.
5. Hansen, J. (1983). Authors respond to authors. *Language Arts, 60,* 970–976; Healy, M. K. (1980). *Using students response groups in the classroom.* Berkeley: University of California/Bay Area Writing Project.
6. Hansen, *op. cit.*

10

Composition Growth in Early Primary Grades

Children learn to write by writing, but they also need help in shaping their work toward increasing models of sophistication. Help comes from teachers' use of direct and indirect instruction and from external models such as good children's literature. Without help to refine their skills, children's writing may grow in length but still be little more than expansions of the "I like" and "I + [action verb]" stories mentioned in Chapter 8. Such writings are called **inventories.**[1] These stories do not present a logical flow of ideas but instead string together unconnected ideas. The "I like" inventories may use "because" clauses for expansion but remain centered on the writers' personal tastes and preferences. "I + [action verb]" inventories will include all the things their writers have done or can do. A third form of inventory that appears as children write more extensively is a listing of all that children know about a particular topic. These, too, are loosely connected strings of sentences tying together what the writer knows and/or has experienced about a topic. Figure 10.1 shows several inventories written by children in early primary grades.

Inventories are primarily expressive writing. For children to move beyond inventories, they must recognize the different kinds of writing (transactional and poetic) and understand the characteristics of each type. Good assignment making and instruction can bring about this movement.

ASSIGNMENT MAKING

Clearly made assignments tell students the topic about which they will write and help them identify whether they should write in the expressive, transactional, or poetic voice. Such assignments let children know the boundaries of their writing task, teachers' expectations, and the extent of experimentation they

I LIke cat's

I LIKe Dogs

Sample 1. What the writer likes

my Story of Aniamals

I Love A ni amals I Li Ke Birds
And fish and Dogs I mostly every
week(Igo to the zoo And I Love seeing
The turtles And snakes And the Monkeys
I LIKe unicorns I Love seeing
Aniamals. ILove Animals I growup
LiKing An aimals. I have two Dogs
two BirdsAnd two cats. I LOve every
Aniamal I Love Them so. Like Bunnies
And I Love horses espelly. ILove
An iamals

Sample 2. What the writer likes

This is a cloud in
the nigth the cloud is
not seen In the day the
cloud seen but we got rained The
sky was blue.

Sample 3. What the writer knows

FIGURE 10.1

Beginning writers sometimes write "inventories" rather than actual stories or reports. Inventories may tell what children like, as in Samples 1 and 2, or may list all that they know about a topic, as in Sample 3. Some inventories may be quite long, but teachers need to help children learn to add substance to their writing.

should seek. In some cases, assignments will also indicate the audience for whom children should write.

Audiences

Audience refers to the people who will read a piece of writing.[2] Children may write to themselves, as in journals, to friends, or to trusted adults. They may also write to the teacher as an evaluator or to the public, as in letters or in writing for public display. What and how children write for each of these audiences will differ because of the level of interest and the extent of evaluation that can be expected. Children can expect their friends and "trusted adults" to be interested in what they have to say and to respond to the message with minimal evaluation. Teachers, the "public," and peers (as part of peer response groups) can be expected to be more critical. If children write primarily for their teachers (and if teachers grade every effort), they may learn to write "safely," to avoid risks and experimentations. They may lose sight of writing as an authentic endeavor and lose the enthusiasm with which they discovered principles of handwriting and invented spelling. Writing may become increasingly "correct," but it soon becomes inauthentic, vacant, and dull.

Topics

Specifying a topic for children's writing can be tricky. Teachers want to give enough suggestion that children do not waste time trying to think up something to write about but also want to leave room for self-expression. Teachers also must make sure that their assignments do not preempt students who have no knowledge of, nor experience with, a topic. A student of mine related the story of her second-grade son, an only child with no young cousins or younger friends. His teacher assigned the topic "a funny experience with a baby." The child racked his brain and could think only of an interchange with a 4-year-old child. He wrote about that, only to be criticized because the child in his story was too old!

When teachers present an experiential topic, they should express a *range* about which children may write, such as a funny experience with a baby *or* with a young child. With options, no child will be left with nothing to write about, no child will panic because he hasn't had a particular experience. All children will know that they can stretch their imaginations to come up with something. Teachers should accept writing that seems a bit "off topic" as long as it clearly represents the child's attempts to approximate the assignment.

Topics for poetic (story) writing should be open-ended and provide options for interpretation and flights of fancy. They must, however, be reasonable. Young children are egocentric and just beginning to see other people's points of view. Far-fetched topics may frustrate children's writing entirely. Temple, Nathan, and Burris (1982, pp. 148ff) discussed many children's responses to an assignment that asked them to pretend to be a vegetable about to go off on an adventure. Some of the stories were inventories; others had more creative elements; but as Temple and his co-authors stated: "The papers are alike in that they don't look very much like stories . . . [partially because] the assignment itself is a difficult one: it is hard to envision a vegetable having an adventure" (pp. 150, 153). This is not to say that imaginative assignments will not work; it is merely to caution teachers that what seems reasonable, even fun, may be too abstract for some beginning writers to conceptualize. Some youngsters, of course, love to play with such assignments as "My Life as a Foot," in Figure 10.2 attests. It was written by a second grader who felt comfortable with writing tasks.

Many teachers use ditto sheets with pictures and one- or two-line "story starters" to motivate children's writings. The disadvantages of these sheets overshadow their cuteness. They negate the idea of the process approach: Everything is there on one discrete sheet to be completed all at once. Children may color the ditto, but there rarely is room for real drawing. The dittos have wide lines for handwriting, but there are usually so few lines that children tend to fit their ideas to the space allowed rather than turning the paper over and writing until they are done with what they have to say. The story starters may be appropriate for the age—"I dreamed . . ." or "My biggest wish . . ."—but the topics would motivate better writing if presented orally, written on the board, discussed, and possibly mapped during prewriting. Additionally, many children do not understand the story starter concept of these assignments and often ignore the opening line altogether.

Purposes for Writing

From their own explorations of literacy, children realize that print is used for many purposes,[3] and they should explore as many of these purposes as possible. They have probably written to communicate information, ideas, or requests to peers and adults; annotated pictures or written whole stories (however short); and made lists to organize or remember ideas. As they begin to write in response to specified assignments, children must learn to shape their own print to particular patterns. To do so takes time, skill, and an understanding of the particular terminology used in making assignments and discussing writing. Think about these words: *story, adventure, plot, settings, characters, fiction, make-believe, poem, rhyme,* and *verse.* These are only a sampling of the kinds of jargon or specialized vocabulary children must know to understand assignments for writing stories. They are examples of the "language of school" that has been mentioned before. The following terms would be used in assignments for transactional writing, writing that explains, instructs, or "gets things done": *report, inform, describe, procedures, facts, thesis sentence, facts,* and *details.* Assignments can only be as good as children's interpretation of what is expected. Clarifying vocabulary may be needed if children are to understand what they are to do.

My Life As A Foot is
not very sweet smelling. Every day
my oner puts on his socks and
that is how it all starts. We an
he gets home from school
I don't smell very good.
and at night I relly don't
smell very good! Oh! I don't
smell very good right know
my oner just came home from
a soccer game. Oh! that is
one thing that is wrog about
being Mr. Smelling Foot. I aways
get kicked.

The E
n
d

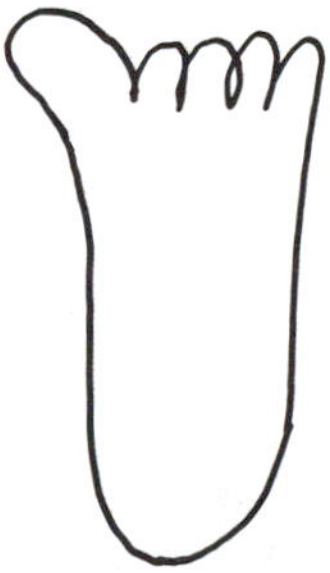

FIGURE 10.2

"My Life as a Foot" was written by a second grader who felt comfortable with himself as a writer. He selected the topic and wrote enthusiastically. Many other second graders would not have been able to imagine this topic, nor to write with such confidence about themselves in another identity. This writer had been writing for several years and had a strong imaginative streak and great confidence in his ability.

This clarification (or reteaching) can be part of the prewriting phase. Explaining and demonstrating what these and other terms mean are important parts of teaching about poetic and transactional writing.

WRITING IN THE POETIC VOICE

The poetic voice includes poems and stories conforming to specific patterns. Some beginning writing verges on the poetic voice (see Chapter 8); but as children write more extensively, they need help learning to fit their ideas into poetic formats.

Stories

Learning how to write stories involves learning how to manipulate in writing the various parts of the traditional story format. As mentioned in Chapter 3, children take information from storybook readings and other media to learn how to tell stories themselves. As they begin to write for themselves, they use the basic conventions of story-writing: *once upon a time* . . . , *happily ever after*, *The End*, and other markers of story-like language. Knowing the parts of a traditional story has been termed knowing **story grammar** or **story schema.**[4] Children realize intuitively that a story is composed of a beginning, middle, and end. Setting and characters are introduced in the beginning, almost immediately after "Once upon a time." An "initiating event" comes next and presents a problem to be solved in the middle of the story. Solving the problem may take several attempts. The ending resolves the problem and possibly pronounces a moral. Characters can "live happily ever after" because of their successful solution to the problem. THE END.

Children may know these story parts intuitively, but if they are going to write real stories with even the barest representation of story parts, they must be able to think up *and* remember appropriate information to fill each slot. Beginning writers, especially those using invented spelling, take a long time to get their ideas on paper. Children who weave wonderful oral stories or participate enthusiastically in prewriting or language experience dictation may not be able to sustain their storytelling in writing. They simply forget what they have to say and resort either to very short stories or to the safety of personal inventories.

Teachers can introduce a specialized mapping technique to help children externalize what they know about story grammar, develop material for each part of a story they wish to write, and remember their ideas. **Story maps** can be divided into sections for children's notes on the component parts of a story. Teachers should introduce story maps in stages so that the task of translating story ideas to writing becomes natural. Table 10.1 presents a sample story map. Children jot down ideas briefly in each category as a memory and organizational aid—complete sentences are definitely not required. They might bring a story map to a writing conference or turn it in for teacher suggestions or questions. Stories can be written from these notes, with some ideas discarded and new ones generated as well. Doing similar maps of children's stories read to or by the children reinforces the concept (this will be discussed in Chapter 13). As skills mature, teachers can introduce more complex maps to reflect story grammar more fully. As an outline, children realize that setting, time, and characters comprise their beginning, with attempts in the middle, and results in the last paragraph. More complex stories with several plot "twists" have more middle paragraphs.

TABLE 10.1
Mapping strategies for beginning writers. Children fill in information to guide them in their writing.

Heading for all maps:

AUTHOR _____ TITLE _____

Categories for poetic (story) writing:

Setting Where?	Characters Who?	Time When?	Problem/Plot/ Action What?	Solution Finally?

Categories for transactional (report) writing:

Topic (Introduction)	What I Want to Know	What I Find Out	Conclusions
	1 2 3		

Descriptions

Many young writers' efforts seem almost "colorless" and devoid of description. Children's word choice is limited or redundant, and writing never really sparkles. Telling children to use "more descriptive words" is meaningless, unless children understand what these words are. A strategy called **showing writing** can help.[5] The underlying idea is that some writing "tells," while some writing "shows" what is going on. Teachers need to explain this concept, possibly by contrasting dull, flat prose with more descriptive, imaginative writing. If both pieces are equally clear, the difference in word choice should be obvious. Children can see, for example, that the word "run" merely "tells," while "saunter," "gallop," "charge," and "amble" all "show" the action. Children should also come to realize that the quantity of description is important in story writing, too. To say a house is "big" conveys some information, but to describe it as "huge, facing the sea on one side, the street on the other, with green shutters, three chimneys, and roses climbing the front porch" is better.

To use showing writing, teachers assign a "telling sentence," such as "The pizza was good," "I was scared," or "The room was messy." Children expand that sentence into several "showing" sentences or paragraphs. Initially, teachers need to brainstorm possible expansions, but as children learn the technique, they need little prewriting discussion. Showing writing can be used for homework or for 15- to 20-minute in-class assignments. Stories should be shared from time to time but rarely revised; this writing is for fun and practice. Attention to descriptive words and details will spill over into children's oral language and reading work as well. Figure 10.3 has three showing writing efforts from the sentence "The room is messy."

Psychological Components of Writing

Temple, Nathan, and Burris (1982) discussed the elements missing from children's beginning stories, stressing especially that children "treat the overt action elements of their stories, and leave out the covert psychological dimension" (p. 160). All action, little reaction—internal responses and goals are frequently omitted just, the researchers maintained, as they are on the kinds of television aimed at young children. Clearly worded assignments that direct children to write "how their characters feel and what they plan to do" can coax young writers to consider these dimensions of their stories. Teacher questions during conferences can help, as can specific slots for "feelings" in a story map. Carefully selected children's literature in which characters express emotions, plan solutions, and overcome difficulties can be discussed specifically in terms of "how the author of the book let us know what the characters were thinking."

Drawing before, during, and after writing may be the first indication that children are attempting to include **psychological components** in their compositions. Smiling or sad faces; relative sizes of people, animals, and "creatures";

intensity of color; and crayon, marker, or pencil pressure can all reflect covert dimensions of the story. Discussing the drawings with children can give teachers insight into the extent to which a sophisticated story schema is evolving.

Responding to What Children Are Trying to Do

Writers in early childhood classes demonstrate wide ranges of skills, varied interests, and different levels of fluency. Teachers must remember and respect this diversity and try always to identify and respond to each individual writer and each piece of work. Holistic evaluation, as discussed in the last chapter, can help, as can a keen analytical eye on both children's surface productions and their underlying strengths and weaknesses. Figure 10.4 presents and analyzes representative samples of writing.

Using Children's Literature as a Stimulus for Writing

Children develop much of their sense of story schema and psychological dimensions of stories from children's literature, and good stories can also be used as a stimulus for writing.[6] There are two purposes for using children's literature as a stimulus for writing. The first is that good stories present universal, comfortable themes, to which children easily relate. Children can "adopt" a theme from a book, rework it, and produce their own version of the story. The result may seem highly derivative but that is less significant than that the writers have played with the ideas and parts of a story to produce a "new" effort. They gained practice thinking about and expressing ideas within the safety of an acceptable topic.

The second purpose is to intensify children's understanding of story grammar. Just as they discover basic organizational patterns, children can identify (at however simple a level and especially with class discussion) the psychological components of a well-crafted story. Themes such as individuality can become more concrete through children's literature so that assignments such as "Write a Story About Why You Are Special" are more meaningful. Children's literature and writing as a follow up to reading will be discussed more fully in Chapter 13.

TRANSACTIONAL WRITING

Writing in the transactional voice is writing designed to get something done—to transact some business between writers and readers. Many children begin to write by composing notes; they understand about mail, and they have seen adults writing letters. Children's notes are, of course, very personal, but they are still a primitive form of transactional writing. A student reported that she had been gently encouraging her kindergarten son to write on his drawings, but he maintained he could not spell. When a tooth came out and he misplaced it, he became very upset because he could not exchange it for money from the

Sample 1.

A very messy room
Once there was a house. And
it looked very nice on the
outside but ugly on the inside. The bed was broken and
the wallpapper was wripped. And
the shutters were down. And
it just much uglyer than ugly.
Mabey people thout it was prey
but they beleav there eyes when
they got in. But then some -
one bout the house and fixe
it up.

Sample 2.

The Messy Room

There was a big earth
qwace. It messt up the
hole room then it was
over. When I came in
the room was messy. I
saw the chair was on
the floor the paint
was scracht the toys
were on the floor and
so were the cloths my
curtins were on the
floor and even my bed
was messt up and one
more thing it was messt
up in the first place
before it happend so its
the End.

FIGURE 10.3

Second graders wrote in response to the "telling sentence" *The room was messy.* Notice
the extent to which each child used detail; notice also that one child used a script format
to respond. Perhaps he was reworking a dialogue from real life!

Sample 3.

Me: Who did this to my room?
the messiest
room P

MOM: A Fox?

DAD: A Raving lunatic?

MOM: A Shiek?

Me: I still dont understand Who
did this to my room?

DAD: Maybe   Tom & Jerry?

MOM: The people in Russia?

randy: My brothers?

robbie(y) My Dog   did.

Me: Get the city pound !

Me: My friend's dog did the messy

job in my room.

randy: They will clean it up.

FIGURE 10.3
continued

Sample 1 The Magic Broom

One day a cat found a broom from a witch. The witch went and got the broom. She saw the cat. Then she turned the cat into a frog. The frog bouced away Into an opened window. He went into the pond. then the witch went with the broom. She met a man. The man got a buchet of water. He pord it on the witch. Then the witch melted. They End.

Analysis

Simple, straightforward first grade story with a good command of basic mechanics and spelling; child might have meant the cat to "steal" a broom from the witch, which would have made it more exciting; some action but no character development to involve the reader in the story.

Sample 2 The Mean Salerie [Celery]

Once there live a mean old calerie. He didn't like people to buy him. Then a little man past buy. He said to his wife "I am going to buy salkerie for the picnic." Suddeny the salerie bit the man. The man said to the casher thta there are bugs in the salerie. No there are not bugs in the salerie said the casher. They called the ditectives they said this salerie has eyes, mouth, and a nose. They took him to inspect him. They put it in a talbe a mose come out of the hole and ate the salerie.

Analysis

Some confusion between English and Spanish syntax; verbs shift between present and past tense; punctuation is weak; child knows about quotations but does not use them consistently, story is very creative and develops a "psychology" for the celery; ideas and actions progress logically to a good solution to the problem.

Sample 3 A Crazy Robot

Once upon a time my dad bought a robot. Dad bought it at robot publiching store. I was jeles [jealous] cause he treated me like a ghost! He always said "Bring me a glass of water and a steak" but he told it to the robot. Once some visitors came. I said "Go bring 19 glasses of orange juice and 19 steaks. He went in the kitchen he jumped and I disconected a little bit of things and after he got the plates he threw them the meat was raw. My dad said "STOP thet crazy robot!" So I stopped it. It said "Crazyyyyy, crazyyyyyy I am a crazy robot." So we kicked it out.

Analysis

Child enjoyed writing the story to such an extent that he lost control of his skills in the middle and used a long run-on sentence; story has emotions (jealousy), a problem to solve, and a logical solution, right down to kicking the robot out; details, such as the raw meat, strengthen the story.

FIGURE 10.4

Samples of children's writing. Sample 1: English speaker, first grade, no drawing. Sample 2: English-Spanish bilingual, second grade, no drawing. Sample 3: Bilingual child, third grade, no drawing. Sample 4: English speaker, third grade, with drawing. Sample 5: English speaker, end of first grade, no drawing. These stories were written as part of regular class work with self-selected topics; all are presented exactly as written.

Sample 4   The Amanginary [Imaginary] Land

I was in a little girlscout troup, and I was just tagging along not paying any attention and all of a sudden my troup turned, and sense [since] I was not paying
any atention I didn't notice and kep on going the wrong way. Then I noticed that
nobody was in front of me. I looked all around me but I couldn't not see anything or anyone. I decided to sit down and think. Then I decided to go left. I
finally saw something. I walked up to it, it was some kind of round red thing
just handing there. Then a dust devel [dust devil, swirling dust cloud] came and
swooped me in the red thing. Before I could catch my bruth I saw myself falling
threw the air, then thump! I landed on a strange planet, and boy I was pretty
thirsty so I went to look for some water, I saw a lake, and I saw the prettyest
thing I ever saw. It was a unicorn with wings. I went over to it and asked her
what her [inserted with an arrow] name was. Unis she said so I told her my
name to. We became very good freinds and she told me how to get back home
and when we got to the place, I asked her if she would come whith me and she
said yes, so we went home and lived happily ever after. THE END.

Analysis

Story progresses logically but lacks details and emotions to let the reader
"see" the action; "land" implied in the title stays "imaginary" and does not
materialize; writer could benefit from "showing writing" activities and needs to
read her work out loud to get a better sense of the flow of language and its relation to punctuation.

Sample 5   The little ants trip aroundtheworld

Once upon atime about 3000000000 years ago there lived a ant she was about
eight years old. her name was anne. now annes mother told her when she was
six that when she was eight she could take a trip around the world! Now that
she was eight she asked her mother. now that I am eight since I am borad may I
take a triparound the world. Shurre honey said her mtoher. Oh goody! said
anne. I'll start righet now. So she got packed. Bye mother see you in a millyon
years. Now anne was verry carfl when she saw another ant get swalod up by a
frog! she pantid herself green and hid in the gress till the frog left. Who, I shure
glad I brout paint with me. espeshilyif frogs were here. Then she went for a little
walk. Then she saw a giant something. then she remembered that her mthoher
said those are hamr les things those are called peple. I better run I'm blocked. it
is flooding. Ive got no place to go. no place to run. Thers giant oceans all round
me. Help! [written large] just when the water went over her head, her duck
friend shierly came to recque her. thanks shierly. I better get home. want to ome
with me! were havein roasted crumbs shirly said wht kind of crumb. chesse and
french bread mixed together. shure and they lved haply ever after. The End.

Analysis

This is an imaginative, creative story full of details and ideas; writer shows
an awareness of feelings and point of view and a clear sense of components of
story grammar and ability to manipulate them; story has specific episodes (leaving home, the frog, the water, interaction with Shirley); child feels comfortable as
a writer and subordinates mechanics to content; this child, although only in first
grade, had done considerable writing and is supported in her efforts.

FIGURE 10.4 *continued*

Tooth Fairy. His mother offhandedly suggested that he write the Tooth Fairy a note explaining his situation. *That* form of writing seemed acceptable; he drew a picture of a tooth and wrote a note stating: "I swulod mi tut." The Tooth Fairy made the appropriate exchange. Business had indeed been transacted.

Letter Writing

Children easily become familiar with letter-writing conventions, and teachers should take advantage of this knowledge to build skills in transactional writing. Encouraging children to write to each other, making assignments that they write to communicate specific information ("What you did over the weekend"), and sending letters to sick classmates all work well. A classroom post office provides additional motivation. Teachers should write to children and expect written replies. A note might read: "Dear Sam, I hear you have a new baby in your house. That's great! Write me back and tell me how she looks." Sam will probably tell more than how the baby looks, but the teacher has requested a specific transaction that the writer will undoubtedly address first. Writing to people outside the class demonstrates the practical aspects of letter writing. Figure 10.5 shows letters written to the late E. B. White in appreciation for his fine children's books.

Children can also learn the basics of persuasive or argumentative writing through letters. Children must understand the difference between this kind of letter and more familiar "friendly" or thank-you notes. Direct instruction will be needed to help children understand that the topic is of interest *to them* but not necessarily to the recipient of their letter, that the recipient may have a different point of view about the topic, and that the recipient must be addressed with appropriate formality and civility. Finally, children must recognize that their purpose is to influence their audience with good ideas and logical reasons. Figure 10.5 also shows letters that are clearly political in nature.

Procedural-Sequential Writing

Children need to learn to write descriptions of processes such as caring for classroom gerbils, the growth of plants, or the preparation of food. Language experience charts about such topics, often with a rebus, have provided children's first exposure to this kind of reporting. Their first independent efforts are often mere lists with no connecting prose. These are efficient but need to be fleshed out with explanatory or descriptive text. As children begin to write their own procedural reports, they must remember the importance of sequence and thoroughness. Maps or outlines that stress first, second, third, and so forth help children organize their writing. Children should be helped to generalize the format of **procedural-sequential writing.**

Writing to Inform

Conveying information is a major purpose of transactional writing. Usually considered "report writing," this form of communication is often not required until

to mr. E. B. White,
I want to tell you How
much I enJoyed reading
Stuart Little, Charlottes weB
and trumper of the Swan
thank you for Writing These
FabbaLas Books!!

June 3,1976

Dear, Mr. E.B. White,
I liked your books, The
Trumpet of the Swan,
Stuart Little, and Charlotte's
Web. I like Stuart Little
the best. If you wrote any
more I diden't read them
yet.

Sincerely. Jessika

Brooklyn, New york
June 1975

Dear Mayor Beame
It is not fair to have
me in a class with 40
class mates. well, I think
we should have the same
amount as it is now.

I hope you will put the
money for our school out
frist and cut down on
So ming else
age 6   from John

Dear mayor Beame
                   BUDGET
If we have Buoit cuts
then we will have too
many papele in our class-
room and I won t be
a bel To work

SUSANNO

Jan. 21,1984
Dear : president
I will like you to help the poor
And to put the prices down.
And the persons that don't have
work to give them work. That's
what I think you should do.
And to be nise to others.

I will like you to do
all this things. Because
you will make my
family happy.

FIGURE 10.5
Letter writing introduces children to transactional prose. They must form their ideas and write them with an awareness of their particular audience. The E. B. White letters were written before the author's death; the letters to Mayor Beame were written during the New York City fiscal crisis; the letter to the President is more recent.

189

middle school. It can, however, be introduced earlier, as long as children are asked to convey information they actually possess or can easily accumulate. The first step in teaching children **writing to inform** is to stress the difference between facts, opinions, and fantasy. For children in early childhood grades, the distinctions may be very fuzzy. Facts can be proven; opinions are what one personally thinks or feels; and fantasy is what one makes up.

The first exercise in collecting facts might be to observe an object, possibly a tree in the school yard. Work begins by generating questions children would like answered about the tree: size, name, description, age. They can "research" the tree for additional factual information. From their data, the map is filled in and a report can be compiled, either individually, in pairs, or even as a language experience chart to model the process of putting facts together. Writing reports differs from procedural writing in that a more global, descriptive approach is used. Figure 10.6 shows how an observation assignment was organized into booklet form.

The next step is for children to select a topic to "research." The topic should be of interest and should not be so broad as to stagger young researchers. Children should already know something about the topic, there should be ample material at the appropriate level for them to learn something new, and they should care enough about the topic that they will not grow bored before finishing their work. Chapter 13 discusses this writing-reading task in greater detail. Report writing can be the vehicle for introducing children to real library work, to the card catalog, to encyclopedias, and to other reference books for specific purposes. Children might select a book that has difficult text but excellent illustrations and use that to supplement other sources.

Teaching children to extract information from sources without copying whole paragraphs is difficult. Children need to become accustomed to the process and must build confidence in their ability to take notes. Having a list of questions to answer and/or a map to fill in helps because it provides an intermediate step between source material and the child's writing and results in less direct copying from resources. Because they have thought of what they want to write, the children focus their reading to find needed information rather than reading extensively and then trying to organize their thoughts.

When they write their reports, children should combine the topic map and a basic "factual report map." They should start by preparing a topic map such as those already discussed. The topic, as stated before, goes in the center with ideas written on radiating spokes. Children should be taught that the basic outline for a factual report includes "introduction," "middle," and "conclusion." A spoke can easily be included in the topic map for "introduction" and "conclusion"; and each of the other spokes with its details will represent the content of a paragraph to go in the "middle." Initial efforts will be sketchy, probably with each spoke being translated into one sentence, but the basic outline will guide children as their skills improve.

Mon. Oct. 6, 1986

today one of
my seeds is
starting to get
green.

page 1

Oct. 9, 1986

Today two of
my seeds you
can see the
lea fo

page 2

Oct. 10, 1986

today one of
my seeds is
a plant.

page 3

Oct. 14, 1986

today three of
my seeds are
groing to plants.

page 4

Oct. 15, 1986

Today one
of my plants
is 18 :centim
eters.

page 5

Oct. 24, 1986

today my
plant is
bigger than
the rooler.

page 6

Oct. 29, 1986

today I
have new
leaves com-
ing out.

page 7

FIGURE 10.6

This child's task was to keep a "Plant Journal" and observe the growth of her plants. She made daily notations and drawings to record growth. She had to attend to and describe detail to keep her journal. (Figure 13.2 shows a later effort from this same child, completed after several months of extensive writing practice in her second-grade class.)

TEACHING GRAMMAR AND MECHANICS

Oral language is the most powerful means of teaching children correct grammar and the mechanical aspects of writing. Writing that sounds "wrong" or "funny" or does not "make sense" frequently sounds so because of grammatical or mechanical errors. Also, because major marks of punctuation (commas, periods, question marks, exclamation points, semicolons, colons, quotation marks) indicate pauses that have direct parallels in oral language, oral reading may reveal errors that might go unnoticed in writing that is read silently. Teachers' first step in teaching children to write standard English is to speak correctly at all times. When children hear standard forms, they learn to use them themselves and eventually transfer them to their writing. Teachers can reinforce children's awareness of standard forms through good oral reading. For example, reading dialogue with changed voices and appropriate pauses is a good introduction to the concept, if not the mechanics, of producing dialogue in writing.

Lucy McCormick Calkins (1981b) wrote, "When children write, they reach for the skills they need. When children ask the questions and raise the dilemmas, [mechanical] skills are learned in context—young writers need time to run into their own problems, to ask their own questions. Only then can skills be learned in context—for the context is not the subject matter, but the child's questions, the child's need" (pp. 89–90). The balance between direct instruction, indirect instruction, and children's own needs produces mastery.

Punctuation

Children do need to formalize their knowledge of punctuation—how to make the different marks, what each does, and what they are called. But this information will make sense only when children have gained the basic concept of punctuation use through frequent writing. A study contrasted two third-grade classes, one stressing traditional instruction in grammar and mechanics, the other providing extended writing periods three days a week. At year's end, children in the writing class could identify, define, and use more than twice as many kinds of punctuation as children in the other class. The writers knew apostrophes, commas, quotation marks, colons, paragraph signs, and carets. The researcher (Calkins, 1981b) concluded: "When children need punctuation in order to be seen and heard, they become vacuum cleaners, sucking up odd bits from books, their classmates' papers, billboards, and magazines. They find punctuation everywhere, and make it their own" (pp. 95–96).

Language experience can introduce punctuation. Transcription demonstrates punctuation use, and spirited rereading of LEA stories reinforces its importance. Teachers can start by emphasizing full stops—periods, question marks, and exclamation points. Next, they should stress internal punctuation—commas, dashes, apostrophes, quotation marks. Names and uses should be presented, but teachers must remember that *using* the marks correctly is more important than *remembering names*. The first grader who called exclamation points *out loud marks* and used them correctly was well on her way to mastering punctuation.

Instruction followed by silent, independent drill activities will not guarantee that children realize that punctuation gives their writing its "voice." Moffett and Wagner (1983) suggested an outstanding alternative to traditional seat work. They recommended that teachers "not try to cover and explain very much [about punctuation]. . . . The main procedure . . . simply narrows [student's] listening while reading toward a focus on the relation of intonation to punctuation" (p. 483). They recommend that teachers develop worksheets of passages that have been reproduced with no punctuation or capitalization. These could easily be dittoes of LEA stories or paragraphs from children's books. With the passage in front of them, children listen to a live or taped reading of the passage that emphasizes normal punctuation, breaks in thought, pauses, and so forth. The children's task is to match the auditory rendering with the printed copy and to insert capitals and punctuation where needed. They compare their work with peers' and finally see the original. "They see for themselves how difficult it is to read a text without punctuation and how punctuation helps render meaning" (p. 483). Like the neutral stories recommended for revision practice, this is another example of how teachers can make the abstractions of writing more concrete for young learners. Because the exercise reinforces the connection between oral and written language, it is more useful than drill exercises done silently.

Grammar

To repeat, oral language is the key to children's mastering grammar. Hearing standard grammar, spoken and read, conditions students to identify nonstandard constructions in their own and others' writings. Reading can help, too, but so much of children's beginning reading material is so simply written that the models it provides are less sophisticated than the writing children themselves may want to attempt.

Children's first language experience dictation and first writing will reflect their speech community, which may employ nonstandard constructions as part of regular speech. Just as teachers should shape LEA stories to standard speech, they should help children shape their writing to standard usage. The trick, of course, is to avoid judgment or criticism of the child as an individual language user. As teachers reread LEA, they might say, "Listen to how I am going to read this . . . This is how we would *write* this in school." Children gradually realize that there is a specific way of communicating *in writing* in school, a more formal "voice" that differs from the way they themselves may talk. Children who begin to "talk or write like a book" recognize this on a general level; the recognition deepens as they identify the finer, grammatical distinctions of subject-verb agreement, irregular plurals, irregular past-tense verbs, and use of negatives and auxiliary verbs, and so forth. Students gradually develop "an ear" for standard grammar, an intuitive sense that often precedes mastery of the names of these particular grammatical elements.

The question most often raised concerns whether grammar should be taught in isolation and drilled through practice activities and seat work. Several careful research studies have found that drill work does not lead to mastery.[7] Better ways of teaching grammar are individual instruction during conferences, **grammar logs** or journals, and sentence combining. Conferences have already been discussed as quick, close, focused student-teacher interactions, during which clarification and instruction can be provided about an immediate grammatical problem. Teachers tell students how their usage is nonstandard and the reasons for the difference. A grammar log can be used to help children record their "deviations" from standard usage and to help teachers keep track of individuals' growth. The log might be set up with three columns for "personal grammar," "school grammar," and the reason for differences between them. The personal grammar is the deviation from standard usage or school grammar. Initially, the teacher explains and records a simple reason for the difference; gradually each child should record the reason in his or her own words. Children develop a personal reference to help them learn standard usage. A "spelling log" can be used to keep track of repeated errors, such as omitting silent letters or reversing vowels in diphthongs or digraphs.

Sentence Combining

Sentence combining helps children understand the many ways that simple ideas can be formed into complex sentences.[8] Like other writing activities, it can be introduced orally. Simple sentences are presented, and children are guided to combine them into increasingly complex expressions. Teachers introduce the wide range of transitional words and conjunctions available for sentence combining to give children alternatives to *And, And so,* or *And then.* When introduced or done orally, sentence combinations should be written down to demonstrate internal punctuation. Gradually children learn to combine simple sentences with *but, and,* and so forth, and to embed adjectives and to place them in series. They also learn to use participles (e.g., *We see the boy. He is reading,* becomes *We see the boy reading).* With practice, children can embed adjective and adverb clauses in their sentences to produce long, descriptive, information-packed sentences. As they realize that sentences too packed with words are too hard to comprehend, they begin to achieve balance and will eventually make decisions about sentence length. This is the beginning of learning about "style." Because sentence-combining activities are done orally and are shared, they generate discussions that make learning fun.

As children gain experience with the approach, independent sentence-combining activities can be assigned. Unlike drill-and-practice worksheets, sentence-combining exercises seldom have only one right answer. Children should be encouraged to combine simple sentences as creatively as possible and to compare their individual results with others who have done the same assignment. Some combinations may be more "correct" than others and some children may make errors in attempting to manipulate the various parts of their new sentences; but "errors" in activities such as this can be the raw material for new growth.

Sentence combining helps children improve their writing and also influences their oral language and reading. Because they are more attentive to the way words and phrases go together, they often try out longer and more complex oral sentences. Attention to the specific meanings of conjunctions, adverbs, and other transitional terms in their writing carries over to reading, and children become more aware of the often-neglected "little" words they encounter. Because these words are often quite significant, this kind of awareness is important.

Paragraph Structure

The mapping strategies presented in this chapter and in Chapter 9 help children organize their thoughts and learn appropriate paragraph structure. As they fill out a map, they recognize ideas, facts, and information that go together—the basis of paragraphing. They should realize that as they translate notations on a map to a written effort, each spoke can become a separate paragraph. There is no magic number of sentences to put in each paragraph, but children should be reminded that if each paragraph has *only one sentence*, they should be seeking more information on a topic or providing more detail or description. For example, if a child is writing a story in which most paragraphs contain only one sentence, the young writer should question whether she is providing enough information to "show" her ideas. A report comprising one-sentence paragraphs should prompt its writer to wonder whether the reader will be left with many unanswered questions about the topic. Teachers can model this kind of self-analysis during writing conferences so that looking critically at paragraph structure becomes part of the revising process.

Stories or reports that are one long paragraph also need self-analysis and revision. A reverse mapping process can help straighten out these papers; children sort out their many sentences by creating a new map that reflects what they have written. As they untangle their writing, they can see which sentences belong together as distinct paragraphs and which ones need additional information to convey their messages.

Learning paragraph structure—sticking to the point *and* providing enough information—is also helped by wide reading experiences. Children who write and also read different kinds of material gain insight into the "writers' craft." They attend to what "works" and what does not; they realize what is easy to understand and what causes comprehension difficulties. Because they think of themselves as writers, they look at what they read critically and learn by observing how *other* writers apply their own skills. Reading and writing become mutually reinforcing.

SUMMARY

Children learn to write by writing in classrooms in which teachers are more interested in the "process" of learning to write than in neat, perfectly spelled final products. Yet, because writing growth requires that children gain control of specific kinds of skills, teachers must shape and direct writing efforts through assignments and instruction. Achieving a balance between free and structured writing fosters growth and allows each child to progress at an appropriate, developmental pace.

The instructional strategies presented in this chapter—mapping, showing writing, Moffett and Wagner's punctuation activity, and sentence combining—make children active participants in learning. None of them points to specific right answers, as workbook and drill activities can do, and all help children become more sophisticated, experienced manipulators of writing language. They learn to make and evaluate decisions about written communication. These activities give form and substance to the "process approach" to writing and help children along the developmental continuum from prewriter to skilled writer.

REVIEW QUESTIONS

1. Be sure that you can define each of these terms:
   audience (for whom children should write)
   grammar log
   inventories (as a kind of writing)
   procedural-sequential writing
   psychological components of a written effort
   sentence combining
   showing writing
   story grammar or story schema
   story maps
   writing to inform
2. Find a simple children's book and summarize it for setting, initiating event, attempts to solve problems, consequences, and reactions. Next, analyze several examples of language experience stories or children's writing to see how much they reflect the elements of story schema. Suggest ways teachers can help children draw upon what they know about story schema. Suggest ways teachers can help children draw upon what they know about story schema to make their writing better.

3. Develop a list of "telling sentences" that would be appropriate for young writers. Use some of the "telling sentences" with young writers and analyze the results. What kinds of discussion are generated as prewriting? Do the children seem to like the activities? Do they want to share their stories orally? How do their teachers respond to the activities?

4. Select two stories in Figure 10.4. List questions you, as the teacher, would ask during a conference. Write another list of questions peers might ask the writer during a peer response group. Develop three entries for a grammar log that each of the writers might keep. What personal grammar would you, as the teacher, point out, and how would you discuss it with the children?

5. Develop sentence combining worksheets on three levels of difficulty. Try them out and analyze the results. Develop short paragraphs for punctuation and capitalization practice on three levels of difficulty. Try them out as well.

6. In what ways do the suggestions presented in the section on "Teaching Grammar and Mechanics" fit within the process approach to composition growth?

7. After reading Chapters 8–10 on the development of composition, write a brief essay to discuss the progression from expressive writing with invented spelling to competent, skilled writing in the poetic and transactional voices. Defend the position that in a supportive, literate environment, this progression is a natural part of literacy development.

NOTES

1. Temple, C. A., Nathan, R. G., & Burris, N. A. (1982). *The beginnings of writing.* Boston: Allyn & Bacon.

2. Britton, J. (1970). *Language and learning.* Harmondsworth, England: Penguin Books.

3. Cochran-Smith, M. (1984). *The making of a reader.* Norwood, NJ: Ablex.

4. Stein, N., & Glenn, C. (1977). An analysis of story comprehension in elementary school children. In R. Reedle (Ed.). *Multidisciplinary approaches to discourse comprehension.* Hillsdale, NJ: Lawrence Erlbaum.

5. Caplan, R., & Keech, C. (1980). *Showing-writing: A training program to help students become specific.* Berkeley: University of California/Bay Area Writing Project.

6. Stewig, R. (1980). *Read to write: Using children's literature as a springboard for teaching writing* (2nd ed). New York: Holt, Rinehart & Winston.

7. Calkins, L. M. (1981a). When children want to punctuate: Basic skills belong in context. In R. D. Walshe (Ed.). *Donald Graves in Australia: "Children want to write."* (pp. 89–96). Rozelle, New South Wales: Primary English Teaching Association.

8. Strong, W. (1976). Close up: Sentence combining: Back to basics and beyond. *English Journal, 56,* 60–64.

11

The Beginnings of Reading

The three previous chapters discussed the development of writing skills in young children. Chapter 5 raised the question of whether reading or writing skills develop first and suggested that for some children, the desire to write does, in fact, emerge first. Often, the two skills develop simultaneously and are mutually reinforcing. Graves (1978) stated, "children who are used to writing for others achieve more easily the necessary objectivity for reading the work of others" (p. 24).

Parents sharing planned literacy events with their offspring let them know how writing and reading "feel" without actually providing direct instruction in literacy skills. Early childhood teachers who adopt a similar approach provide an atmosphere in which children who have already formed some ideas about literacy can try out their guesses, refine them, and grow. In that same atmosphere, children who have had little exposure to books, reading, or writing will begin to explore the materials, tools, and behaviors that have enriched their classmates' home experiences. Like parents who want to encourage their children's interests in writing and reading, teachers must support, nurture, and still challenge all children.

There is no real "preliteracy" curriculum; instead, careful structuring of experiences, skillful choice of materials and activities, and shared joy in learning about literacy allow individual children to "take what they need" from what their teachers provide. Teachers will do well to heed Dorothy Butler and Marie Clay (1979) who, writing for parents, stated: "There is clear evidence that it matters more what a child brings to the task of learning to read than what the [first grade] teacher has to offer him" (p. 17). It falls to preschool and kindergarten teachers to provide the raw materials from which children gain what they need to "bring" to later literacy instruction.

A DEFINITION OF READING

To understand how children learn to read successfully, it is necessary to understand what reading actually is. In her book, *Reading: The Patterning of Complex Behavior*, Marie Clay (1979) gave this definition:

> I define reading as a message-gaining, problem-solving activity, which increases in power and flexibility the more it is practised. My definition states that *within the directional constraints of the printer's code, language and visual perception responses are purposefully directed in some integrated way to the problem of extracting meaning from cues in a text, in sequence, to yield a meaningful communication, conveying the author's specific message."* (p. 6)

The definition is full of information, but may need some explanation. "Message-gaining" and "problem-solving" are essential components of reading in that readers must know that print conveys a message that should make sense. Children must also realize that meaning will not just jump out at them; they must work to make sense of it themselves. This work is a form of problem solving in which readers use as many cues provided in the text as they need to obtain meaning. The cues include letter-sound correspondences, word meaning, and sentence structure, which together help children achieve the major goal in reading: comprehension.

The "directional constraints of the printer's code" are the pattern of writing as it moves from left to right, from the top of the page to the bottom. These constraints may seem arbitrary to children accustomed to scanning their environments in whatever ways please their wandering, curious eyes and to filling pages with color and shapes to reproduce the pictures they see in their own imaginations. Young readers must remember to swing their eyes back from far right at the end of a line to the far left to begin a new line or, even worse, from the right bottom of a page to the top left of the facing page. Adults should not underestimate the difficulty some children have in remembering which way print does, in fact, move on a page; children have so many more important things to concentrate on.

"Visual perception responses" are identifications of the graphic image in print and should lead to a language response—the recognition that the graphic image stands for a word whose meaning the reader already knows. Young readers must "attack" printed text to pull together all the pieces of the language puzzle. They must consciously try to identify words they see, determine *individual* meanings, and search out the *total* meanings of phrases and sentences. Sequence, young readers must realize, is crucial. Letters are in a particular sequence in each word, and words are sequenced within sentences. The order matters in recognizing individual words and in making sense of longer pieces of text. The sequence must follow the left to right, top to bottom format as well. Using a finger or hand to point to or mask words is often beneficial as beginners attend to their task.

The cues from which readers extract meaning are many and varied. For young readers, they include pictures, letter-sound correspondences, individual word meanings, and grammar and sentence structure. Learning about all the possible cues is the gist of learning to read, integrating cues marks growth in reading, and using the fewest number of cues to gain meaning is the mark of successful reading. The more teachers know about the complexities of reading, the better able they will be to appreciate what young children do as they become readers and to provide safe opportunities for children to discover answers to their own questions about literacy. Discovery, rather than teacher-directed instruction, provides the foundation for growth.

READING READINESS

Texts on developing reading skills usually include a chapter on *reading readiness*. The term is a familiar one, with diverse definitions and uses. Clay (1979) summarizes the two most common, traditional definitions of "readiness" as (a) the point in time (differing from child to child) when children become "ready" for formal reading and (b) the period of time during which children change from being non-readers to being readers. Inherent in the concept are a developmental sequence and the accumulation of necessary skills and concepts.

The third widely accepted aspect of reading readiness is an instructional one. Teachers in kindergarten or first grade often speak of "teaching readiness"; they present concepts and skills needed for beginning reading and reinforce their instruction with activities and worksheets emphasizing directionality, same and different, whole-part relationships, left and right, and so forth. Most commercial reading programs begin with a readiness segment, which may include work on handwriting, vocabulary, alphabet skills, and possibly beginning phonics.

Problems with the Concept of Reading Readiness

The idea of reading readiness emphasizes the many different skills and concepts needed for beginning reading and suggests that teachers *can* influence children's literacy acquisition; however, the traditional conceptualization of reading readiness and readiness activities is flawed.

There are two specific flaws in traditional thinking about reading readiness, flaws that can seriously inhibit children's successful literacy acquisition. The first flaw is that children bring little information about literacy to their first encounters with reading instruction, that they are "empty vessels" when they reach school. Research on children all over the world has indicated that preschoolers observe print, make guesses about its purpose, and experiment to try to figure out how it works. Teachers who fail to acknowledge children's hypothesizing about literacy are missing the most vital component of any "readiness curriculum." Children must be allowed to build on what they know and to clarify their ideas.

The second flaw is one of timing. Teachers can, indeed, influence children's level of readiness and can compensate for literacy-poor homes. But the influence teachers exert comes less from structured lessons than from the literate classroom environment, the use of literacy events, and the on-going commitment to the idea that young children enter school already engaged in literacy learning that prepares them to take advantage of what teachers offer. Current research on literacy acquisition points to the need to broaden the concept of readiness to reflect the entire continuum of language growth. An updated concept of readiness would stress that children can take command of much of their own literacy learning because they want to understand and use the varied forms of communication; it would view literacy acquisition as a natural progression in learning the communicative processes. As with oral language acquisition, teachers assist children in acquiring literacy through **scaffolding** and **modeling,** as well as through direct instruction. Pushing too early or waiting too long are equally counterproductive for children growing up in a world full of print.

Some New Terms

The first new term has been mentioned before. The term, **emergent literacy,** acknowledges the importance of children's attention to the varied uses of print in the environment. It emphasizes the continuum of language growth from oral language through mastery of reading and writing and focuses on what children themselves do to become literate. The second term has also been mentioned before; it refers to what teachers can do to encourage emergent literacy. Instead of the traditional concept of readiness, teachers might think of Lev Vygotsky's *zone of proximal development*. Vygotsky (1962), as cited in Chapter 5, used this term for the "discrepancy between a child's actual mental age and the level he reaches in solving problems with assistance. . . . What the child can do in cooperation today, he can do alone tomorrow. Therefore," Vygotsky maintained, "the only good kind of instruction is that which must be aimed not so much at the ripe as at the ripening function" (pp. 103–104).

Emergent literacy is indeed a "ripening function." Bombarded by print and curious about how it works, young children seem to develop their own "readiness" curriculum. The **appropriate teaching point** means that teachers, alert to what children have mastered, provide opportunities for expansion and refinement of skills. The concept *does not mean* that children should constantly be given work that is just a bit too hard for them; but neither should the work be too easy.

Appropriate work builds on what children know, and today's children know tremendous amounts about writing and reading. Instruction at the appropriate teaching point balances planned, formal lessons with spontaneous responses to difficulties children encounter in solving literacy problems. Teachers capitalize on literacy events, by which children can strengthen their skills through purposeful tasks within a supportive atmosphere that acknowledge the difficulties of learning to read and write. Teachers avoid instruction that would encourage rote memorization or imitation of literate behaviors, even though, as Vygotsky cautioned, such teaching often seems to produce more immediate "results." He might well have been criticizing the overuse of workbooks and dittos when he wrote: "Persistent training . . . can induce [children] to perform . . . complicated actions, but these are carried out mechanically and have all the earmarks of meaningless habits rather than insightful solutions [to linguistic problems]" (pp. 103–104).

Realities of Learning to Read

Early childhood teachers contemplating students' emerging literacy growth must keep several realities in mind. The first reality is that learning to read and write is a complex, difficult task that no child will accomplish without considerable struggle, work, and energy. Children need confidence in their abilities, stamina, and support for what they are doing. The second reality is that learning to write and read usually takes a long time, as children process information and build their own models of how literacy works. Teachers may think that their preschoolers or kindergarteners just are not learning about literacy, that efforts to create meaningful literacy experiences are wasted. This simply is not true! Children may show no evidence of learning for long periods of time and then suddenly delight and reward those around them with some demonstration of how everything is "falling in place."

The third, related reality is that youngsters need and benefit from repetition of experiences. Given their choice, children may want the same book read to them every day for a week (just like children at bedtime). Suppose the book is *Frog and Toad Are Friends* by Arnold Lobel. Also suppose that a week after reading the book, the teacher introduces a science unit with tadpoles in a tank and notices several children conferring busily over one of the books placed in the science area. They walk toward her, holding the book in front of them, and announce that they can "read the book." Their proof lies in their pointing carefully and correctly not to the pictures but to the labels for pictures of frogs and toads. Repetition of the Lobel book has paid off in interest in the science unit and the important realization that *f-r-o-g* and *t-o-a-d* are the same in two entirely separate contexts.

Finally, teachers should be responsive to children's interests and attention levels. When children begin to lose interest, a literacy lesson or activity should stop. Equally, when teachers feel themselves becoming frustrated, when they begin to think "This is so easy, why aren't the children getting it?", it is also time to give everyone a chance to rest. Learning about writing and reading should be fun, stimulating, and enjoyable, with children growing in awareness and teachers marveling at the enthusiasm with which this learning takes place.

HELPING CHILDREN REFINE THEIR EMERGING LITERACY SKILLS

Teachers who recognize the concept of emerging literacy and accept the idea of the appropriate teaching point approach the task of helping children become literate in very specific ways. First, they determine the extent to which children possess skills needed for literacy instruction to make sense.

Identifying Necessary Skills

Clay (1979) has summarized the skills necessary for children to begin to read. Most will develop through normal maturation and can be readily observed by sensitive teachers. First, children must be able to produce and understand oral language and have adequate vocabularies and command of sentence structure. Second, children must be able not just to see but to distinguish differences in and comprehend the meaning of what they see. Observing environmental print and practicing beginning writing skills have sharpened children's visual perception. Third, eye-hand coordination must be developed to the point where children can track print across and down a page. Snuggling next to an adult who points to words while reading, following a teacher's hand across a LEA chart, and controlling one's own scribbling, drawing, and writing all develop eye-hand coordination.

Children must be mentally mature enough and have had enough experiences to be able to coordinate what they hear in oral language with what they see in print. They must know that print conveys messages and that the messages should make sense. Children's attention to environmental print and to stories read to them has helped them understand that the written communication is purposeful and symbolizes oral language.

Finally, children must be motivated to learn to read and write. This motivation seems to be almost innate in most children at first, but children differ in the extent to which they sustain motivation to attempt what they may perceive as a difficult or meaningless task. Their home environment may not value reading and academic pursuits, or older siblings may have had difficulties learning to read. Understandably, these youngsters may assume they, too, might fail. Teachers need to demonstrate the value and pleasure of reading and writing and help children develop what should be a natural inclination to learn to communicate in these new ways.

Figure 11.1 presents a checklist to assess the extent to which children have mastered essential skills and are motivated to refine emerging literacy. The checklist can help teachers determine clusters of children who seem to be at the same developmental levels. Clustering children allows teachers to provide informal literacy events at their students' appropriate teaching points. Assessing children's levels also enables teachers to identify children who might work well together for independent projects or activities. A child who has begun to read might be paired with a classmate to study a topic of mutual interest. As the reader gains information from library books and shares with her partner, she is modeling the reading process, helping her friend to increase his store of sight words, and demonstrating some of the benefits of real, purposeful reading.

So, What Should You Do?

In the home with the close interaction between parents, child, and book, "instruction" is truly individualized. Don Holdaway (1979) says this produces a "visual intimacy" conducive to learning within a "storybook learning cycle." Individualized instruction in an early childhood classroom is a fine ideal—but one that is usually beyond even the most competent teachers because of high pupil-teacher ratios. Additionally, completely individualized instruction sacrifices the valuable child-child interaction that helps so many children adapt successfully to school.

The word *instruction* often implies lecture, hardly the behavior parents use when they share books with children. Like parents, teachers must aim to support children's natural growth. Two distinct methods support emerging literacy by providing information and assistance at children's appropriate teaching

Questions about Books

1. Does child seem interested in or curious about books?
2. Does child know how to handle books?
3. Is child aware that books convey meaning?
4. Does child enjoy listening to stories?
5. Does child know how to listen to stories and respond to questions about them?
6. Does child reenact storybooks?
7. Does child ever draw about stories he/she has heard?
8. Is there indication that the child has books at home?
9. Does child track print when read to him or her?
10. Is tracking left to right?

Questions about environmental print and writing

1. Does child know some environmental print, even if he/she reads a supermarket logo as *Food Store?*
2. Does child seem to know any sight words?
3. Has child begun to "write," even if the writing is scribbles?
4. Does writing reflect pseudo-letters that child wants to read?
5. Is there evidence of higher levels of invented spelling?
6. Is child's drawing orderly or merely random?
7. Does child attend to art activities long enough to finish them?
8. Does child seem to like to work with art materials, pencils, and pens?
9. Is there any indication of awareness of left to right orientation in art or writing activities?
10. Does child recognize own name, even if he/she cannot write it clearly?
11. Can child identify letters of the alphabet in sequence and in isolation?
12. Can child write letters of the alphabet reasonably well in sequence and in isolation?
13. Does child know any of the sounds?

Questions about vision, dexterity, and so forth

1. Does child seem to be able to focus near and far?
2. Can child hold pencils and crayons comfortably and use them efficiently?

FIGURE 11.1

Checklist for evaluating young children's interest in and preparation for reading. Ask these questions about each child. If answers are "no," determine if the child is fearful and reluctant or merely immature. Balance the profile that emerges about each child against age, family background, previous school experience, and general health. Evaluate children as individuals, but also evaluate overall class situation to determine how best to support emerging literacy for all children.

3. Can child use scissors?
4. Has the child demonstrated hand dominance?
5. Can child sit still for a reasonable time?
6. Can child stand still and walk in line for a reasonable time?

Questions about concepts and language

1. Does child have names for colors, shapes, and so forth (names may be in English or in child's first language if not English)?
2. Does child seem fluent in expressing wants and needs (within normal range for age and sense of pragmatics)?
3. Can child stick to the point when carrying on a conversation?
4. Does vocabulary seem appropriate for age and experiential background?
5. Is child interested in and capable of learning new vocabulary?
6. Does child understand terms for time, space, causality?
7. Is the word order in child's sentences relatively correct and stable?
8. Is the order of syllables correct in most polysyllabic words (not "coster-roller" for "roller coaster")?
9. Does child seem to have control of most of the consonant and vowel sounds of his/her dialect and language community?
10. Is articulation mostly clear and easy to understand?
11. Does child seem able to understand and carry out simple oral directions?
12. Do there appear to be any hearing problems?

Questions about emotions

1. Does child seem overly shy?
2. Does child seem fearful?
3. What is child's apparent level of energy, stamina, and general health?
4. Can child attend to task happily?
5. Does child take reasonable risks or is he/she easily intimidated?
6. What are child's expectations for school?
7. What are parents' expectations? Are they reasonable and age-appropriate?
8. How supportive are the parents?
9. How assertive or passive is child?

FIGURE 11.1
continued

points. Because both approaches approximate parent-child interaction with scaffolding and modeling, teachers provide appropriate "assistance" as children learn to read: Today they read with the teacher and their classmates; tomorrow (or next week or next month), they will read alone. The two approaches are (a) shared literacy experiences with **big books** and "storybook reenactments" and (b) the language experience approach to the teaching of reading.

Shared Literacy Experiences

A "literate classroom environment" has books, writing materials and tools, environmental print, art supplies, comfortable places set aside for browsing through books, other early childhood equipment, furniture, and supplies—and even more books, some of which may have been made by the teacher or by the children themselves. Free access to books helps children link their beginning hypotheses about literacy with the "real thing."

Student-teacher sharing of books is as important as intimate child-parent sharing, and teachers should attempt to approximate the intimacy as much as possible, even within the bustle and noise of a good classroom. It is through the close, triangular relationship among children, an adult, and books that children who have not had books in their lives learn that reading is enjoyable, meaningful, and important. They learn what a story is and how it is put together. Children whose homelife has been enriched by books feel immediately comfortable and receptive to whatever "instruction" evolves from this familiar, **shared book experience.**

The term *shared book experience* is central to beginning reading instruction in New Zealand. Don Holdaway and Marie Clay have familiarized reading and early childhood teachers with the sensible methods used to introduce New Zealand children to the wonders of reading, and Holdaway's concept of a "preschool **bedtime story learning cycle"** translates the closeness of parents and child sharing a book into a workable classroom approach. Storybook reading is the first stage in this approach and should be a regular part of every early childhood class. Good storybook reading must be an active process that includes talking about pictures and text, making guesses about what will happen, comparing stories read on different days, and at times engaging in specific follow-up activities like drawing or role playing, as in the Directed Listening-Thinking Activity discussed in Chapter 3. Discussion should be mutual, with teachers asking questions and encouraging listeners to do the same. Questions may elicit recall or seek to identify concepts, words, or ideas that children do not understand so that confusion can be clarified immediately. Just as storybook reading is supposed to teach children that reading is enjoyable, it should also teach them that reading makes sense. Children failing to gain this insight while they are still at the listening stage may encounter difficulties later when they themselves begin to read.

The best books for successful storybook reading with young children are those with relatively simple stories and good, related illustrations. Topics should be appropriate for young learners—familiar enough to make sense but challenging enough intellectually to maintain children's interest. Large, clear print is also desirable because it is easier for children seated around a teacher to see. Wordless picture books work well, too, especially with small groups of children. Children "read" the pictures and provide the story themselves.

Traditionally, the teacher is seated, holding the book, surrounded by a circle of children sitting on the floor or on chairs. While efficient, this method quickly loses the "visual intimacy" of the bedtime story setting. A story-time circle should be small and informal, with children snuggling as close as possible to the teacher so they can then see the pictures and print and the teacher can observe individual's responses to the story. If there are multiple copies of a book, children can follow along, turning the page each time the teacher does. Of course, children may want to sprawl on the floor and may even fidget no matter how small the circle is, but the objective of storybook reading is to convey pleasure in reading, not to teach children to sit perfectly still. The trade-off teachers must make to achieve this intimate arrangement will be repetition; in order for a class to accept the "small circle" reading situation, they must be confident that everyone will get an opportunity at some point during the day (or maybe the next day) to hear the story. Aides or volunteers can take turns as storyreaders, as long as they understand the techniques for sharing literature with children. Children from higher grades make excellent storybook readers.

Storybook reading provides a bridge between oral language and book language and is the first stage in children's learning to read independently. It introduces learners to two important concepts: (a) Book language is similar but not identical to oral language, and (b) the individual words on the printed page each have a recognizable oral equivalent. Striving for a balance between instruction and informality is the key to reinforcing these concepts. Pointing out individual words helps but can be awkward when print is small. If certain words are emphasized by larger or different colored print, they should be called to children's attention, as should words like *Wow* or *Bang* or animal sounds that often receive special graphic emphasis. Teachers can use their voices to demonstrate individual words. For example, a description of a caterpillar "sliding—slowly—sneakily—silently—across a branch" should be read with particular, suggestive emphasis. Preparing for storybook reading allows teachers to develop and perfect these oral effects.

The books teachers share with children should be readily available for quiet, independent browsing and for children's own initial attempts at reading. Having multiple copies of books helps, and inexpensive paperbacks make this possible for at least some of the class favorites. Paperbacks themselves can be cut apart, laminated, and rebound for longer use. Shared-book experiences can lead to more lively follow-up activities as well. Children should be encouraged to act out stories in dramatic play or with puppets and to draw or paint their favorite characters or scenes. As they rework the ideas, they are learning rudimentary comprehension strategies—how to extract meaning from text. More structured, teacher-directed activities work well, too. Teachers might assign a few children roles for a dramatization or puppet show to be presented to the rest of the class. By planning and discussing, children are again strengthening their comprehension skills. They may even have to refer back to the story to clarify points of disagreement. Group art activities such as murals, dioramas or papier mache can also be used as follow up. These are all viable preludes to the "book reports" older children write and strengthen beginners' understanding of school-related reading tasks.

Big Books

Don Holdaway wrote (1979), "Reading to a group of children in school has little instructional value simply because the print cannot be seen, shared, and discussed. The parent is able to 'display the skill in purposeful use' and at the same time keep before the [child's] attention the fact that the process is print-stimulated. Teachers can do the same by using enlarged print for the experience of listening to stories and participating in all aspects of reading" (pp. 64–65). Big books are available commercially, and directions for teacher-made big books are outlined in Figure 11.2. Big books should be made only of favorite books, with proven appeal. Predictable books or caption books are also good material for big books, as are books that invite "audience participation" so that children can easily "read" along with the teacher. Appendix 1 suggests many suitable predictable and caption books, and Chapter 12 elaborates upon using them for formal instruction.

Big books are effective because children need, benefit from, and enjoy repetition. Teachers should introduce big books soon after reading the regular form of a story so that all children can respond to the questions "Who can tell me what this book is?" Because the print and format are larger, children can easily participate in this sharing session and recognize that the pictures may be somewhat different but *the words are the same*. Running the hand under each word, pointing out space between words, emphasizing special words, and stopping at the ends of sentences are all easier with the big book format. Words that begin with the same letters as class members' names can be pointed out, or children may even be asked to find words that begin like their names. Informal instruction is easy and effective with big books. As teachers point out about "words that begin the same" or "long words" or "words like *slither* that sound funny," they are not interrupting the enjoyment of the story. The "lesson" reinforces children's enjoyment, strengthens their appreciation of the story, and increases their understanding of how books work.

Big books' versions of stories can be used with groups for several days if children are enjoying them and also must be left out on their chart stand or in a convenient place after actual student-teacher sharing has stopped. Just as children turn to a standard copy of a story for added enjoyment, they will also review a big book. Individuals or small groups "play school" with the big book or merely "read" to each other. The larger format of words in these familiar stories invites independent study and sharing and encourages the kind of familiarity from which children develop their first sight vocabularies. In this way, the large format print of big books becomes almost like environmental print and strengthens emerging concepts about reading.

Teachers may want to make original big books for their classes to introduce or reinforce units of study, commemorate special events, or record on-going class activities. These should be introduced enthusiastically and used with pride. Children delight in the idea that the teacher made a book especially for them and receive the effort warmly. In response to a big book written by a university student, a child wrote: "I think it's fun haveing a big book and a litle book becas you can rede awt of the tine wune and see the pichrs in the big wune. Big books are easyer to rede."

Storybook Reenactments

Children retelling the contents of a storybook as though reading themselves is a common sight whose value is often minimized. When children reenact a story, they may or may not think that they are "reading." As in play-writing, children try out a behavior they have seen around them; they are getting the "feel" of a skill they want to master.

Having books available is the strongest inducement to children to reenact what has been read to them. Unfortunately, many teachers "protect" their books by keeping them out of children's reach. Available books invite browsing and reenactments; older children in a group "read" to younger ones, children "play school" with books, and individual children amuse themselves through private reenactments. These behaviors are positive and well worth the price of a few dirtied pages on favorite books.

After reading a story to a group of children, teachers should invite individuals to "read the story to me, please" to determine what children have figured out about literacy. Researchers[1] have classified such storybook reenactments in three ways: (a) descriptive comments governed by pictures but not telling a story, (b) real storytelling governed by pictures, and (c) real storytellings governed by print. In the first level of response, children merely comment as though the action conveyed by the pictures was taking place in the here-and-now, or they label and comment on the pictures. Children may appear to be commenting primarily to themselves and may skip or recycle story parts; but they are becoming familiar with book format and handling, attending to pictures closely enough to label and comment, and at low level, translating "book language" into oral speech. Doing this in the intimacy of one-on-one interaction with an adult affirms children's guesses about how books "work" and makes book handling a pleasurable part of the school experience.

Materials:

Chart tablets or sheets of large, heavy paper
Magic markers with strong colors
Children's art work
Rings or other devices to bind books together
Laminating equipment (optional)
Chart stand or easel

Procedures:

1. Decide on the contents of the big book; it may be an original book or duplication of a commercial book.

If using a commercial book:

2. At first, reproduce the pictures as closely as possible; using an overhead projection machine helps those whose art skills are weak.
3. Later, rough sketches or children's drawings can be used in place of duplications of original illustrations.
4. Duplicate the text in neat, clear handwriting; try to keep the same number of words per line of text that children will see in the book but definitely match text in original to pages in big book so that children can make a one-to-one correspondence between the original and the new book.

If using an original idea:

5. Keep text and illustrations simple; make sure it will be relevant to the children.
6. Write text horizontally, usually across the bottom of the page (see diagram).
7. As children become familiar with big books, use their drawings to illustrate.
8. Use pictures cut from magazines or other illustrations for books, especially if they are going to be laminated.

FIGURE 11.2

Big book versions of familiar children's books or original big books written by teachers or teachers *and* children are easier to read than regular-sized books. Children like to use big books to play school themselves. Big books should be made sturdy enough to withstand several years' use.

For either kind of big book:

9. If the book is in chart tablet form, display it on a chart stand or easel; punch holes in tops of pages of books made from large sheets of newsprint or tagboard, reinforce the holes, and use rings to hang them from chart tablets.

10. If books are smaller than chart tablet size and will be handled by children, laminate pages for durability; punch holes in pages, reinforce if necessary, and use rings, string, or yarn to bind together.

Displaying books:

1. Hang books on chart stands when presenting them to children; leave chart stands in clear sight so children can reenact the story.

2. Use an easel or chalk tray as support for books that cannot be hung; leave these readily available for individual and small group browsing and reenactment.

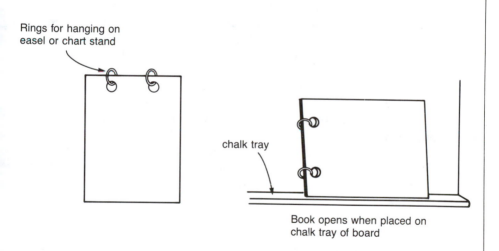

Rings for hanging on easel or chart stand

chalk tray

Book opens when placed on chalk tray of board

FIGURE 11.2
continued

Reenactments that draw cues from pictures are of several types. Children may use "book-like" or "speech-like" language in retelling or a combination of both. Book-like reenactments contain phrases from the original and story patterns that sound book-like but were not in the actual model. When the patterns are new, children are probably drawing upon the realization that language in books is different from regular speech; they are demonstrating the same awareness discussed previously as children's attempts to "write like a book" with terms such as *Once upon a time*. The content of children's reenactments may or may not match the content of the original story, and the total reenactment may or may not present a coherent whole. Usually, however, children will use story-reading intonation in their retellings as evidence of their sense of themselves as "reading" the book to their audience.

The third kind of reenactment are those that are governed by print. Many children do learn to read on their own[2] and do attend to print, match letter-sound combinations, and do so with comprehension. Variations of this actual reading behavior are reenactments in which children read those words they recognize, often from the environment, laboriously sound out some of the words, and skip others. This beginning knowledge of letter-sound correspondence may come from "Sesame Street" or other media or from the same hypothesis forming that is leading to invented spelling. In either case, it is clear that children are beginning to figure out some aspects of reading and need encouragement and support in their effort. These beginners do not, however, need correction and instruction at this point: Acceptance of what they are doing, answers to their questions, and enthusiasm for their reading will provide momentum for more growth. The value of storybook reenactments is that children can get support and help at an appropriate level and do not have to muddle through the beginnings of reading in frustrating aloneness. Here, indeed, is Vygotsky's idea of the child receiving help today in preparation for independence tomorrow.

Two final variations of the print-governed reenactment provide different information about young children. The first is an almost verbatim recitation of the story, coming primarily from memory. This is not the same as memorization of nursery rhymes because, while children may not visually track the actual print, they seem aware that there *is* a match between what is on the page and what they are saying. The second variation also indicates that children know about print-oral language matching; children refuse to "read" because "I can't read yet." Either behavior is acceptable within emerging literacy, but both can cause problems later on when reading is actually expected. Dependence on memory and fear of trying to read are both discussed in the next chapter.

LANGUAGE EXPERIENCE APPROACH

Among methods for encouraging prereading skills and beginning reading, the language experience approach (LEA), already mentioned as an aid in teaching writing, ranks very high.[3] LEA (not to be confused with the general idea of children's experiences with language) can be defined as a method for encouraging reading growth that, in its early stages, uses materials developed by transcribing children's dictation. The process is simple: As children dictate, their teachers transcribe; then they guide learners in sharing or actually reading their stories. LEA can be used with individuals or with small or large groups. LEA is often recorded on chart tablets, which like big books, are easy to see, and lend themselves to children's rereading.

LEA involves all the language channels, both receptive and expressive, and is totally accepting of children's developmental levels. LEA builds upon the "experience-language-cognitive wealth that children bring with them to school . . . [and] provides a sound, all-embracing foundation on which to construct and develop reading ability" (Stauffer, 1980, p. 17). This approach works because it is intrinsically motivating. Children like to see their words written down and are fascinated with the process of reading these words. It works because it builds upon children's experiences in and out of school.

LEA in Preschool or Kindergarten

The language experience procedures can be the core of any preschool or kindergarten literacy program. (Chapters 12 and 13 extend the use of LEA even farther.) You have already encountered the term *literate environment* to describe the tone, attitude, and physical set up of an early childhood center or classroom. It is easy to see how a literate environment accommodates language experience. Classroom labels and charts developed with children's help are actually part of the foundation of language experience because they emphasize that just as one can *say* the name of a learning center or piece of furniture, so, too, can one *write* the very same name.

Commentaries on children's work, either individually or in groups, is another introductory use of language experience. Children will frequently dictate a line or two about a painting or drawing or will welcome teacher's labeling of objects in a picture. A daycare director, writing in a log kept on one child's progress through a semester, reported transcribing the girl's story about Mickey Mouse: "She was thrilled—she giggled through my reading. When I copied her dramatic voice inflection, she hugged me. I certainly intend to do this again more often—talk about instilling a sense of positive self-concept!"

Daily routines with the calendar can incorporate LEA when teachers make a calendar with large spaces left for each school day. Near the end of each day, the children discuss the day's happenings and dictate a few statements to be recorded on the calendar. Teachers then read back the dictation to the children and perhaps make additional comments or discuss what will happen the next day. This use of the calendar is a true language experience activity, for it involves discussion of common experiences, dictation of ideas, recording of ideas, and sharing, as teachers read the daily summary. Children learn the routines of language experience through daily practice and understand what is expected of them when asked to participate in longer dictation sessions resulting in a group story.

Chart Stories

The most common use of LEA is the chart story. Children and teachers share the act of composing and reading a story, often about a shared experience. If children were going to take a trip to a greengrocer to get fruit for fruit salad, for example, the teacher might generate a set of class rules through discussion and then record them on an LEA chart. When the children returned to class and have made and enjoyed their fruit salad, they could write a story about their trip. "Who," the teacher would begin, "can suggest a name for the story?" The name, appropriately referred to as the *title*, is written at the top of the chart. The children dictate what they want to say while the teacher records these ideas. The teacher might provide prompts such as "What else happened?" or "What did we do then?" if the children's memories lag. After the chart is completed, the teacher reads it to the children, pointing to each word. Individual children can find their names or any words they recognize. The completed story might be posted on a bulletin board, kept in a "Big Book of Trips," or even dittoed off for each child to have a copy to illustrate and keep.

Children could also draw pictures of their trip and dictate comments for the teacher to write. These could be bound into a book. Individual pictures and a group story could be sent to thank the people at the greengrocer for their help while the class visited them. Neighborhood stores and services frequently display these kinds of thank-you notes—good public relations for them and certainly a delightful surprise when young authors happen to catch sight of their efforts at a later time.

Guidelines for Preschool and Kindergarten LEA

Simple guidelines guarantee success with LEA in preschools and kindergarten. At this age, children are just beginning to gain a sense of story, and concepts such as sequence are only weakly developed. Children's dictation can be confused, unsequenced, and redundant and teachers must guide their dictation carefully. In guiding the activity, teachers can reinforce concepts of time and sequence, for example, by inserting, "Who can tell me what we did *first* . . . What did we do *after* we saw the fire engine? . . . Tell me what we did *after* we left the store *but before* we got back to school . . . *before* we made the fruit salad, what did we do?"

Two ways of taking dictation are possible, and both have advantages. Especially when the approach is still new to the children, teachers may use direct or indirect quotations so that children see their names recorded on the chart. Thus, teachers might ask the children what they saw and then record their statements this way: "Billy said, We saw tulips in a garden. Ana said, We saw a fire truck. Rachel said that we all saw her mommy waiting for the bus." Inasmuch as this is not a grammar lesson, quotation marks are not necessary. This method can produce long but boring chart stories; however, teachers can compensate for the redundancy by reading the story with inflection and enthusiasm and by acknowledging each child as his or her statement is read. The children see that what they say can be written down, and they see their own and each other's names actually used in print. They may even be invited to "read" what they or someone else said (probably from memory and not always perfectly).

The second method involves more summarizing. Teachers must have a clear idea of what to include in the story and guide the dictation toward that format. Direct questioning elicits comments about one aspect of the experience, which the teachers then summarize. In response to the question, "What did you like best?", the teachers might record: "Sam and Maria like seeing the fire truck racing down the street. Rebecca and Debbie like the smells of all the fruit at the fruit store. Bobby and Isaac enjoyed eating the fruit salad best of all." Taking this kind of dictation is more difficult because children have to concentrate on the questions and wait while several people respond. Yet, the approach allows teachers to help children realize when they have repeated someone else and models good sentence formation and varied vocabulary (note the use of "liked best" and "enjoyed" above). Children see their names included in this kind of story and gain the same sense of "That's what I said, right there in print!" They may go back to point to their names in the story or to any other print they think they can recognize. The resulting story is more fluent, coherent, and "book-like." Teachers may intersperse a few simple pictures with the children's dictation to add variety and can help children actually read their stories. As teachers point to the words and pictures in a chart story and say the words, the children can chime in by reading the pictures. This combination of words and pictures is called *rebus writing*. This technique is good for class recipes, too, as shown in Figure 11.3, the recipe for fruit salad.

One final guideline for using language experience with preschoolers or, indeed, with any children: Neatness counts! Teachers should make any transcription as neat and attractive as possible. Handwriting should be dark, clear, and large, with adequate spacing. Language experience represents genuine authorship for young children, and teachers must demonstrate respect for the young authors.

CHILDREN'S CONCEPTS OF WORDS

Before children can learn to read, they must understand what *words* are. Environmental print has taught them the beginnings of this **concept of words**—that a graphic representation stands for some oral utterance. Children must learn that there is a one-to-one match between print and speech and then must learn to attend to the boundaries of print they see in texts. Listening to children's speech gives some indication of why this concept is difficult. The child who says, "Momma, Iwanna glasamilk anacookie" may be a long way from understanding that the utterance is made of ten distinct words—Momma, I want a glass of milk

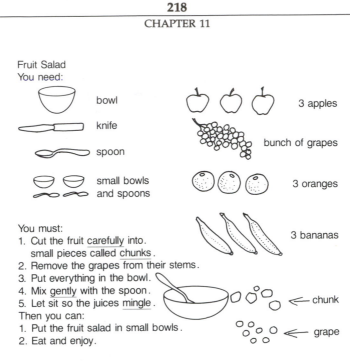

Fruit Salad
You need:

bowl

knife

spoon

small bowls
and spoons

3 apples

bunch of grapes

3 oranges

3 bananas

You must:
1. Cut the fruit <u>carefully</u> into.
   small pieces called <u>chunks</u>.
2. Remove the grapes from their stems.
3. Put everything in the bowl.
4. Mix <u>gently</u> with the spoon.
5. Let sit so the juices <u>mingle</u>.
Then you can:
1. Put the fruit salad in small bowls.
2. Eat and enjoy.

← chunk

← grape

FIGURE 11.3
Words and pictures can be combined for a rebus approach that children can read easily.
This rebus recipe could be used in a cooking experience after a trip to a grocer to buy
fruit. Children who are familiar with cooking procedures would feel confident as they
read this recipe. Words that are underlined would be stressed to make sure children
understood them.

and a cookie—not the four of the oral utterance. Beginning writing shows some
print-speech awareness, but initial efforts may be so skeletal that it is difficult to
know exactly how children have conceptualized the transfer from speech to
print. Young writers may also run their words together with no "white space" to
indicate word boundaries or arrange their print vertically.[4]

There are numerous strategies to help children discover the essential relationships between print and speech. Writing words for songs and poems on
chart tablets and again taking the time to point to each are essential as this kind
of material is introduced. Teachers can ask children to "echo read" the material:
Teachers point to words and read a line first, then they point and read again as
children chime in. As children memorize the material, they develop an auditory
trace and also realize that there is relationship between what they say and the
print itself. One researcher referred to this as "putting the written message 'in
children's ears' before requiring them to read" (Morris, 1980, p. 108).

Shared book and language experiences also provide excellent opportunities to demonstrate print-speech correspondences. Teachers point at words as
they read; children themselves point at words and at the "white space" between

words. Children listen to text and track it visually, and eventually they recognize words as distinct units that represent something they know and can themselves say. If children do not make this conceptualization, beginning reading instruction, especially phonics, will be frustrating and confusing. One researcher asked, "How can children benefit appreciably from intensive work with isolated phonic sounds if they are not aware at some level that these sounds are part of a meaningful conceptual frame—the word? . . . Many beginning reading problems could be avoided if children were simply given more time in a supportive language environment to work out the conceptual complexities of the writing system on their own" (Morris, 1980, pp. 108–109).

SUMMARY

Books in a preschool serve two distinct purposes: children's exploration and self-discovery and student-teacher sharing. As children look through books, they not only gain pleasure, but also skills in handling books, the ability to interpret picture clues, and some basic information about how reading works. At first tentatively but with increasing confidence, they hypothesize that certain combinations of letters make certain words over and over again. Final confirmation of this important fact may still be a long way off, but an emerging "model" of how literacy works is supported.

Teachers who share books with children can guide young learners toward specific discoveries and can clarify misconceptions or wrong guesses about literacy. Big versions of favorite books and language experience stories make these interactions even more meaningful because informal lessons come close to the intimacy of parent-child sharing a story at bedtime.

Young children, those often not even considered "ready" for reading, gain a feel for favorite stories, and create and "read" back their own texts. They gain a sense of what words are. From these experiences come affirmation of themselves as literacy users and determination to refine their emerging skills for more sophisticated reading tasks. Then, at some point, in a burst of understanding or slowly and methodically, children realize that no longer will it be just the fast-food restaurant signs, package labels, or environmental print in the classroom that they can read; they will be ready to move on to more sophisticated reading tasks.

REVIEW

1. Be sure that you can define these terms:
   appropriate teaching point
   "bedtime story learning cycle"
   big books
   concept of *words*

emergent literacy (update your definition to include new information)
modeling (as the term applies to reading)
scaffolding (as the term applies to reading)
shared book experience

2. Look at Marie Clay's definition of reading on page 200. Restate it in your own words in no more than a sentence or two.

3. Think about Butler and Clay's statement that what children bring to learning to read is more important than what a first-grade teacher presents to them. List all the positive characteristics or behaviors children can bring and state why they are important. Then list all the negative characteristics or deficits that children might bring and suggest what preschool and kindergarten teachers do to compensate for the negatives.

4. In what ways do children's discovery of writing and invented spelling represent a form of problem solving that occurs prior to their learning to read?

5. Find a children's story that would be appropriate for a big book. Make the big book and present it to a group of children. Record how they react. If possible, leave the book in their classroom and note whether they return to the book for storybook reenactments.

6. Find another book to present to young children. Read it to several children one at a time and invite each child to reenact the story. Observe their behavior as they "read the book" and tape-record what they say. Notice how much prompting you have to do. Analyze the tape-recording to determine what kind of storybook reenactment each child presented.

7. Visit several preschools and kindergartens and "survey" their libraries. Are there enough books to encourage browsing? Are the books appropriate for the children? How do the teachers feel about prereaders using books on their own?

8. In your visits, determine the extent to which language experience is used to develop prereading skills and concepts. What opportunities for LEA use are being missed? Ask the teachers how they feel about LEA. If possible, conduct some LEA sessions yourself to see how the children respond.

NOTES

1. Sulzby, E. (1985). Children's emergent reading of favorite storybooks: A developmental study. *Reading Research Quarterly, 20,* 458–481.

2. Cochran-Smith, M. (1984). *The making of a reader.* Norwood, NJ: Ablex; Durkin, D. (1966). *Children who read early.* New York: Teachers College Press.

3. Stauffer, R. G. (1980). *The language experience approach to the teaching of reading.* New York: Holt, Rinehart & Winston.

4. Morris, D. (1980). Beginning readers' concept of word. In E. H. Henderson & J. W. Beers (Eds.). *Developmental and cognitive aspects of learning to spell: A reflection of word knowledge* (pp. 97–111). Newark: DE: International Reading Association.

12

Moving Toward Skilled Reading

This chapter discusses how children progress toward skilled reading. No *particular* grade level is designated because some children "emerge" into reading in kindergarten, while others do not; school districts themselves differ in when they begin formal instruction. This book maintains that "real" reading emerges from "play" reading, language experience opportunities, and beginning writing within supportive, literate environments. Structured preschool reading instruction is not necessary. In fact, "before school instruction begins, [some] children may combine memories for words, recalled visual cues from text, picture clues, and their own ability to predict from the language of that text, and begin to read independently" (Genishi & Dyson, 1984, p. 166).

READING INSTRUCTION

Specific reading instruction helps most children solidify emerging literacy concepts into useful behaviors and skills. Children need visible demonstrations or models of how actions are accomplished. Clay (1979) stated that "children become ready for formal reading at different times and as a result of different rates of maturing" (p. 11) and stressed that they will learn to read only in the presence of print and print use. Children can *see* people writing, physically moving a pen or pencil, and producing marks on a surface; they often have an auditory memory trace to help them read their own and others' dictation; and they can easily read environmental print, with its short, information-laden messages and direct concrete representations. But understanding how people actually read, silently, with few picture clues is different: Children cannot see inside others' heads to understand the "patterning of complex behavior," as Clay has called reading. Because there is no external model of this cognitive behavior, the abstract task of learning to read *can* be very difficult.

Clay (1979) maintained: "Reading instruction places new demands on the child. He must use his old preschool ways of responding in novel situations and he must discover or invent new coordinations [between oral and written language]. The initiative for this active learning comes from the child" (p. 11). Children need to organize their previous understandings about literacy and add new insight to what they already know. Commercial reading series can confuse this organization, but fortunately teachers do not have to abandon language experience and shared books for rigid, uninteresting reading curricula. Even with structured commercial programs, early childhood reading instruction can continue spirited interactions with print.

A Look at Traditional Instruction

Reading instruction has long been structured around commercial **basal readers,** sequenced books and materials for all elementary grades. The major characteristics of basal readers include sequenced readers that progress in difficulty throughout the grades, supplementary material such as workbooks and dittos, and teachers' manuals to help guide instruction and assessment of progress. Basals advocate a balance of direction instruction, independent practice, and silent and oral reading; but actual reading often accounts for less time than the skills assignments in workbooks.[1] This reflects "the prime myth" in reading, which, "is that reading instruction should consist exclusively of teaching phonics, vocabulary, and grammar . . . [even though] there is little evidence that children learn their working vocabularies from reading exercises. [Reading should be] a way into worlds unheard of and undreamed, the worlds of Maurice Sendak and Dr. Seuss, of Snow White and E. B. White, even of the comics and the television advertisements" (Bruner, 1984, p. 194).

Sentence structure in basals can be as much as 1½ years below that of children's oral language, and controlled vocabularies with specifically selected words prohibit the wide variety of expressions children themselves utter and use in beginning writing.[2] Sentences "look like real language and yet they do not correspond to any real language form. . . . They also sound like real utterance in spite of transmitting no information and lacking any communicative content" (Ferreiro & Taberosky, 1982, pp. 274–275). Having learned to expect meaning from print, children may "act as if any nonsense could come out of a text, as if the text were a hybrid, as beginning texts truly are, halfway between real language and tongue twisters." Replacing dictation, writing, and children's literature by this "hybrid" language can be truly disheartening; when children cannot connect their own language and the language in basals, their sense of themselves as language users can be undermined. Their writing efforts often begin to echo the simplistic basal "style" and lose the vitality common in most beginner's compositions.[3]

Simplified in vocabulary and sentence structure, basal stories are often simplistic in content as well. Anticipating that they will read for meaning and fun, children find little in their beginning readers to comprehend. This seems to be an American trait, as European basal series and books used in New Zealand present more interesting, real-life situations to which children can actually relate.[4]

Basal teachers' manuals are designed to guide skills instruction, enrichment activities, and on-going assessment. In practice, however, teachers' most consistent use of basal manuals is for post-reading comprehension questions, which are often the most limited aspect of a manual and do not encourage the thoughtfulness children expect from a directed listening-thinking activity or big book presentation.[5] Still the basal reader, used carefully, can play an important part in children's continued literacy growth. The whole language approach recommends a flexible stance that can accommodate commercial materials, as long as children are allowed to build on the language competencies they bring to school.

ALTERNATIVES TO TRADITIONAL INSTRUCTION

Researchers remind early childhood teachers that traditional, structured programs *can* work for children with more advanced understandings of school-related interactions (pragmatics) and of literacy in general.[6] For beginners, however, flexible alternatives are essential for real growth. Teachers' behaviors, attitudes, and expectations; materials in the classroom; and methods of instruction and assessment define "alternatives" to basal programs within whole language classrooms.

Characteristics of Classrooms and Teachers

An environment rich in print, where children see significant adults reading and writing—this is a recurring theme in this book and is as relevant to early primary classes as to preschools and kindergartens. Children know—because they engage in experiences that demonstrate this—that reading involves seeking meaning from the printed text. Teachers recognize that "the developmental [literacy] learner attempts the skill in a bumbling cascade of errors which the teacher receives with remarkable tolerance" (Holdaway, 1986, p. 43). Teachers encourage children to seek and accept help but provide assistance without moralizing, criticism, or comparisons to peers. Teachers demonstrate their love of literacy, and this modeling can compensate for home environments where literacy is not valued or practiced. Early primary grades are by no means too late to introduce children to the pleasures of reading and writing.

Cueing Systems and Diversity

Good beginning reading programs accustom children to using three kinds of information or **cueing systems** to gain meaning from what they read:[7] (a) semantic constraints of text (word meanings); (b) the syntactic constraints (grammatical structure); and (c) the phonological constraints (letter-sound correspondences). Young writers have actively manipulated these constraints in their stories, but they may need help transferring their knowledge to reading new material.

Children must also develop a "set for diversity" in interpreting written language, especially as they encounter standard spelling. Invented spelling helped children discover the regularities of language; and as they read, they often stumble over more irregularities, such as silent letters. Children must approach reading aware of the variability, prepared to try several different approaches to unfamiliar words, and guided by the knowledge that reading *ought* to make sense. Strategies discussed for teaching the spelling of irregular words help children develop this flexibility (see Chapter 7).

Assessing Children's Knowledge About Print

The best means for assessing children's knowledge of print and literacy skills is focused kidwatching. Unfortunately, paper-and-pencil tests, whether informal or standardized, are more common, in spite of two severe limitations. First, tests can be scary to children, and frightened test-takers may not give a true indication of what they know. Second, paper-and-pencil tests assess only selected parts of the total behaviors needed for reading and writing and may miss important skills and concepts children actually do possess.

Checklists can make teachers efficient kidwatchers. Inviting children to reenact stories is another strategy. Assessment should begin early in the school year, as soon as teachers feel they have adequate rapport with the children. To use storybook reenactments for focused kidwatching, teachers engage the class in a shared book experience. Next, one at a time, children are invited to "read" the story to the teacher. Teachers then observe how children attack the total task and also point to specific words to see if children can read them at sight or figure them out. Inability to identify individual words means reading is still closely tied to auditory memory and the child needs help generalizing skills to wider reading tasks. Teachers should ask comprehension questions, although answers to these questions will also reflect memory of the shared book experience.

If children read the story and discuss it with comprehension, teachers should invite them to read another, unfamiliar book. Observing the child again, teachers try to identify reading strategies most readily employed. Young readers who depend on letter-sound correspondences may sound out each word they encounter. Laborious sounding out indicates that the child has not learned to use **sight words** and needs to expand his range of reading strategies. Alternatively, children who have a vast storehouse of sight words may stumble over an unfamiliar word and not know how to "attack" it; they need a different kind of help to broaden reading strategies. Provided their comprehension is adequate, both children should most definitely be considered readers, rather then "reenacters."

These assessment strategies can work throughout early childhood, with children's literature and with basal readers. Teachers may even pull selected passages from a basal to get a rough assessment of placement within a series. The key is to assess children's *entire* interaction with reading, including familiarity with books. The child whose only experience with books has been with a basal reader may view reading in terms of structured questions and worksheets, while the child who has always had books around (even if not at home) will be more comfortable and confident. Figure 12.1 summarizes what teachers should look for in assessing children's beginning reading.

Assessing Word Attack Strategies and Memory

Some children may be able to "read" and still not understand what they have read because they lack the connection between meaningful oral language and print. Using letter-sound correspondences, these children go from print to oral utterance quite accurately, but asked what they read, they cannot respond. First graders who have been praised for "reading" but never questioned about content and older children whose comprehension has never been fully assessed are often dubbed *word callers* and may be headed for real problems. Butler and Clay (1979) warned, "There is considerable evidence that the majority of 'failed' readers see reading as the task of saying the words aloud correctly, one after the other, and not as a process of 'getting the message.' On the other hand, young children who are becoming good readers can often be seen almost swallowing the print whole, keeping the sense going by a miraculous mobilization of all the resources at their disposal—an exhilarating experience" (p. 6). Early assessment of this behavior is essential.

Youngsters may also have memorized children's books or stories in basal readers and can "read" text entirely from memory by coordinating auditory recall and picture clues. Some memorization is expected in familiar books, and some is desirable because it provides an auditory "trace" against which children compare what they are saying. Children must realize that there should be a match between what they *say* in oral reading and what they previously *heard* or *might have heard* in normal speech. Lacking a match cues them to go back to the text to reapply word attack skills or to self-correct. Basal readers favor children with good auditory memories; the simple text can be easily committed to memory.

Teachers need to be alert for children such as Cecily, who was one of my first-grade students: Cecily was Black, from a low-income family, and had had few experiences with books. She was proud, full of enthusiasm, and confident that she could read. The first story on the Bank Street Preprimer read "One house. Two houses. Three houses. Many houses are in the city." After several weeks of prereading work, Cecily picked up a preprimer and read the first story flawlessly. She seemed to make rapid progress, but I began to watch her closely because even to me as a beginning teacher, something seemed strange: Cecily

Knowledge conventions of reading

1. When children are handed a book:

   ☐ do they hold it correctly?
   ☐ can they point out the front and back of the book?
   ☐ do they realize that there is a correspondence between the print and what one reads orally?
   ☐ can they point to individual words in lines of print?

2. Are they familiar with these words and what they mean:

   ☐ author?
   ☐ illustrator?
   ☐ print?
   ☐ pictures?
   ☐ words?

3. Can they respond to these questions or commands?

   ☐ Show me where a person should start reading.
   ☐ Which way does a person go when she finishes a page of the book?
   ☐ Tell me about the pictures in the book.

Book-reading behavior (whether children are actually reading or reenacting a story)

1. Do children track print correctly?

FIGURE 12.1
Determining what children know and how they feel about beginning reading. Teachers should observe children as they read or handle books.

didn't stumble over words, she seemed too confident, she didn't use her finger. Opening the book at random, I asked her to read. She panicked. I pointed to individual words, and she told me that "wasn't really reading." She could not read words in isolation and had difficulty reading whole passages of text (consisting of no more than five words) unless she started at the very beginning of the story. Cecily, I discovered, had memorized two preprimers by listening to her second grade brother, still a beginning reader, labor through the same books at home. Conceptualizing reading as associating pictures and an auditory memory trace and then reciting text, she was convinced she could read. She was shocked and hurt that I did not agree with her way of reading, but extensive language experience and work with supplemental readers finally helped her unlearn her faulty habits and start over in a way that allowed her to use her memory powers productively.

2. Do children use their fingers correctly in following their reading?
3. Do children use pictures appropriately to aid reading?
4. When reading, do children seem to use many word attack skills in a flexible manner?
5. Can children use context clues?
6. Do they self-correct when reading orally or do they seem unaware of errors?
7. Do they depend on teachers for all unfamiliar words?
8. Do they mumble read when reading silently?
9. Do they seem to hold books too close or too far away? (Vision check is advised.)

Attitudinal Signs

1. Do children seem happy and relaxed when reading with the teacher either in small groups or alone?
2. Do children volunteer to read during reading group?
3. Do children use reading as a free-time activity?
4. Have children talked about going to the library?
5. If the class goes to the library, do children seem familiar with the place and its purpose? Do they check out books?
6. Do children mention reading books at home or bring books to share with the class?
7. Do children seem able to finish books they select in class?
8. Do children seem to turn to books as reference material when needed for class projects? Do they bring books from home for class projects?

FIGURE 12.1
continued

MAINTAINING THE MOMENTUM OF EMERGING LITERACY

Rather than thinking of themselves as the people who teach children to read and write, teachers should take responsibility for helping children maintain the momentum of emerging literacy skills. Becoming a skilled reader means learning to use all print cues in organized, efficient ways by attending *selectively* to semantics, syntax, and letter-sound correspondences. Most adults do not think about their reading behaviours much; they centre their attention on attaining meaning. There is a test in that last sentence: Two words are spelled with British spelling. Did you catch them? Or did you read for meaning, guided by the semantics (no hard words) and syntax (straight-forward sentence structure). Or, perhaps quotes from Clay and Holdaway have accustomed you to British spellings. Children, who know so much about language, must continue to search for meaning and to become efficient processors of text.

Gaining meaning from text is reading with comprehension. If children know how to listen with understanding and know how to get meaning from environmental print, half the lessons of reading comprehension have been mastered. They know they should seek meaning. Learning to read well is a total, holistic process, in which children construct ideas about the way reading and writing work. Beginners' constructions are incomplete, inefficient, and possibly full of misconceptions, but they must be the starting point for focused instruction, and they are stronger if children understand they should read for meaning.

Instructional activities should be supportive; that is, they should help children move from play to real reading with a minimum of effort.[8] Subskill instruction is part of the student-teacher interaction during this beginning period because gaining control of ways to "attack" unfamiliar words makes readers efficient. But subskill instruction should never overshadow children's search for meaning and enjoyment from books. The rest of this chapter discusses instructional strategies for the initial and later stages of reading growth.

Shared Literacy Experiences in Early Primary Grades

Big books and storybooks can be the core of a supportive approach to beginning reading. The previous chapter discussed how big books give children the feel of reading; more directed use of these materials refines skills. The approach is widely used in New Zealand, where handling books, listening to teachers read, producing LEA texts, and seeing teachers read and write themselves bring visual and auditory cues together for young learners.[9] Committees of New Zealand teachers have developed the *Ready to Read* series of books mentioned in Chapter 11. Neither vocabulary nor sentence structure is rigidly controlled in the series, although words of high frequency in children's oral language and literature predominate. Controlled text, it is reasoned, seduces children into thinking that all texts are regular, a misconception they discover only too quickly. Small groups of children working together with the teacher are the basic instructional "delivery system" of the approach, although whole class and individualized instruction have their role as well. The approach is adaptable to any early childhood classroom.

Grouping for Instruction

Most adults remember reading groups, and groups remain a cornerstone of traditional instruction. Groups may or may not have specific names, like "Robins" or "Superpersons"; but they are bound together by reading "in the same book," and group members receive the same instruction whether or not they already possess the skills. Grouping in itself is not bad when it allows teachers and children to meet together with some intimacy to discuss stories or refine skills. Unfortunately, interaction often centers at skill practice.[10] Also unfortunately, groups become fixed, and movement out of or across groups rarely occurs. Once a Robin, always a Robin, children feel bored and demoralized when they figure out that the Robins do not "read as well" as the Bluebirds.

Grouping need not be lock-step; flexible grouping is, in fact, an essential characteristic of classes in which children move smoothly from shared book experiences to independent reading. Initial groupings should be of approximately the same level, but membership is not fixed. As children's independence increases, they should move to different, more challenging reading tasks. Those still needing support and reinforcement should not be made to feel inferior or "left behind."

The purpose of grouping, besides the obvious goal of efficient delivery of instruction, is to tap the energy and intelligence of group members. Groups of children playing with literate behaviors in dramatic play try out and share emerging hypotheses about reading and writing. Grouping in early grades should serve a similar purpose: Children should be encouraged to cut through teachers' "language of instruction" to explain concepts and skills to each other.

Teachers must be willing to give some of the "control" of instructional groups to participants; children must feel comfortable enough to discuss, share, and question what is presented. As children process ideas for oral sharing, they increase their control of reading skills. What they say—correctly or incorrectly—gives teachers diagnostic insight into children's progress toward mastery.

Groups for Supportive Reading

The first kind of group is called a **supportive reading group,** which helps children acclimate to working together for instruction, handling books, and attending to instruction. Handing children a book and telling them to open to the first page may be efficient, but it will not nurture a love of reading. Supportive reading groups start with an enlarged print version of a story, which teachers read clearly and naturally, pointing to each word and emphasizing any unusual words or features of the text. Asking children if there are any words they know comes next and acknowledges that they may know some sight words and can already read. Next, if possible, children should browse through the regular-sized book to note similarities and differences between this and other books, identify sight words, and become familiar with the pictures. This process need take no longer than five minutes. Teachers then read the book as children read or "echo" words they know. Discussion follows, accompanied as appropriate by dramatics or other activities. Copies of the book are left out for additional browsing. Needless to say, these groups are small, no more than five children.

Instruction should remain low-key, although teachers are constantly assessing children's emerging skills. The objective is movement from teacher-directed to student reading with no sacrifice of the support that teacher direction has fostered. The transition should be smooth and natural, with no one point when reading skills move from "play" to "real." Teachers never really withdraw support from beginning readers. They continue to challenge children to exercise skills, stretch what they know, and apply knowledge in new situations—all at the "appropriate teaching point." Through supportive groups, children discover that they *do* know some of the words and guessed right on others. These discoveries increase children's confidence so that they can gain more from shared reading and move effortlessly to more focused group instruction. Figure 12.2 (pp. 232–233) summarizes this procedure.

Big Books and Enlarged Print for Reading Groups

Big books allow small groups of children to share reading. Remember the child who wrote, "You can see the pichrs . . . big books are easyer to rede." By pointing to individual words, teachers demonstrate the movement of print on a page and reinforce the one-to-one correspondence between graphic images and their oral equivalents. Needless to say, children should be encouraged to point when they read from a big book and also when they read normal-sized texts. The behavior decreases with growing competence.

Big books do not have to be the only form of enlarged print in a classroom. Holdaway recommends both overhead transparencies and slides of pages of actual books projected on the wall. Transparencies should be lettered in the teacher's best handwriting or made thermally from xerographic copies of pages of actual books. Print, again, is large and masking devices can be used with transparencies to isolate specific letters, words parts, whole words, and phrases for study and discussion.

Masking, Oral Cloze, Caption, and Predictable Books

Enlarged print and overhead transparencies lend themselves to use of sliders or masking devices. Pointers can be used when slides are projected on the wall. **Masking** or systematically covering and uncovering words is better than using lists of words or flash cards because masking gives children a discrete image to focus on without isolating words from a meaningful context. Beginners can easily memorize the graphic image of a flash card and not realize that the letters stand for a word in their vocabularies. This memorization produces a form of word calling that does not promote reading with comprehension. Figure 12.3 (p. 234) shows how print can be masked.

Masking involves a strategy called *cloze,* which is based on the idea that readers search for meaning in print and can fill in missing words if they are reading with comprehension. Guided by sight words and letter-sound correspondences, children read as teachers unmask text and use semantics and syntax to predict "what words will come next" in particular sentences. They learn to predict story lines, and teachers can stop at appropriate places to elicit guesses about "what action will happen next." This method of slowly unmasking text and modeling self-questioning and predicting comes close to externalizing the unseen, mental processes of reading. Teachers are in control of what children see and demonstrate the predicting children should do in independent reading. Random, wrong guesses indicate comprehension difficulties, while wrong guesses that are semantically or syntactically correct should be discussed with "Yes, that word *would* fit here; but the word the author used is ____; they mean the same thing, don't they?"

Oral cloze is *not* the same as *open sentence* activities, which feature a sentence with a blank spot and several words from which children are to select (and often circle) "the one that belongs in the blank." These encourage children to attend to small, fragmented parts of a sentence—which word would go between these two other words?—or merely to guess. Cloze activities are open-ended, do not always have just *one* right answer, and can lead to good discussions of why

Materials:
> Multiple copies of children's literature or basal reader and enlarged print version of what children will read.

Procedures, Day 1:

1. Teacher presents the enlarged print version of the material and reads it in a normal, conversational voice, pointing to each word as he/she reads, emphasizing words like POW with both voice and comments.
2. Children are invited to point out or guess any words that they might know by sight.
3. Children look through regular-sized copies of the book for about five minutes; they should note and discuss the pictures and words they know. This gives them a chance to coordinate the teacher's oral reading and the regular text.
4. The teacher reads the text again as children follow along either on the enlarged print or in the regular books; children are encouraged to echo the teacher's reading as much as possible; teacher should note who does not seem able to track the print in the text or the enlarged print and who can echo read most of the text.
5. If the story is appropriate, the children may act it out or draw about it; these activities reinforce their understanding of the story and increase comprehension.
6. Copies of the material are available for browsing.

Procedures, Day 2:

1. Steps 1-4 are repeated at a more rapid pace.
2. Echo reading behavior should increase during this session. Children should be called upon to read words, phrases, or whole sentences either

FIGURE 12.2
Structuring a supportive reading group.

certain words do or do not "work" as answers. Children gain more intellectually than from one-answer-only worksheets.

Caption books and predictable books[11] are especially good for introducing masking. Children easily figure out what the books are about, can call out a caption, or chime in with a repetitive chant or story line, and they soon can read the books independently. Appendix 1 lists caption and predictable books, and teachers can easily compose books specifically for their own classes.

Oral cloze can encourage attention to letter-sound correspondences. For example, as teachers approach a word starting with a blend, they stop the masking process and say, "Now, see if you can figure out this word. I'll give you a clue." Unmasking only the blend elicits guesses about the word. Children must from their books or from the enlarged print version; approximations of the correct text are accepted.

3. Teacher provides appropriate low-key instruction by pointing out words that have a specific sound, represent a particular part of speech or grammatical principle or other aspect of reading.

4. Teacher observes the extent to which children participate and determines who needs advanced work and who needs continued close support.

5. Copies of the material are available for browsing and rereading; peer reading and story reenactment are encouraged.

Procedures, Day 3:

1. A new book may be presented in the same fashion, or children may continue to work on the previous material.

2. From time to time, a familiar story is reviewed for fun and to reinforce past learning.

Alternative procedures:

1. A similar process can be used with dictated language experience stories; teacher may or may not ditto the LEA story for individual children, but the basic procedure of supportive reading is followed.

2. Again with or without dittoed copies of the enlarged print material, supportive reading strategies can be used to introduce poems, information on charts, posters, or bulletin boards, or song lyrics; children follow along as the teacher reads and read as much of the material as they can on their own.

3. Either of these alternatives can be used with small groups or with the whole class; the echo reading process allows even weaker readers to participate.

FIGURE 12.2
continued

use both their knowledge of letter-sound correspondences and the preceding words to ask themselves what word would fit *and* begins with the indicated blend. Doing this successfully demonstrates the true utility of **phonics** and **context clues.**

Varying the Kinds of Reading

Children in whole language classrooms read extensively, as part of daily routines. Children also write and read their own and others' stories and apply awareness of letter-sound correspondences to editing or "cleaning up" their work. As long as there is a good selection of books in the class, sustained silent

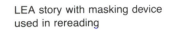

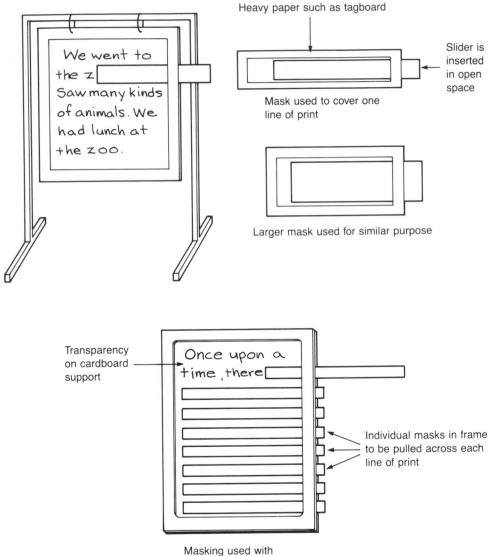

FIGURE 12.3

Masking devices can be used to cover individual words, single lines, or large pieces of text. They can be used with stories presented on chart stands or overhead transparencies. Teachers uncover text as children read orally or silently. The amount of text uncovered depends upon the instructional objectives: to reinforce phonics skills, to demonstrate context clues, to encourage prediction of story line, and so forth.

reading (SSR) can be initiated, even with prereaders. This is a counterpart to sustained silent writing (SSW) discussed in Chapter 8. Of course, beginners will not be reading silently; but the transition from whispered to mumbled to silent reading does occur with time. Children must realize that SSR is a time for quiet enjoyment of books; and, as reading abilities grow, time devoted to SSR increases and silence is demanded.

Through extensive assigned and free-time reading, children discover that they *do* possess reading skills, that their "play" is now real. Children must make two discoveries if they are going to progress successfully in reading. They should have discovered the connection between reading and the words in their own listening and speaking vocabularies. They should also discover that their visual memory for specific graphic images transfers to larger contexts; that is, that *dog, DOG,* or any other form of the word can be counted on to be the same word. Children know this concept in terms of environmental print, but they must discover this reliability of visual memory has broader application than consistently identifying their favorite fast-food restaurant.

Reading in diverse situations helps children trust their visual memories, depend on them, and transfer memory for individual words to new situations. Their visual memory must be accompanied by an auditory trace (how words sound) and by awareness of meaning. Again, consider yourself a kidwatcher as you read about a child in the same class as Cecily: Russell, also Black and also from a low-income family, had been read to considerably and was enthusiastic about school. Gaining familiarity with the neighborhood was part of the first-grade social studies curriculum, so we took frequent walks and wrote LEA stories about them. Near the school was a factory outlet store for athletic shoes; one day, on a neighborhood walk, we noticed several pairs of old sneakers that had been tied together and thrown over a lamp post outside the store. This was a wonderful sight for first graders: Who had done it, why, how many shoes were there? "Big kids" and "to be slick" answered the first two questions, but the number of sneakers was hard to guess. Russell, who had been reading the same preprimer as Cecily, settled the debate by firmly stating: "MANY! MANY SNEAKERS ARE ON THE LAMP POST!" The rest of the class concurred. The children had been encountering the word visually and auditorily, but until Russell used the word itself purposefully and correctly, *many* of the children had not really realized what reading was about.

LANGUAGE EXPERIENCE IN EARLY PRIMARY GRADES

The value of language experience extends throughout the early primary grades, where material developed through LEA capitalizes on children's experiences and interests and reflects their individual language patterns. As stated in the previous chapter, LEA builds upon the "experience-language-cognitive wealth that children bring with them to school . . . [and] provides a sound, all-embracing foundation on which to construct and develop reading ability" (Stauffer, 1980, p. 17). Using group and individual chart stories as "basal material" has been shown to be as effective in promoting reading growth as more traditional approaches,[12] and their use has a definite place within whole language instruction.

Chart stories are appropriate instructional materials because they reflect children's vocabularies and semantic and syntactic development. The wealth of language available for young learners to use is monumental, yet the average first-grade reading program presents approximately 400 words.[13] Syntactic variety may also be limited, although children are able to produce and understand even relatively complex sentence patterns. Language experience has particular value for second-language learners and for those who speak a nonstandard dialect. Because LEA allows children to use their own regional or code-switching dialects, reading materials do not present the semantic or syntactic conflicts that basals, written in Standard English, might pose for young learners. Teachers in bilingual classrooms can take dictation in children's dominant language and help them produce appropriate, relevant basal material that fully reflects their own language community. Teachers shape dictation toward standard use and provide a bridge between "home" and "school" language.

Language experience seems to be good for teachers as well. There is indication that teachers trained in using LEA "tend to modify their classroom climate toward less authoritarian relationships" with children and increase the value they place on children's language skills (Spache & Spache, 1977, p. 138). Teachers who value children's language skills will bring their classrooms closer to the nurturing home environment that has been praised as ideal for developmental literacy learning.

Word Banks and LEA

Developing a "key vocabulary" or **word banks** is another aspect of LEA. Each day, children request one or more words, which are written on cards to be stored on key rings (hence, key vocabulary) or in word banks made from coffee cans, shoe boxes, or any other sturdy container. A box of some sort is best because dividers can be inserted to separate words alphabetically or according to designated categories, such as "Words for Things," "Words for Actions," "Words that Describe," and so forth. Periodically, teachers "quiz" children on their word cards, and words that cannot be recognized should be discarded. Teachers can also supplement personal words with cards for "function words" such as *and, the, is, are,* and so forth. These words are often difficult for children to remember at sight but are necessary for word bank activities. Teachers can also provide special interest, seasonal, or thematic word cards to encourage writing and word recognition.

Children may study their cards, trace words with their fingers, and use them as flash cards to test themselves and their friends. Such activities reinforce recognition as children see the word, say it to themselves, and study its shape. Tracing the word with their fingers provides a tactile-kinesthetic reinforcement, as does writing the words on separate pieces of paper or the chalkboard. The total process of seeing the words, saying them out loud or silently, and writing or tracing helps children take ownership of their key vocabularies through purposeful independent study.

Children can also use their word cards to construct phrases and sentences. Sentence constructing may take two forms. First, children may formulate a sentence on their own and then look for the word cards needed to construct it. In this case, they may have to ask for some new words for their word banks. Forming sentences, they realize the value of function words teachers have provided and may request additional ones as their sentences become more complex. The second way to construct sentences is to spread out many different word cards and build a sentence from this "raw material." This can be a good collaborative project as children discuss what word cards say and how individual words work in different sentence structures. Additional challenges can be introduced as children are charged with making long sentences or silly sentences. A variation of this activity involves copying sentences from LEA charts on sentence strips, cutting up individual words, and having children reconstruct sentences they have dictated.

Teachers must stress that children read these sentences orally and that the sentences can always be changed. Children may also be asked to write their sentences, and this often produces competition over who has constructed the most, the longest, and the best sentences. By showing off their sentences to each other, children are actually teaching their private collection of words to their peers. Word banks also become children's personal dictionaries as they add words they need for composition.

WORD ATTACK INSTRUCTION

Instruction in the subskills of reading is supposed to help children identify unfamiliar words. It is based on the ideas that total reading behavior can be broken down into parts and that children learn to read by learning the fragments separately. This is akin to saying that parents teach children "Mak - mak - mak - Dah - dah - on - on - lds—McDonalds!" rather than pointing to the sign as they drive into the parking lot. This is not to say that subskill instruction has no place in a whole language classroom; in fact, there may be more total direct and indirect instruction than in traditional classes, as children work to master subskills through their on-going literacy activities. Mastery of reading requires awareness of why the skills are important, which comes from practice with real reading tasks rather than work in worksheets, in workbooks, or most recently on computer drill-and-practice software. Practicing skills in context teaches children to integrate what they know and what they are learning.

It is also important to remember that instruction has its own "language" full of jargon and specialized terms. As teachers guide children to understand reading, they must clarify terminology through explanation and examples. Children may learn concepts and skills before they master related vocabulary but misunderstandings of what terms mean can lead to faulty interpretation of instruction and confusion in applying skills. Figure 12.4 (pp. 239–241) details this jargon and the concepts it represents.

Phonics

Phonics is an instructional approach stressing the sounds (or phonemes) letters make in conjunction with other letters. Traditionally, instruction starts with beginning consonants, introduces vowels, and builds to include the 44 sounds of the English language. Constance Kamii, a scholar in early childhood education, maintained that children learn to do phonics activities *"if they are already at a relatively high level of development,* but they also learn to become mentally more passive and wait to be told what to do and think. Children who are not developmentally advanced enough to learn phonics," she cautioned, "learn to submit to adult power and often lose confidence in their own ability to read" (Willert & Kamii, 1985, pp. 6–7). Young children want to see logic and rules (like Jenny, in Chapter 7) and often are not developmentally ready to understand the diversity of letter-sound correspondences. Additionally, many beginners cannot say or hear all phonological possibilities because of physiological immaturity. For them phonics can be very frustrating.

Children can progress in learning phonics generalizations through a combined program that uses creative writing, games, sight words, language experience, and spelling instruction. Anyone who has seen young children writing cannot doubt that these beginners have discovered many letter-sound generalizations and can use phonics expressively, that is, to produce text. What children may not know is that spelling and sounding out words are two sides of the same behavior. This realization develops from broad experiences with print production and from analysis of the way words are formed.

Games can be a good introduction to phonics analysis and should start with rhymes and word families. Rhyming words demonstrate phonics: They rhyme because the first sound of the word is changed. Word families are groups of words created by adding different first sounds to a base word—*at* becomes *bat, cat, hat,* and so forth. Oral or written lists of words in the *at, ot,* or other families (even the ones that can produce nasty words!) are fun. Children decide if words are "real" or not; in fact, many beginners generate long lists of word family variations and systematically cross out the nonwords. This practice may drill words in isolation, but it is expressive rather than passive and is essentially self-correcting. Children can move from word families to generating words with letter cards, sets, or blocks. As children create words in this way, teachers

Phonics

Vowels: the letters, *a, e, i, o,* and *u* are vowels; *y* is sometimes a vowel.

Long vowels: the vowel "says its name"; long vowel sounds may be made by the letter itself alone in a word or in combination with other letters; see digraphs, below.

Short vowels: the vowel sounds in *cat, egg, sit, cot,* and *cut* are short.

Vowel digraphs: two vowels together are digraphs when one vowel is sounded and the other is silent; usually, the first vowel is voiced, but not always, as in *build* and *fruit*; usually, the voiced vowel is long, as in *boat,* but this is not always true, as in *bread*; examples:

ai (pain); *ay* (hay)
ea (weather, bread, each); *ee* (tree); *ei* (weight, either, receive)
ie (piece, either)
oa (boat); *oe* (toe); *ow* (low); *ou* (tough)
ue (true, blue); *ui* (build, fruit)

Vowel diphthongs: two vowels together, whose sounds make one *new* sound different from the sound made by either individual vowel; these can be very difficult, especially for dialect speakers; examples:

au (haul); *aw* (hawk); *ew* (few); *ey* (they)
oo (book, school), *oi* (soil); *ow* (cow); *oy* (boy)

R-Controlled vowels: vowels or vowel combinations that are followed by an *r,* are neither long nor short; again, children who speak dialects that drop or add *r* sounds have trouble with these sounds; examples:

star, ear, tire, ore, or, and *oar,* or *lure*

Silent vowels: vowels that are not voiced are silent; examples:

sail, where the *i* is silent
sale, where the *a* is long and the final *e* is a "placeholder" to indicate that the previous vowel "says its name."

Medial vowels: vowels that come in the middle of words, also called "middle vowels"; example:

C-V-C Combinations: *c-v-c* refers to the pattern of words that begin and end with a consonant (single, digraph, or blend) with a *short* vowel in the middle; examples: *cat, fish, dog.*

C-V-C-E Combinations: these demonstrate the "silent *e*" principle, as in *cape, bake, hope.*

Consonants: letters that are not vowels (or functioning as vowels) are called consonants.

Initial or beginning consonant sounds: the first consonant in a word; the "initial consonant sound" may be made by single, double, or triple combinations of consonants, as in *sit, shut,* or *school.*

Medial consonants: consonants in the middle of a word.

Final, end, or terminal consonants: consonants at the end of a word.

Consonant digraphs: two adjacent consonants that make one sound that differs from the sound of either consonant by itself; these are the last elements to appear in children's invented spelling; examples:

ch (church); *sh* (ship); *th* (that); *wh* (what)

FIGURE 12.4

Terminology and understandings for phonics and other word-attack instruction (pp. 239–241).

gh (cough)

ph (graph, phone)

Silent consonants: these consonants make no sound; examples:

b (lamb); *p* (psalm); *h* (ghost); *w* (wring); *l* (walk); *k* (knife)

Consonant blends or clusters: two or more adjacent consonants whose sounds *glide* together while the individual sounds remain somewhat distinct; think of words b-b-b-lend, c-c-c-luster, or g-g-g-lide to help remember rules about consonant blends; children use blends in their invented spelling; blends can appear at the beginning, middle, or end of words and should be taught in clusters according to the first letter of the blend; teaching them as part of spelling instruction is effective; examples:

b-blends: blue, brown

c-blends: clown, crown

d-blends: dress, dwell

f-blends: flower, from

g-blends: glue, grow

p-blends: plate, pretty

s-blends: skill, slow, small, snail, spin, story, swam, school, screen, shrink, splash, squash; past, crash

t-blends: tree, trash, twelve, three

n-blends: friend, sing, sink

r-blends: work; hurt

Hard and soft consonants: *c* or *g* followed by *e, i,* or *y* usually makes a "soft" sound as in *city* or *gem*; "hard" sounds are those of *cat* and *game*.

Morphemic and structural analysis

Roots or stems: these terms refer to whole words onto which an affix is added (e.g., *like* is the root of *likes, likable, dislike,* or *likelihood)*; they can also refer to Greek and Latin roots, the smaller word parts from which many of our words are built (e.g., the Latin *multus,* meaning many, is the root for *multiply)*.

Knowing the concept that affixes can be added to words is useful for word attack, but memorization of extensive lists of "word parts" serves little purpose for beginning readers; it forces them to look too closely at individual words and can slow them down; instruction as part of spelling is best.

Affixes: word parts that are added onto the beginnings or ends of words are affixes; they change the meaning of the words in specific ways.

Prefixes: elements added at the beginning of words; 15 prefixes account for more than 80% of all common words that have prefixes (Herr, 1982); examples:

Negatives: *dis-, im-, in-, un-*

Directional: *ab-, ad-, de-, en-, ex-, pre-, pro-, re-, sub-*

Combinational: *be-, com-*

Suffixes: these word parts are added to the ends of words; examples:

Plural markers: *-s, -es*

Verb markers: *-s* for third person singular, *-ed, -d, -t,* for past tenses

Adjective or adverb markers: *-er* for comparing two things, *-est* for comparing three or more; *-less* (meaning *without), -ful, -full* (meaning *full)*

FIGURE 12.4

continued

Noun suffixes: *-er, -ist, -or* (meaning *one who*); *-tion, -sion, -ment, -ness* (meaning *state of*)

Compound words: two little words put together to make one, new, longer word; children enjoy compound words because they can usually figure them out and feel proud to read big words; but care must be taken that children realize that some compounds have a cumulative meaning, as in *luncheon*, while some may be more deceptive, as in *hot dog* or *eggplant*. Compound words make good spelling lists.

Contractions: one word made by deleting letters from two other words, inserting an apostrophe to show the deletion, and then use to stand for the two other words; contractions are most easily learned in conjunction with oral language work. When children write contractions, they often forget which letters to leave out and where to place the apostrophe (e.g., *is'nt* for *isn't, hsn't* for *hasn't*, etc.). Some regional dialects omit additional letters in oral use of contractions, causing additional confusion as children try to spell them in their writing. Spelling instruction is the best place to study and learn contractions.

Teachers must remember:

1. Children need extensive repetition and practice in varied situations before knowledge of these concepts and skills becomes automatic.
2. Children need to tie these concepts and skills to their oral language and learn ways their oral language may mislead them.
3. Practice that reinforces these concepts through auditory and visual channels is best; writing further reinforces these skills so long as children are using the skills purposefully rather than on fill-in-the-blank worksheets.
4. Many of these concepts and skills can best be introduced through structured "word study" as part of spelling instruction.

Children's steps for figuring out unfamiliar words independently

1. Look at the word carefully and say the sound of the first letter, blend, or digraph. Then read to the end of the sentences to see if you can figure the word out from context clues.
2. If that technique has not worked, attack the word by trying vowel sounds: a vowel in the middle is most often short; a CVCE construction usually indicates a long vowel and silent *e*, if two vowels are together, often the first vowel is long, except in *oi, oy, ou, ew,* or *ui*.
3. Say the word again after applying the vowel rules; if it still does not make sense, read to the end of the sentence to try context clues again.
4. Try consonant rules next, remembering especially hard and soft *c* and *g* rules and silent consonants.
5. Say the word one more time after applying the consonant rules; again read to the end of the sentence.
6. If the word still does not make sense, write it down to ask the teacher or to look it up in the dictionary at a later time.
7. GO ON READING because context clues later in the passage may help you figure out the word.

FIGURE 12.4
continued

should point and ask what they say. Because these are words in isolation rather than in a story, correction and instruction are appropriate.

Teachers can add an auditory component to shared book and LEA sessions with masking strategies or simply by asking to "find words that begin like your name or like the day of the week or that end with a vowel." As children scan print, they sample words and test whether each meets the criterion. Beginners may just point to the word for the teacher; the more skilled read it themselves. As teachers themselves say these target words, they should use a normal, not an exaggerated, tone.

Spelling instruction, as discussed in Chapter 7, provides excellent opportunities for phonics instruction and encourages children to transfer skills from writing (expressive) to reading (receptive). Spelling instruction is analytic and should demonstrate the breaking down and putting together of words.

Structural and Morphemic Analysis

Spelling is also the best way to illustrate structural and morphemic analysis, the study of small parts of words such as root words, prefixes, suffixes, and inflected endings. Through spelling, children come to recognize that word parts have consistent meanings that will help them figure out unfamiliar words. For example, *un-*, *dis-*, *non-*, and *anti-* all mean approximately the same thing. Learning word parts as "mini-sight words" is a useful tool for word construction in spelling and word identification in reading.

Context Clues

Context clues involve using the words around an unfamiliar word to come up with a "ball park" meaning that is *good enough* to allow reading to continue. Success is based on the same psychological principle that allows cloze activities to work: Readers seek meaning by trying to obtain as much as they can from available information. Children use knowledge of all cueing systems to figure out the word. Masking and other cloze activities are on-going demonstrations of how context clues work.

Children's first context clues may be pictures. Teachers can lead children in discussing the pictures and seeing how they relate to the text. "Look at the picture" is often a good clue when a child encounters an unfamiliar word. If the picture stimulates a different but appropriate word, teachers acknowledge the attempt with "Yes, but, what *other word* would work? Look at the first letter of the word you don't know."

As children encounter unfamiliar words in their reading, teachers should encourage them "to read to the end of the sentence" to see if they can identify the word. This simple behavior is often enough for even beginners to put the available information together. If that fails, they should run through the steps included at the end of Figure 12.4. These word-attack strategies must become second-nature if children are to develop into strong, independent readers.

Miscues

When children read orally, they often deviate from actual text with omissions, insertions of words or word parts, or substitutions of new words. At times, readers will catch themselves and self-correct; at other times, they will continue reading. It is useful to think of these deviations from text as **miscues** rather than errors. Miscues may or may not change the meaning of what is read, and this important fact should guide teachers in correcting or interpreting children's oral reading.[14] Deviations from text may also be real errors or nonsense words, but in many cases, children who feel comfortable with reading will catch their errors and self-correct.

According to researchers, the most important single indicator of reading competency is the semantic acceptability of the miscues. That is, has the reader substituted a word of the same part of speech or left out a word whose loss does not detract from the meaningfulness of the sentence? Even young readers search for meaning, and they will often go back to correct miscues that diluted the meaning of what they read. This indicates that they are monitoring the semantic aspects of what they hear themselves reading. Examples would be a child's reading "I want to go to my house" for a text that stated "I want to go home," or "The dog was big, grey, floppy-eared, and friendly" for a textual description of "big, tall, grey, floppy-eared, and very friendly." In neither case was the meaning lost.

Analysis of children's miscues gives teachers insight into how young learners are processing text and whether children need more focused instruction or are progressing in a normal, developmental fashion. Teachers must understand that children who speak nonstandard dialects or who are reading in their second language will frequently "translate" standard text into their own dialect or use code-switching in their oral reading. Children who normally drop consonantal endings from their words, for example, will do so in oral reading, too, and by no means does this indicate weak phonics skills. So long as comprehension is adequate, acceptance of nonstandard oral reading is absolutely necessary if children are to progress with reading. The key is comprehension, no matter what the oral, surface utterances might be.

TRANSITION TO SILENT READING

Beginning readers have difficulty reading silently. Reading groups are often at least half oral work, and reading conferences are always conducted out loud. To suggest that children read "to themselves" before they have learned how to do this can result in their merely staring at their pages. Just as finger pointing gives a visual assist, vocalization seems necessary to help monitor and maintain comprehension.

Children will be receptive to suggestions that they whisper or mutter, and gradually, their voices will taper off as silent reading begins. Teachers must be prepared for a low hum as children read independently and do other work. It is normal and usually indicates a productive class.

SUMMARY

Being part of children's mastery of beginning reading skills is exciting. Teachers need to provide support as well as direct instruction during this important period of learning and need to show their patience and understanding for the difficult task. Instruction that helps children bridge the gap between "play" and "real" reading is best because it allows young learners to continue to test and refine their hypotheses about literacy. Varied reading with many different kinds of material increases children's appreciation for books and gives them purposeful opportunities to practice their skills.

REVIEW QUESTIONS

1. Be sure that you can define each of the following terms:
   basal readers
   context clues
   cueing systems
   masking
   miscues
   oral cloze
   phonics
   sight words
   supportive reading groups
   word banks
2. Discuss how oral cloze strategies allow for both teacher control and student input in reading instruction.
3. What important roles does memory play in beginning reading growth? In what ways can overdependence on memory be harmful?
4. To what extent do you think language experience could be the total reading program in an early primary class? What advantages and disadvantages would you anticipate from its use?
5. Discuss the difference between a miscue and an error when children deviate from text in their oral reading.
6. For what reasons is it important that teachers keep their reading groups flexible? What are some of the reasons for moving children from one group to another?
7. Develop several oral cloze activities and try them with children in early primary classes. Tape-record their responses for analysis and determine if the children seemed to enjoy the activities.

8. Interview several early primary teachers to find their criteria for grouping children. Observe their reading groups. How do the children respond? What are the rest of the children doing while the teacher works with one group? What suggestions for improvement could you make?
9. Why is supportive reading important? How can supportive reading strategies help children make a natural transition from prereading to competency?
10. Understanding the concept of miscues is essential for supporting children's emerging reading skills. In what ways does acceptance of miscues represent the same teacher attitude that welcomes invented spelling?

NOTES

1. DeFord, D. (1981). Literacy: Reading, writing, and other essentials. *Language Arts, 58*, 652–658.

2. Powell, M. (1973). Acquisition of a reading repertoire. *Library Trends, 22*, 177–196.

3. Eckhoff, B. (1983). How reading affects children's writing. *Language Arts, 60*, 607–616.

4. Ready to Read Series. (1985). *Reading in Junior Classes.* New York: Richard C. Owen; Bettelheim, B., & Zelan, K. (1982). *On learning to read.* New York: Vintage.

5. Durkin, D. (1984). Is there a match between what elementary teachers do and what basal manuals recommend? *The Reading Teacher, 37*, 734–745.

6. Ferreiro, E. (1984). The underlying logic of literacy development. In H. Goelman, A. Oberg, & F. Smith (Eds.). *Awakening to Literacy.* (pp. 154–173). Portsmouth, NH: Heinemann Educational Books.

7. Gibson, E., & Levin, H. (1975). *The psychology of reading.* Cambridge, MA: MIT Press.

8. Holdaway, D. (1979). *The foundations of literacy.* Sydney: Ashton Scholastic.

9. Holdaway, D., *op. cit.*

10. DeFord, D., *op. cit.*

11. Burris, N. A., & Lentz, K. A. (1983). Caption books in the classroom. *The Reading Teacher, 36*, 872–875.

12. Stauffer, R. G. (1980). *The language experience approach to the teaching of reading* (2nd ed.), New York: Harper & Row.

13. DeFord, D., *op. cit.*

14. Goodman, K. S. (Ed.) (1979). *Miscue analysis.* Urbana, IL: ERIC Clearninghouse on Reading and Communications Skills.

13

Reading, Writing, and Thinking

What follows is an example of kidwatching, where the "kids" are graduate students. A recent graduate class of mine included several students who had to take early childhood coursework to maintain new positions, even though they really wanted to teach upper grades. These unwilling teachers volunteered that they were apprehensive about teaching little ones: "You can't talk to them," "All they do is cry," "They just need babysitters." Several other students became furious and proceeded to elaborate on young children as sophisticated thinkers and motivated learners. Because the class concerned the development of literacy skills, I directed the discussion toward how and what children learn about literacy and how reading and writing instruction in early childhood classes is also instruction in how to think. The early childhood enthusiasts among the class greeted my comments with "Oh, yeah. . . ." and argued my points persuasively. This chapter presents the point of view that reading and writing instruction should be integrated and should help refine children's thinking skills. It also presents strategies to integrate reading and writing instruction to increase children's reading comprehension, writing skills, and enjoyment of literacy.

READING COMPREHENSION

Children explore their world to find meaning, learn oral language to communicate meaning, and eventually experiment with reading and writing to increase their abilities to receive and express meaning. Yet, beginning instruction in both reading and writing often neglects children's search for meaning and concentrates on mastery of individual subskills. Even instruction in upper grades may not emphasize reading with understanding. Comprehension is tested but rarely taught; children read and teachers ask questions with no intervening step in which teachers model or discuss how comprehension is accomplished.[1] That intervening step is all important in helping children transfer what they know about gaining meaning to the specialized tasks of gaining meaning from extended text. Prereaders have learned many letter-sound correspondences and the basic conventions of how printed communication works. Their basic understanding is that one reads primarily to gain meaning. As skills mature, children must learn sophisticated strategies to move beyond surface understanding of print so that they can gain fully from diverse reading tasks.

Influences on Reading Comprehension

Comprehension requires readers to attempt to gain the meaning that authors have stated or implied in their texts. Because authors are usually not present when their work is read, readers themselves must work to combine what they already know about a topic with what authors have written. Reading comprehension is complex; it is "building bridges between the new [text] and the known . . . [by means of] a dialogue between writer and reader" (Pearson & Johnson, 1978, p. 24). The "known" includes all that readers know about language processing (reading skills and vocabulary) and about the topic presented to them. The "new" includes what authors know about their topics and how they present that information. The "new" may include new information, concepts, and terminology that readers can learn and add to their knowledge base. If young readers lack sufficient background experience, they will find the "new" material hard to understand. A good example is a child reading the political satire of "Doonesbury." The words may be simple; but lacking experience comprehending satire and knowledge of the political-social inferences, the child may be totally lost. Textually, the "new" may also include challenging sentence structure and unfamiliar words that make children's "communication" with authors difficult. In these cases, reading skills and vocabularies have not matured enough for children to read the text with ease.

Prereading activities and instruction help children tap their background experiences for new reading tasks. New vocabulary may be taught, or vicarious experiences and discussion develop necessary concepts. Direct instruction and supportive reading groups can encourage youngsters to apply reading skills in increasingly challenging tasks. Children must never lose sight of reading as an active process requiring involvement with print and resulting in meaning.

Levels of Comprehension

Many lists summarize the levels of behaviors that collectively can be termed *reading comprehension*. Basal reader comprehension work presents questions that, especially for beginning readers, often concentrate on the lower levels and do not challenge children to sophisticated interaction with texts. Teachers need to understand the levels of **comprehension** so that they can model appropriate strategies for reading with understanding.

The lowest level of comprehension, often called **literal comprehension,** requires readers to interact only with what authors state directly. Literal comprehension may be little more than recognizing and recalling sequence, relationships, specific facts, or details. In oral reading groups children with strong auditory memories can often answer literal questions correctly simply because they have listened carefully and can remember accurately. Correct answers may deceive teachers and students into a false assessment of actual skills. Children should be asked to integrate the surface-level components and summarize or restate the basic message conveyed in writing, in addition to answering literal-level questions. These literal questions are sometimes termed *Right There* questions because the answers are directly stated, right there in the text.[3]

The second level is often called **inferential comprehension,** reading to infer what authors have implied or stated indirectly in their text. Information needed for comprehension is presented in the text, but readers must "read between the lines" to get the authors' actual message.[4] Readers may get a hunch about what authors really mean or think about the content. Students have exercised inferential comprehension when they have thought about hidden meanings or relationships or have used their imaginations in interacting with text. Inferential questions ask readers to "Think and Search," that is, think what is asked and then search through the actual text to find answers.

The third level, **evaluative comprehension,** also requires extensive thinking about what one reads. Readers judge what they read against external criteria such as information provided by teachers or additional reading sources or against internal criteria such as their own experiences with the topic. They evaluate material for accuracy, worth, completeness, or usefulness (for example, as a source of information), and judge authors to determine how authoritative or truthful they are. Determining the difference between reality and fantasy or fact and opinion are frequent evaluative comprehension tasks for young readers. Judgments in evaluative comprehension also require children to "read beyond the lines," and instructionally, it is said to present "On My Own" questions.

The final level, aesthetic or **appreciative comprehension,** also involves "On My Own" reading tasks. When readers decide if they liked what they have read and when they show awareness of the literary techniques used to develop characters and setting and advance plot, they exercise appreciative comprehension. When young storybook listeners or readers become angry at a character in a story or cry over a sad turn of plot, they have shown appreciative comprehension. To respond emotionally or intellectually, readers must understand the gist of what they read at the literal level and also use inferential and evaluative comprehension to piece the elements of text together. Youngsters may not be able to tell why they respond as they do, but allowing them to express positive and negative responses is important in fostering reading growth. Figure 13.1 gives sample questions at all four levels.

Main Idea Comprehension

Getting the **main idea** of a selection is a common reading task and is often classified as low level, literal comprehension. Main idea comprehension is actu-

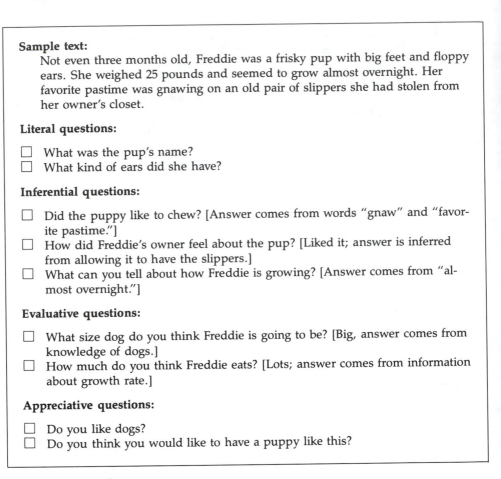

Sample text:

Not even three months old, Freddie was a frisky pup with big feet and floppy ears. She weighed 25 pounds and seemed to grow almost overnight. Her favorite pastime was gnawing on an old pair of slippers she had stolen from her owner's closet.

Literal questions:

☐ What was the pup's name?
☐ What kind of ears did she have?

Inferential questions:

☐ Did the puppy like to chew? [Answer comes from words "gnaw" and "favorite pastime."]
☐ How did Freddie's owner feel about the pup? [Liked it; answer is inferred from allowing it to have the slippers.]
☐ What can you tell about how Freddie is growing? [Answer comes from "almost overnight."]

Evaluative questions:

☐ What size dog do you think Freddie is going to be? [Big, answer comes from knowledge of dogs.]
☐ How much do you think Freddie eats? [Lots; answer comes from information about growth rate.]

Appreciative questions:

☐ Do you like dogs?
☐ Do you think you would like to have a puppy like this?

FIGURE 13.1
Levels of comprehension and sample questions.

ally complex and can be confusing. Researchers[5] have suggested that children need to learn to distinguish between topics and main ideas and that they can understand the broader nature of topics earlier than they can understand main ideas. Early reading material increases the confusion. It is usually narrative (poetic mode), the common basal story. Stories do not have real main ideas, and while they may stick to the point, they do not have "main idea sentences" in every paragraph. To try to teach main idea with narratives can be frustrating, even though many basal reader teachers' manuals ask such main idea questions. Teaching children to understand and identify topics is more beneficial because stories can be *about* something. Topics of stories are "all the literal events . . . which tell what it is about." (Aulls, 1986, p. 99). Thus, teachers should ask open-ended "What is it about?" questions and accept broad, categorical responses that are not expressed in complete sentences.

Gradually, children encounter more expository writing (transactional mode) that conveys information, until, by the time they reach middle school, their reading consists mostly of exposition. After understanding how to extract events and significant details from narratives, children can learn to identify topics in expository prose and then find single statements of the main idea. The process is developmental and goes from easiest to more complex skills. Graphic aids such as mapping, drawing, discussions, and writing activities can reinforce learning of main ideas and topics.

Metacognition

Cognition is thinking; metacognition is deliberate thinking *about* thinking. Children can learn to think about reading in the same way they previously thought about invented spelling. Learning *how* to think about reading gives children control over their reading behavior, helps them monitor comprehension, and allows them to select among their various reading strategies for the on-going task of gaining meaning from print.

The metacognitive tasks in reading are (a) self-knowledge, (b) task knowledge, and (c) self-monitoring.[6] Self-knowledge is knowing one's strengths and weaknesses as a reader. For example, a child who finds reading quietly under his breath helpful with difficult material should be encouraged to use the "trick" in independent reading. Self-knowledge also includes how children see themselves as readers. Supportive reading groups encourage a positive reading self-concept as they help children bridge the gap between play and real reading.

Task knowledge involves understanding that various strategies can be used in reading, that some work better than others in particular situations, and that good readers try to match strategies to reading tasks. Strong readers are flexible in their selection strategies—if one fails, they automatically try another. Young, inexperienced readers gain insight into the many strategies available to them through modeling as teachers "talk through" the process of figuring out an unfamiliar word or applying other skills. Drill and practice activities can fragment reading so that young readers fix on only one strategy or do not gain a sense of the way in which many behaviors fit together for successful reading. Oral cloze and masking activities introduce children to the diversity of reading strategies, and instructional procedures discussed below further their understanding.

Knowing whether one is comprehending and knowing what to do when not comprehending are aspects of self-monitoring. Skilled readers check progress through self-questioning; teachers model this behavior by asking questions throughout reading. Skilled readers know when and how to recycle material to gain more understanding; young readers must learn to do this, too. For them, recycling may be reading out loud to get the sound of the words in their ears, finger pointing, or asking the teacher or peers to talk about the topic being read. Children should not be daunted to realize that they are not comprehending; they should merely adjust their reading behavior and try again.

Metacognition develops from teachers' efforts to externalize reading processes so that the abstractions of processing print become as concrete as possible for young learners. Metacognition or thinking about reading is not too hard for beginning readers; rather, awareness of what they should be doing as they read makes learning to read easier.

INSTRUCTIONAL STRATEGIES FOR READING COMPREHENSION

Children learn to comprehend various kinds of texts by reading widely in diverse materials and also benefit from carefully planned, purposeful teacher directed, instructional group activities. In such groups, "active teachers will be as explicit as possible in their explanations of [reading] rules and their key concepts. They will also provide verbal models of how to use rules, as strategies, to arrive at the learning goal. Lastly, active teachers will be collaborators who guide student practice and give feedback focused on the process of fusing rules as well as the product" (Aulls, 1986, p. 104). This can be thought of as the process approach to reading comprehension, and in many ways, the approach is similar to the process approach to composition.

As children move beyond the supportive reading groups, instruction becomes more focused and routine. Children must learn the pragmatic aspects of reading groups: listening carefully, attending to specific tasks, using proper turn-taking behavior, and curtailing inappropriate, irrelevant comments. As Chapter 3 stated, some children may genuinely not know what good listening manners involve. Praising those children who participate in an appropriate manner is more useful than criticizing those who do not, for learners quickly see what gets recognition.

Children must also be able to use metacognition and talk about their thought processes in terms of the specific task at hand. That chore can seem so staggering that children may become shy and withdrawn in reading groups. Starting lessons by calling on children who can be expected to answer correctly can help. By providing "opportunities for several children to perform flawlessly" and clarify verbal behaviors, teachers help shyer children increase expertise in the pragmatic, social-interactional aspects of reading groups (Mason & Au, 1984, p. 200). This suggestion does not mean ignoring quiet, shy children in favor of their more confident peers; it means instead that children knowledgeable in the "language of instruction" help model processes for discussion and interaction. Children who are uncertain about expectations and behaviors have an extra chance to witness group interaction.

Beyond supportive reading, two other kinds of groups are beneficial in early primary grades: **reading conferences** and **directed thinking about reading activities.** Both include teacher modeling and discussion, but they differ in the amount of direct explanation and instruction teachers provide.

Group Reading Conferences

We have already discussed writing conferences wherein teachers and individual students discuss a work in progress. A variation is peer response groups, in which children read each other's work critically and make suggestions for revision. Student writing can be seen as the first "basal" for teaching high-level comprehension skills. Critical reading skills developed by reading one's own and peers' work transfer to commercial material when children realize that printed material has also been written by authors. One researcher (Newkirk, 1982) quoted a second-grade author-reader's realization: "Before I ever wrote a book I used to think there was a big machine, and they typed the title and then the machine went until the book was done. Now I look at a book and know that a guy wrote it. And it's been his project for a long time" (p. 457). Realizing that there is a person behind a written piece, children should be encouraged to ask questions *as though asking the author* and should feel free to identify flaws, inconsistencies, or inadequacies in what they read.

Reading conferences may be student-teacher interactions or small group sessions. Rather than offering specific skills instruction, they give children opportunities to learn to form questions about the content of what they read. Nevertheless, these conferences readily become mini-lessons as teachers clarify the means of comprehending a story (for example, understanding an embedded flashback or use of figurative language) and children share their perceptions and strategies with each other. In discussing *what* they have read, children also share *how* they have accomplished their reading, thus cutting through the "language of instruction" to present workable explanations of reading individual skills.

Hansen (1983) proposed a progression of conferences culminating in students' response to books written by professional authors. At first, children discuss a work in progress, question its author, and offer suggestions. Second, the group discusses a finished piece of writing so that the author can determine how well he conveyed a desired message or story.

In the third kind of group, a child reads a peer's finished work; group members question the reader about the work, and she must speak for the original author. The original author is also present if needed, but he should remain as silent as possible. This procedure models the steps in moving from passive to active reading. Children ask questions about the work, and the reader must infer answers based on what she has in front of her. When she can answer, she has successfully interacted with the author's work; when she cannot respond, all involved realize that sometimes authors leave out so much information that complete comprehension is impossible. Children gain awareness that readers must form questions they would want to ask the author—What did you really mean? Why did you use *that* word?—but that they must pose them to themselves as active readers. The tone during such an interaction should be kept as informal as possible.

Through conferences, participants learn to question the printed word. Hansen's fourth kind of conference—children talking about a professional author's work—can work as a reading group activity even if children are only beginning to understand the dynamics of peer response groups. This kind of conference could be introduced before actual peer response groups are used. One child reads a story or selection from a basal to the group, and participants pose to the *reader* those questions they would want to ask the real *author*. Answers to some questions can be figured out; others cannot. As participants find answers, they are learning to use inference and analysis skills to deduce information not included in the surface of the text. They dig beneath the actual words to find what authors really meant or felt or wanted readers to realize. Hansen has stated that children often focus on information authors omit or on style. They may conclude that authors thought readers would know certain data or simply miscalculated a stylistic decision, both perfectly acceptable judgments. Children cannot do anything (except, as Hansen suggests, write to the author); but they have learned about reading and about writing as well.

For this approach to work, teachers have to model the procedure before a child assumes the role of author-substitute. Teachers prepare a short but meaty storybook or a selection from a basal reader. The story should not be too difficult but must offer some challenge in content and style. Children must have their own copies, whether original or clear copies. Teachers read the story straight through, and children then pose questions they would want to ask the author: Why did the author use a specific word? Why did a character behave in a certain way? Why was information included or left out? Children may just brainstorm initial reactions but soon generate their own questions and get the "feel" of active involvement with their reading.

Children can soon engage in their own reading conferences, two or three students reading and discussing a book or basal story, sharing their thoughts in a student-teacher conference and possibly writing their questions in a group report or review. Even if not all of the children are reading on the same level, peer interaction about content and style offers valuable learning experiences. Children learn about critical reading and also about the social interactions (pragmatics) of intellectual discussions. Individual reading conferences are discussed later in this chapter.

The "Directed-Thinking-About-Reading" Activity

Basal reader groupings have been mentioned, along with the criticism that children often spend more time on skills worksheets than in actual reading. These teacher-centered procedures are frequently called *Directed Reading Activities* (DRA). A variation of the approach is the *Directed Reading-Thinking Activity* (DRTA) or the *Directed Thinking About Reading Activity* (DTAR), the term that will be used here. The emphasis, as the names imply, is on thinking.[7] DTARs work with children grouped according to ability or interests and have value in teaching word attack strategies as well as comprehension. Sardy (1985) wrote, "The one basic premise of the Directed Thinking about Reading (DTAR) approach . . . is that students must be taught to distinguish between authorship and authority. They must learn to view the text as a set of problems to be solved rather than as a final word on a subject. They must learn that they are entitled to criticize and evaluate a text for the extent to which it succeeds in communicating to them as individual readers" (p. 214). The DTAR is more teacher-directed than the conferences discussed above and can include direct skills instruction. It can also be used as the framework for long-term group activities such as unit projects.

The DTAR concept is based on several assumptions that material to be read is worthwhile and that it can be understood.[8] It is further assumed that students, even young ones, know how to think and have knowledge about the world and about reading behaviors. Teachers must find material about which students can make predictions while reading and should encourage them to reread, check predictions, and monitor their comprehension.

The introductory phase of a DTAR is similar to the prewriting phase in composition and has several distinct goals, the first of which is to establish a purpose for reading. If the title is a question, children should speculate on possible answers; if the title is evocative, children should guess what events the story *might* contain. Teachers should guide purpose setting with direct statements and open-ended questions. They might say, "Today, we are going to read a story about a very brave child who lived a long time ago. He was an orphan. What do you think it would be like to be an orphan? Would he have to be brave? What do you think an orphan's biggest wish might be? Well, this orphan *did* get to live with a family that was going across country to Oregon in a covered wagon. What do you know about travel in a covered wagon? Yes, like on television. What do you think could happen?"

Readers need to draw upon their experiences to ensure comprehension. Purpose-setting discussion is the start, but some selections and some children require more elaboration. The title may suggest what a selection is about; but if a title is vague, teachers must provide a key word or phrase to activate what children know about the topic. **Mapping** strategies similar to those used in prewriting can be used to guide prereading discussion. Most early primary reading material will be narrative (poetic mode) or expository (transactional mode); that is, their purpose will be to tell a story or to convey information.[9] Maps for narratives should target the broad topic the story concerns, while those for expository prose bring together information about specific topics. The "orphan traveling west" story might lend itself to a concept map on bravery and a topical map on westward travel.

Except for special, difficult, or technical words, the prereading phase of a DTAR does not present vocabulary or subskills instruction unless absolutely necessary.[10] Using their skills in context gives children practice with real language problems to solve. Presenting vocabulary that children *ought* to be able to figure out on their own deprives young readers of still more opportunities to practice skills. "Calistoga" and the names of Indian tribes might be introduced prior to the westward travel story; but in most cases, children should apply their emerging skills to figure out words themselves.

Previewing is the second step in a DTAR. Beginning readers may just look at the pictures, but children who know how to skim will work quickly through the story. Instruction in skimming should be given at separate times, so children know it is different from word-by-word reading. This second step should be kept relatively short.

The third step is directed reading. Ideally, children read silently, but teachers monitor the reading by assigning only a few pages to be read before questioning. Oral reading may be interspersed for variety, assessment, or clarification of difficult passages. Oral reading can also be used to enhance enjoyment. During oral reading, teachers provide encouragement with comments like "Read to the end of the sentence," or "Use context clues," or "That *w* is silent," when children encounter unfamiliar words, or "Read the sentence again, you missed a word," or "Look at the picture, it will help," when children seem to be getting lost. Such encouragement helps children tap their vast storehouse of word attack and comprehension skills. Encouragement may even be merely telling a child a puzzling word so that she can get on with the reading. Teachers quickly get a sense of who among a reading group will always stop at unfamiliar words and look appealingly for help; these children lack confidence in their own abilities and need a tough kind of support to develop and trust strategies to do it on their own.

Teachers ask questions so that children summarize, evaluate, and refine their predictions about the story, and interact thoughtfully with the action, facts, and ideas they are encountering. Other questions ask readers to focus on specific aspects of the text at the word, phrase, sentence, or paragraph level. Teachers may ask for definitions, synonyms, or restatements of particular words or phrases or may elicit suggestions of "better words" than what the author has selected. Balancing questions about content, style, and mechanics assesses the full range of children's comprehension and makes them more aware of the variables to be considered in gaining meaning.

Questions in a DTAR are used sparingly and are directed only at complex, interesting, or puzzling aspects of text to help children "communicate" with authors and learn to generalize skills to other reading tasks. They are teaching, not testing, questions; and often teachers may have to answer them themselves to model a skill so that children will attempt it independently. Instruction does not intrude on the story but clarifies a "problem to be solved" within a meaningful context, at the appropriate teaching point.

In step four, at the end of the reading, children review their initial predictions to see which were right. Teachers' questions check on comprehension of the total selection and again must be used for teaching, rather than testing. Children should be able to substantiate answers with reference to the text; and when they seem to have trouble comprehending, teachers should guide them back to the passage that provides a direct or indirect answer. Wrong answers can be as significant as right ones in shaping instruction. Teachers' pointing out specific words needed for literal comprehension, explaining implied meanings for inferential comprehension, and talking through an evaluative comprehension puzzle (such as identifying fantasy) are modeling appropriate behavior for children so that they will be better prepared to solve similar puzzles on their own.

Teacher questions are only one form of post-reading activity. Children might draw, paint, do a puppet play, or act out the story themselves. Group oral retelling reinforces comprehension and provides opportunities to go back to check literal information or points that had to be inferred from text. Writing summaries is a literal comprehension task, but children may also write to change the ending, add a new character, or put themselves in the action.

The DTAR makes as concrete as possible the invisible mental processes of reading. We want children to think about what they do when they read, to learn to gauge their understanding, to employ a wide range of strategies, and to master this "patterning of complex behavior." A DTAR takes time, both in teacher preparation and presentation, and the approach should be used only for basal reader selections or children's literature that can withstand analysis.

THE READING-WRITING CONNECTION

Reading and writing are different sides of the same process, and both involve thinking. "Composing is critical to thought processes because it is a process which actively engages the learner in constructing meaning, in developing ideas, in relating ideas, in expressing ideas. Comprehending is critical because it requires the learner to reconstruct the structure and meaning of ideas expressed by another writer" (Squire, 1983, p. 582). Clay (1979) maintained, "[The] building up process [of writing] is an excellent complement to the visual analysis of text [in reading], which is a breaking down process" (p. 124). In early grades, oral language binds these processes together by allowing children to test their ideas and by providing means for teachers to model appropriate thought processes.

Unfortunately, the close connection between reading and writing is often ripped apart in the early primary grades by emphasis on subskills and by fragmented drill-and-practice activities.

Writing Across the Curriculum

The term **writing across the curriculum** is often used for the approach to planning that exploits every opportunity to use children's writing.[11] This approach is not as common in early childhood classes as it should be, probably because many teachers do not recognize just how early children can begin to write. Writing across the curriculum allows children to write in varied ways, in all their curriculum areas. They can write factual reports, letters, diaries, or logs. They can write fanciful, imaginative efforts *as long as the writing presents information accurately.*

In writing-across-the-curriculum programs children learn to view writing as a means of communicating information and to recognize writing as a tool to organize and test their thinking. As they write about a topic, they may identify conceptual or informational gaps that additional reading and thought can fill in.

Informative writing must always be authentic; that is, it must come from the processing of facts. Too often, teachers ask children to "write" as a follow up to content-area work but have not provided enough information to produce a valid writing experience. If information is merely spoon fed to children and their follow-up writing assignments simply ask them to feed the information back to their teachers, the writing experience is invalid. Consider a second grader who had been "studying" Germany, Korea, and India in social studies and was to write a report about those countries. She was confused about the assignment—she could not write from personal experience, so she started her paper bravely and honestly. Realizing, perhaps, that her paper was considerably different from those of her peers, she tried to pull herself into line. She wrote: "I don't no abwt germany but I am riten abwt germany. I want to go to germany. To see wat it is like." Contrast that with Figure 13.2 which shows pages of a second grader's report about trout.

Writing across the curriculum gives children opportunities to process information as both fact and fantasy, in a variety of ways. A unit on Thanksgiving, for example, could lead to a factual report on the Pilgrims or Indians, a letter from Plymouth colony, a description of the first Thanksgiving dinner (with drawings), a thank-you note to Squanto, a script to reenact the first Thanksgiving dinner, a report on Thanksgiving celebrations in other nations, or a recipe for cooking turkeys. A few children may find some of the assignments "silly"; others may have trouble handling a full "research report"; but because there are varied opportunities for writing, the whole class—avid story writers to meticulous fact seekers—can accomplish something. Through assignments like these, children gain valuable practice writing in different modes, for different purposes, and to different audiences.

This approach places writing at the very center of the curriculum, and answers teachers' frequent questions about when they will find time to allow their children to write. They find time as part of instruction, as a follow up to instruction, and as a means of evaluating learning. A diary, for example, would

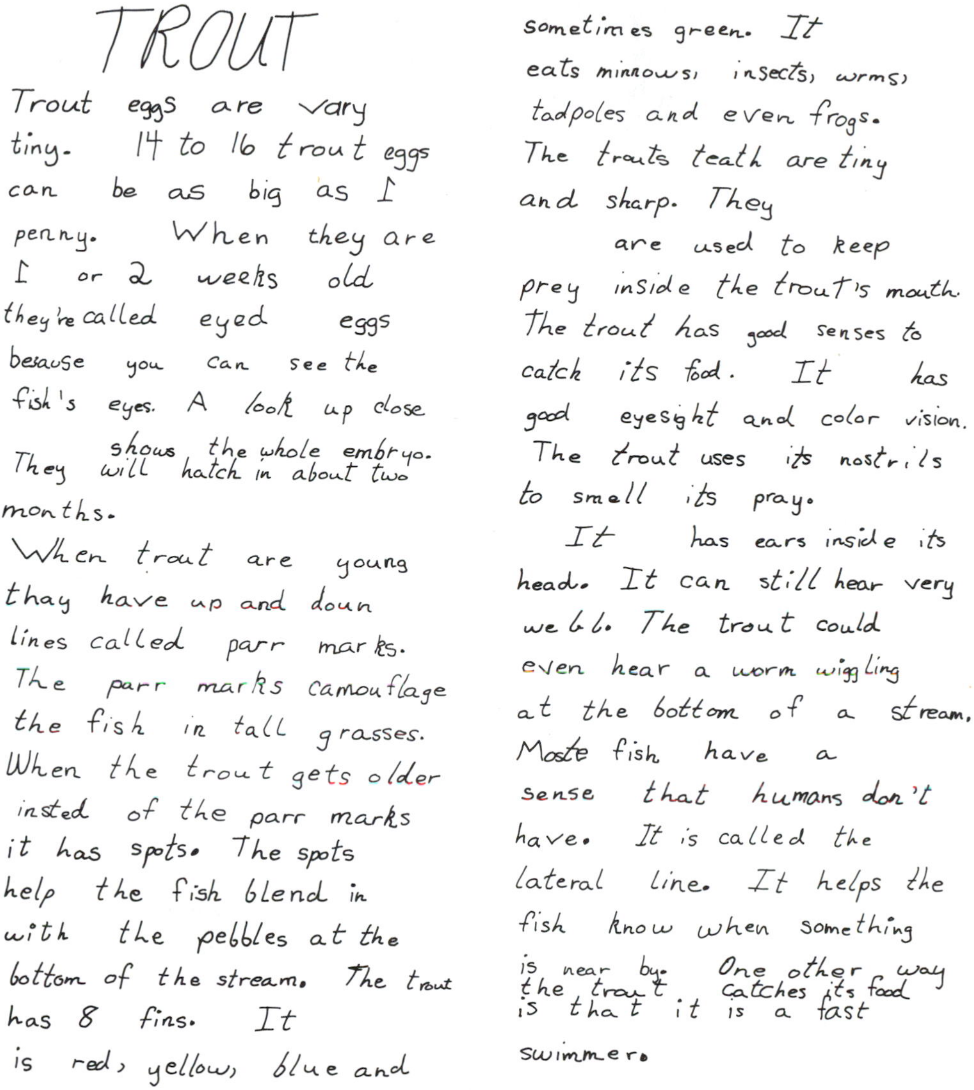

TROUT

Trout eggs are vary tiny. 14 to 16 trout eggs can be as big as 1 penny. When they are 1 or 2 weeks old they're called eyed eggs because you can see the fish's eyes. A look up close shows the whole embryo. They will hatch in about two months.

When trout are young thay have up and down lines called parr marks. The parr marks camouflage the fish in tall grasses. When the trout gets older insted of the parr marks it has spots. The spots help the fish blend in with the pebbles at the bottom of the stream. The trout has 8 fins. It is red, yellow, blue and sometimes green. It eats minnows, insects, wrms, tadpoles and even frogs. The trouts teath are tiny and sharp. They are used to keep prey inside the trout's mouth. The trout has good senses to catch its food. It has good eyesight and color vision. The trout uses its nostrils to smell its pray.

It has ears inside its head. It can still hear very well. The trout could even hear a worm wiggling at the bottom of a stream. Moste fish have a sense that humans don't have. It is called the lateral line. It helps the fish know when something is near by. One other way the trout catches its food is that it is a fast swimmer.

FIGURE 13.2

As a research assignment, this second grader wrote about trout. Her report was enclosed in a booklet decorated with a rainbow-colored fish.

provide more insight into what its young writer really had learned about Plymouth Colony than would most paper-and-pencil tests. If the diary went on about cooking dinner in an oven, going to movies, and shopping at supermarkets, the teacher would know that its writer had failed to understand the realities of the Pilgrims' lives.

DTAR and Writing Across the Curriculum

Stauffer (1980) distinguished between group and individualized directed-thinking-about-reading activities. Individualized DTARs differ from group work in that children are grouped according to their interests and may be at different skill levels. Work may extend over several weeks as they pursue a project and may involve considerable reading and writing. The approach can be used for individual study as well, but valuable socialization may then be sacrificed.

Prior to beginning individualized DTARs, children select topics to which they can commit several weeks of energy and study. Teachers may want to guide the selection based on curriculum requirements or available resources. There must be enough information available to study for this kind of project to work. After topics are identified, children should determine the questions that will direct their work. Stauffer (1980) stressed that the questions must be the children's own: "Because the pupils are learning to ask their own questions, they are learning to be free intellectually. In turn the freedom to question is accompanied by a responsibility that directs activities in the learning process. In a sense, raising questions is an exercise in scholarly self-control and implementation" (p. 242). Especially for beginners, teachers help shape the questions toward a workable plan of study.

Teachers' responsibilities as individualized DTARs get under way include setting goals for end products, supplying materials, and providing assistance. The process of reading and writing to find answers to significant questions is the purpose of DTARs, but children should work toward completing some definite "product." Teachers use their knowledge of children's abilities and attention span to guide them toward such products as an annotated scrapbook or bulletin board, a diorama, a dramatization or class presentation, or possibly a "research report."

Teachers must be willing to provide this research time on a regular basis and to assume a resource role as children work independently. DTARs let children encounter their own "language problems" as they read new material, learn to take notes, and organize what must seem to be vast amounts of information. Teachers may teach some necessary skills prior to research time; but as children work, instruction should be offered only in response to students' immediate needs. Teachers might, for example, help a child use an index, read a graph, or find a definition to a technical term; they might remind another to summarize rather than copy vast amounts of text from an encyclopedia or help organize an outline of a report. Teachers must believe that children can direct their own learning and that they master literacy through purposeful reading and writing.

Long-term individualized DTAR activities should encourage many different kinds of writing, the most common of which is preparation of a "report." Direct instruction about report writing should be offered to the whole class and followed by individual reteaching as groups put their work together. Reports are a form of transactional writing that summarize and convey information accurately. Simple reports need not be beyond the reach of young learners, especially if pictures and graphs are included. A topical map (as already discussed) is the start of a good report. The topic is the center, surrounded by spokes for aspects of interest that will be researched and reported. Individual spokes may represent a paragraph for beginning report writers or longer sections for more experienced ones. For each spoke or subtopic, children should prepare a series of questions they think their readers might like to have answered. Children may know the answers to some of the questions; the others will guide their reading and notetaking.

As long as children understand that spokes on their map constitute paragraphs or sections of their report and know that reports must include an introduction and a conclusion, they can control the basic format. Some areas of the report may lend themselves to pictures or drawings, and their use, along with some annotation, should be encouraged. Individuals in a group can take responsibility for separate sections of a report—some may be writers and some illustrators—or a total group report may be prepared through peer conferencing and revision.

At the end of a long-term DTAR, finished reports, handwritten or typed on a classroom word processor, should be bound together as a published book. Other written efforts, like scripts for plays or outlines of presentations, can also be published by display on bulletin boards. If children's efforts have not led to extensive writing but are instead a series of pictures with annotations, those captions should be read and shared with the same enthusiasm as a full report. It is up to teachers to encourage children to do as much writing as possible within this kind of activity but not to make writing appear to be a burdensome chore.

Reading, Writing, and Math

Learning math is like learning a new language, but it becomes easier when children also draw upon what they know about speaking, reading, and writing. The beginning is stressing that every math principle or problem can be expressed in words as well. Teachers need to state one-to-one correspondence, matching, and beginning algorithms in sentence form to tie mathematical symbolism to oral language. As children work with beginning addition and subtraction, they should be able to state problems with math language (*plus, minus, take away*, etc.) and regular language as well. Given $3 + 2 = 5$, they should be able to state and write, "Three and two makes [is, equals] five." Key terms like *more than, less than* should become automatic clues to the processes needed to solve word problems.

Graphing can help children make these connections and can provide opportunities to read and write in math. The six steps for developing a graph are: (a) deciding on a subject to graph, (b) deciding on the format of the graph and setting up a recording system, (c) collecting data (a high-tech math term), (d) recording data on the graph, (e) reading the graph and analyzing the data, and (f) restating the data in sentence form. Teachers may select topics to graph or may elicit suggestions, but planning the format, recording system, and data collection should thoroughly involve students. Initially, teachers record information on the graph, but gradually, children can do this step as well. When familiar with graphing, children can collect and record data independently. Reading the graph means translating symbolic material into oral language, and analyzing means making some sense out of it. The analysis should lead to a restatement in written form, which is either included on the graph or written on an accompanying chart. Figure 13.3 shows a graph prepared in kindergarten.

Charts offer other ways to present information with symbols and minimal print and are especially good to illustrate comparisons and contrasts. As with graphs, charts enable all children to "read" and extract information from the combined symbols and words so that even weaker readers can participate actively in discussions.

As children gain expertise with graphs and charts, they can write their own summaries and data analyses and compare them. Realizing that graphing is one way to convey information with symbols, pictures, and minimal print, children may include them in formal research reports developed in DTARs. They would give artists and mathematicians opportunities to translate information collected by stronger readers into usable form.

CHILDREN'S LITERATURE, READING, WRITING, AND THINKING

A recent article (Kutzer, 1981) defined children's literature as "that literature which is read by or listened to and enjoyed primarily by children, although not necessarily meant for them" (p. 717). It continued, "A teacher who can combine an understanding of childhood with an appreciation of literary merit is likely to fare well . . . [and can] guide children into critical reasoning. . . . Children who are readers will indiscriminatingly read almost anything; part of the task of adults is to help such children learn to make distinctions and judgments" (pp. 722–723). Children's literature in its rich and varied forms stimulates children to read and to think and can encourage writing, too.

Advantages of a Strong Literature Program

Literature exposes listeners or readers to new ideas and provides vicarious experiences with unfamiliar places, events, and times. Listeners or readers can compare their own experiences to those of the characters they meet to gain insight into emotions, motivations, and behavior. Literature also is a source of pleasure.

Literature also exposes children to "book language," which is structured differently from speech and may be more complex than language in beginning basal readers. First by listening and then by reading themselves, children be-

Are you a righty or a lefty?

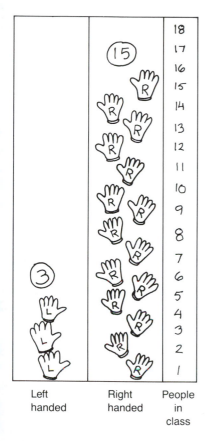

1. We drew our right or left hand.

2. We used our hand to tell if we are a righty or a lefty.

3. There were 15 righties.

4. There were 3 lefties.

5. 15 is more than 3.

   15> 3

6. There are more righties in K–5 than there are lefties.

| Left handed | Right handed | People in class |

FIGURE 13.3
Graphing activities become even more valuable when language experience strategies are also used. Teachers and students discuss the format of the graph, data collection, and data representation. Complete sentences should be used to summarize what has been shown on the graph. This graph was prepared in a kindergarten class; used by permission of Maralee Gorter.

come familiar with book language and can understand its structure. This understanding is necessary if they are to gain comprehension from free-choice, nonbasal, and content-area reading.

Selecting and Displaying Books
Teachers should select a variety of books, new and classic, based on their own preferences, the purposes for which they wish to use the books, and knowledge

of their students' interests and abilities. Veatch's book *How to Teach Reading with Children's Books* (1968) stated: "Get lots of books! Big books, little books, paperbacks, fat books, thin books, fairy stories, cowboy stories, mysteries, silly stories . . . ANY BOOKS THAT YOUR PUPILS WILL LIKE AND BE ABLE TO READ." Veatch recommended at least 100 books for a start—purchased, begged, borrowed, swapped, or "contributed," including poetry, fiction, and nonfiction. Included in the beginning library can be teacher- and student-made books as well. Appendix 1 is a book list for early childhood classes.

A library area attests to the value teachers place on books. Books should also be displayed around the room: science books in the science area; baby animal books near the gerbil cage, perhaps; or "Author of the Week" books along the chalkboard. "Books tucked away on shelves with only their spines showing give a tidy appearance, but are less inviting to prospective readers than those which are featured by virtue of a special placement" (Hickman, 1983, p. 3). "Inviting" children to read is the key, especially if they come from homes without books. Teachers need to be prepared for books to become dirty and torn; fingerprints on a book, a professor of mine once said, indicate good "reviews."

Introducing Books

Teachers' skillful oral reading provides the best introduction to children's literature; having books available for browsing reinforces the introduction. Teachers throughout the early primary grades (and beyond) should read to their classes every day, provide time for browsing, and supplement these activities with such tape-book sets as Bill Martin's *Sounds of Laughter, Sounds of a Powwow,* and *Sounds Jubilee.* Many classics have been recorded, and teachers can make their own tapes of favorites.

Even within a directed listening-thinking activity, there are two styles of reading books to children, each of which reflects a specific point of view about children's literature.[12] The first approach views literature as a work of art, something to be enjoyed and relished: Teachers read and ask questions to encourage appreciation of the oral content, emotions, and flow of language expressed in the story. The second approach views literature as a vehicle for modeling comprehension and higher-level thinking skills, and teachers ask children to predict outcomes, intuit motivations, and conjecture about "What if. . . ." Teachers using the second approach tend to ask more questions and stop more often than do those whose purpose is to enhance enjoyment. Both approaches have value, and teachers should observe their "natural" reading style and work to adopt the other approach as well. Evaluating literature before oral reading helps teachers decide which style of presentation to use. Knowledge of one's students and the amount of time available for reading also help determine style of presentation. Books with many suspenseful moments that invite prediction and emotional responses will take longer than do books to be read for sheer pleasure.

Interacting with Books: The Arts

In *The Read-Aloud Handbook,* Jim Trelease (1985) suggests adding a "third dimen-sion" to a book whenever possible. Among his suggestions are having blueber-ries when reading *Blueberries for Sal* or bringing a harmonica and a lemon for *Lentil*. This third dimension stimulates involvement and can be extended to include many postreading activities as well. Oral storybook reading, big books and supportive reading sessions, and independent reading can all lead to dram-atization, puppets, art, pantomime, or choral or dramatic reading with children assuming various roles. Music can accompany postreading activities, especially if theme can be matched. If children have heard or read stories about the South-west, for example, folksongs or Copeland's *Rodeo* or *Billy the Kid* would be ap-propriate. Art in children's books can influence discussion, especially when the art contributes to setting, mood, or tone. Monson (1982) stated, "It is not impor-tant or encouraged that we teach children to analyze each piece of art, music, literature or drama closely. But it is important that we recognize some of the commonalities among art forms and give children guidance in appreciating them" (p. 256). Feeling rhythm in music can lead to appreciation of figurative language and cadence of writing, appreciation that young children may most easily express through movement, drama, or art. These follow-up activities often reflect higher levels of appreciative comprehension than a child's saying "Yes, I liked that book."

Interacting with Books: Individual Conferences

Veatch (1968) recommended two individual-student reading conferences per week, conducted while the rest of the class is working independently. They need take no more than five minutes per child. Unlike writing conferences, where work in progress is discussed, children come to reading conferences pre-pared. During the conference, children read and talk about their selection, and teachers assess comprehension at all levels. Teachers also determine strengths and weaknesses and identify small groups of children for instruction in the same reading problem. Finally, teachers approve or check projects such as those discussed in the long-term DTAR. Needless to say, children may elect to prepare stories from basal readers rather than children's literature, and within reason, this should be allowed.

Interacting with Books: Book Reports

Traditional reasoning goes something like this: Children should read indepen-dently, but teachers cannot be sure that children *are* reading unless they do some kind of report; children in early childhood classes cannot *really* do reports, so they should fill out a form with title, author, and illustrator of the books they read and write perhaps one what-the-book-is-about sentence. That activity, rea-soning goes, constitutes a legitimate book report for beginning readers. In some schools, if children fill out a certain number of these forms, they even receive a good reader prize. Nonsense!

Book reports—or independent, individual follow-up activities about favorite books—can be much more creative, involving, and stimulating than filling in a dittoed form. Children may do art activities, write factual summaries, write to authors or characters, or do any form of writing-across-the-curriculum activity. Such activities require more than copying names and writing one bland sentence, and they take work and real interaction with books. Some may be time consuming and should be used only with books that children have thoroughly enjoyed and want to think about at length. They encourage children to go back to what they have read, to review and rethink, and then to plan a follow-up activity. Skills practiced in preparing reports like these generalize to other reading tasks. If children are drawing and writing a character sketch, for example, they must think about how the author presented the character and identify the details used to define the person emotionally and physically.

Children's Literature and Writing

Enjoying, discussing, and studying literature can help children become better writers. They become familiar with the skills and devices of writing and discover themes and topics to write about. Two forms of writing evolve: writing about the literature and writing based on the literature. Writing about the literature is not exactly a book report but is a response to a book as a whole or to parts, such as favorite characters or events. If teachers allow drawing as well as writing, even beginners can respond in this way. Often, children will draw and write only the title; this is a start. Figure 13.4 shows responses to literature from a kindergartener and a first grader.

Literature can also be a springboard for writing. Literature provides beginners with direct models, which in shortened versions, are virtually copied. Copies gradually become "liftings" as children personalize another author's ideas or adopt phrases, choice words, or imagery. In time, children edit or revise a story, change plots, settings, or characters, or use only the basic framework and title. This writing is not as derivative as it may at first seem. Far from passive, it involves analysis and reconstruction.

Children should encounter literature expressively and receptively; that is, they should both hear and read it. Both experiences can lead to writing. Figure 13.4 also shows stories written in response to *Alexander and the Terrible, Horrible, No Good, Very Bad Day*. All the writers were fascinated by the "terrible day" theme, but they differed widely in the extent to which they experimented with it. Some generated relatively bland stories with perfectly possible, not really "terrible" events. Others were more creative in their terribleness. Still others reversed the theme entirely. Literature like *Alexander . . .* lets children realize that stories do not have to be only about "nice" things, helps them externalize

The A teams terrible, Horrible, No go Very Bad day. Here's wat happed.

Mr.T got knockedout and Face got shot, Murdok got beeten up Hanabolgot shoped with a sword Amy got robed and tok! her to a hidout Mr.Ts van broke.

Sample 4.

My Wondeful, Most, Good Super Day

You know want happen to day When I wokeup I wokeup bightander lyy befor my Mommy and Daddy soerly it was 5:00 o'dock I gotdresst andate my brefeest and when. I was thow with at my mommy wokeup and mydaddy wokeup too. Then at school and I hadsuger work. I noow want a My Wondeful, Most Good super day. and at lunch a good thing happen I had a good dsert.

He
HAS
A
Cat

Sample 2.

Max was wearing a wild coat.
And mother sent max to bed without any supper.
And maxs bedroom grew until it was a jungle.

FIGURE 13.4

Responses may be a few sentences or complex "reworkings." Sample 1 shows how a kindergartener combined *Green Eggs and Ham* and *The Cat in the Hat*. Sample 2 is from first grade. Samples 3 and 4 rework *Alexander and the Terrible, Horrible, No Good, Very Bad Day.*

feelings, legitimizes discussing them, and affirms that these themes can be written about.

Children can adopt characters from books in series like Hoban's *Frances* or Lobel's *Frog and Toad* and write new adventures. Even commercial instructional materials such as basals can motivate writing. With models of ideas, models of writing style, and permission to "lift" from favorite literature, children are caught less frequently with "nothing to write about."

SUMMARY

Early childhood teachers know that young children think differently than older children, but they recognize the power and importance of young learners' cognitive processes. Teachers know that they should encourage thought, stimulate new ideas, and help children expand their understandings. Literacy learning—mastering the skills of reading and writing—should not be overlooked as a means of encouraging wide-ranging and enriching thinking. Children can apply their emerging literacy skills to new learning and strengthen their grasp of reading subskills and writing mechanics in the process. Teachers' modeling of high levels of interaction with text leads children to think about reading as a process and about what they read as sources of new, exciting information. Writing activities further strengthen children's thinking about text and give them an additional means of reinforcing learning.

REVIEW QUESTIONS

1. Be sure that you can define these terms:
   appreciative comprehension
   comprehension
   directed-thinking-about-reading activities (DTAR)
   evaluative comprehension
   inferential comprehension
   literal comprehension
   main idea .
   mapping (as a prereading strategy)
   reading conferences
   writing across the curriculum
2. Why is it important to help children develop appreciative comprehension skills?
3. Find a beginning basal reader story and develop comprehension questions about it to reflect all four comprehension levels. Compare your questions to the ones in the teachers' manual.
4. For the material in Question 3, develop follow-up activities that would motivate children to think and read more widely about the story's topic or content.

5. What advantages do you see in using long-term DTAR activities? What disadvantages would you foresee?
6. Explain the process of writing across the curriculum. How does it strengthen reading, writing, and thinking skills? How can the approach motivate reluctant learners?
7. Visit several early childhood classrooms and take inventory of the books that are available for children. Discuss reading conferences with the teachers to determine if any form of conference is used. Why do you think teachers might be reluctant to use reading conferences?
8. Find several children's books that could be used to encourage writing. Develop lesson plans to introduce and discuss the books and devise writing assignments to use as a follow up. Use these plans if possible and criticize them.

NOTES

1. Durkin, D. (1978). What classroom observations reveal about reading comprehension. *Reading Research Quarterly, 14,* 481–533. See also: Durkin, D. (1981). Reading comprehension instruction for five basal reader series. *Reading Research Quarterly, 16,* 515–544.
2. Pearson, P. D., & Johnson, D. D. (1978). *Teaching reading comprehension.* New York: Holt, Rinehart & Winston.
3. Raphael, T. E., & Womnancott. (1985). Heightening fourth-grade students' sensitivity to sources of information for answering comprehension questions. *Reading Research Quarterly, 20,* 282–296.
4. Raphael & Womnancott, *op. cit.*
5. Aulls, M. W. (1986). Actively teaching main idea skills. In J. F. Baumann (Ed.). *Teaching main idea comprehension* (pp. 96–132). Newark, DE: International Reading Association.
6. Bondy, E. (1984). Thinking about thinking: Encouraging children's use of metacognitive processes. *Childhood Education, 60,* 234–238.
7. Sardy, S. (1985). Thinking about reading. In T. L. Harris & E. J. Cooper (Eds.). *Reading, thinking, and concept development* (pp. 213–229). New York: College Entrance Examination Board.
8. Sardy, S., *op. cit.*
9. Stauffer, R. G. (1975). *Directing the reading-thinking process.* New York: Harper & Row.
10. Tchudi, S. N., & Tchudi, S. J. (1983). *Teaching writing in the content areas: Elementary school.* Washington, DC: National Education Association.
11. Teale, W. H. (1984). Reading to young children: Its significance for literacy development. In H. Goelman, A. Oberg, & F. Smith (Eds.). *Awakening to literacy* (pp. 110–121). Portsmouth, NH: Heinemann Educational Books.
12. Stewig, R. (1980). *Read to write: Using children's literature as a springboard for teaching writing* (2nd ed.). New York: Holt, Rinehart & Winston.

14

Computers in Early Childhood Classes: Increasing Literacy Growth

Daycare teachers who responded to a survey about the value of the computers in their centers cited children's increased interest in learning, lengthened attention span, peer teaching, discussion and sharing of ideas, and exposure to technology. They reported children becoming more independent and confident.[1] A kindergarten teacher wrote of her conversion from computer skeptic to enthusiast (Burg, 1984): "I'm always on the prowl for the teaching aid that will captivate children. . . . I engage my subconscious in the endless hatching of new ideas for activities that will make children say, 'I want to do that!' [because] I know that when children want to do something, they will become involved, and learning will happen. So why did I reject the computer's potential for children's learning? I wore prejudice, a cloak of uninformed, irrational, and stereotypical thinking. Understanding has removed my fear" (p. 303).

Computers are just beginning to find their way into early childhood classes, and teachers and researchers are just beginning to appreciate their full potential for use with young children.

YOUNG COMPUTER USERS

Children often have unique and possibly outrageous definitions of the term *computer*. One study[2] found that many children think computers are "sort of alive" and attribute a "psychology" to the small, one-purpose computers such as "Speak and Spell" or "Merlin," a toy that plays tic-tac-toe. Even children who could discuss batteries and electricity puzzled about the toys' abilities to be smart enough to "cheat" at games, to talk, and to seem to express emotions when they lost or won. Children may not understand that when computer

271

software displays a smiling or sad face after an answer that it was their own answer that generated the response—unlike one child with whom I worked. After he got an answer right, I asked him where the smiling face came from. He pointed to himself and told me he would make a sad face next. Laughing loudly, he deliberately made an error on the next task on the software, pointed to the sad face, and promptly corrected his mistake. No matter how he might have defined *computer* or discussed its internal workings, he knew that he was transferring skills he had learned through other means to his work with the software his center provided. The child understood the connection between his actions and the computer and knew he was in charge.

Introducing the Computer

To start, teachers might elicit children's definitions and ideas of the purpose of computers and record them in a language experience chart. Older children can write their own definitions, poems, or stories, even science fiction. Children's ideas should be accepted unless they are negative or incorrect or indicate fear. Next, teachers should clarify the purpose of the computer and rules for its use. Computer terminology should be introduced—but with care. Children should be familiar with the terms in Figure 14.1 so they will understand the terms in discussions and directions and eventually use the terms themselves. *The Computer Alphabet Book* (Wall, 1984) provides a computer term and definition for each letter of the alphabet and pictures that teachers can enlarge for classroom display or a big book. For early primary grades, *The Dictionary of Computer Terms Made Simple* from *Family Computing Magazine* (Scholastic, 1984) is an interesting source of exact definitions for young, capable readers. Many other books are available as well.

After talking about computers, children can draw or paint pictures of computers and construct models from boxes and other materials. Workbooks such as *Let's Investigate Computers* (Carratello, 1984) and other descriptive material are

---

Monitor—like a TV screen
Disk drive—where the disk goes
Disk (or floppy disk)—has the program on it
Cassette—similar to a disk, also contains the program
Keyboard—like a typewriter, with letters and numbers and other useful keys
Return key—usually located on the right of the keyboard; often used to make programs advance or to indicate decision making or selection of subsections of a piece of software
Spacebar—located at the bottom of the keyboard, as on a typewriter; used for similar purposes as the return key and also to leave spaces between words in writing text
Arrow keys—usually at the lower right of the keyboard; used to delete (in some programs) and to move the cursor or other indicator
Delete or Instant delete—usually at upper right of keyboard; used to delete letters or words
Cursor—the blinking light that appears on the screen
Console—the main part of the computer (with some computers)
Program—what makes the computer run
Software—another word for program
Load—start up the computer
On/off and Loading lights—on all parts of the computer; these indicate that the computer is on; a light on the disk drive indicates when a piece of software is loading; children should not touch the keyboard then.
Menu—lists the options on a piece of software and may provide instructions for use.

FIGURE 14.1
Important computer-related terms

readily available. Labeling parts of their pictures or constructions reinforces vocabulary. Old computer magazines can be used for collages. As children look at the pictures and ads, they pick out sight words and recognize the packaging from software in their own classes. Scholastic Book Service, other school suppliers, and some of the computer magazines offer descriptive posters that make suitable wall decorations.

The Classroom Computer Center

Many school districts have chosen to invest in centralized computer labs, which children visit at least once a week. While labs are practical and efficient, a classroom computer center is better for young learners.[3] A separate center can be decorated with descriptive charts, computer reference books, and children's computer-related art work. Alternatively, the computer could be placed in the math or language arts center. The computer center should be located near electrical outlets in a part of the room where glare from windows or lights can be controlled at all times of the day. Teachers should check for glare by sitting at children's level and moving the monitor's position.

Assessing Children's Readiness

In determining children's readiness for computer use, teachers must make sure each child can focus on the screen without squinting, is motivated to use the computer, and understands that he or she is in fact the one making choices in response to the computer's prompts, questions, or tasks. Teachers also need to ask whether children are ready for each software package. If concepts or terminology are unfamiliar, the software will not make sense or may be confusing. Mismatches of children and software can lead to frustration, faulty learning, and negative attitudes toward computers. Children themselves will not know why they are having trouble and may end up thinking that the "person" inside the computer is cheating or ridiculing them. The other side of this problem is software that is too easy; boring computer activities are as bad as boring dittos or workbooks.

EVALUATING AND USING SOFTWARE

While there is considerable educational **software** available, even for early childhood grades, not all of it is good quality. Software is expensive to produce, and clear graphics, animation, and ease of operations (*user friendliness*) make prices even higher. Poor software can undermine computer use, and teachers must evaluate software before introducing it to children. As they evaluate software, teachers need to see it as a child might, anticipate problems, estimate attention span, and evaluate attractiveness and value to children. Computer and educational magazines review software, but reviews tend to emphasize good points and should be read with caution.

Finding Good Software

Early childhood software may be of two types: preset or open-ended. Preset (or "canned") software is the common "software package" with limited activities and options. Just as some basal readers are too controlled, some (but not all) preset software offers far too little to justify its price. Because software may seem to meet all criteria and still not work as a total package, each piece must be evaluated as separate parts and as a whole. Flexibility is very important. If parts of a package will work at different times of the school year or with different groups of children (as in a multi-age classroom), the software can still be valuable. As they evaluate software, teachers should determine the concept and skill level of *each part* of each piece of software. The next step is to determine whether children possess these concepts and skills sufficiently to benefit from the software. Much of the early childhood software practices recognition of same and different, seriation, and classification. Young learners first need concrete representations of these concepts; next they can apply concepts with pictures; finally, they can process abstractions. Computer software presents a hybrid situation between pictorial and abstract representation. There are pictures to be viewed, but children may wonder where they came from and whether the tasks presented are really familiar. Teachers also should check for "user friendliness," especially clarity of directions and ease of movement from activity to activity. Software that keeps track of children's "scores" on games is helpful for record keeping. Teachers should check for good, clear graphics, nonsexist or nonstereotypical depictions and language, and the absence of judgmental comments or pictures when children make mistakes. Teachers also need to determine that software will run on their computers, whether a joystick is needed, and whether a color monitor is essential.

Alphabet Software

The simplest form of alphabet software presents a picture and a letter on the monitor; the child must press the corresponding key. The recognition task can be extended by asking the names of the letter and the object and by offering comments about the sound the letter makes or the position of the letter on the keyboard. Other software flashes a series of letters on the screen and children must press the key corresponding to the letter that comes before, after, or in the middle of the sequence. This kind of software increases children's familiarity with the keyboard.

Software that combines letter recognition and basic phonics can be confusing. Children must view a picture or scene, determine what the target word is, segment the initial sound of the word, and press the appropriate key. Some graphics (just like pictures in phonics worksheets) present inappropriate examples. Neither *skate* nor *whale*, for example, is a good stimulus because neither word begins with a *single* consonant. Some of the software can cause further confusion by mixing objects, backgrounds, and actions in what they ask children to view. Several fish swimming across the screen in a prominently featured fish bowl can cause children to wonder if they are to press *f*, *s*, or *b*. Evaluation before use alerts teachers to these problems, and, again, discussion as children work can compensate for inconsistencies or confusion in the software.

Problem-Solving Software

Some software for young children encourages planning, estimation, or higher-level thinking, and places a real premium on language skills. *Facemaker* (Spinnaker) is a good example. Children literally make and animate a face by selecting features and programming actions. Features and actions should be discussed and named. Children can then run their program of facial movements (crying, blinking, ear wiggling, etc.). The facial features, which can be combined in many ways, are very funny and stimulate wonderful descriptions from young children and even follow-up art work. The real value is in motivating close attention, labeling, discussion, and visual memory. The software has a delay feature so that time between movements can be slowed down for even young children to observe and discuss. Older children can play against the computer, which will present increasingly long progressions of movement to remember. If they cannot duplicate the exact order, the computer wins, and they play again. A color monitor is not essential for *Facemaker.*

OPEN-ENDED SOFTWARE

The most common forms of open-ended software for early childhood classes are Logo, story generators, and word processors. These allow children to exercise thinking skills, creativity, and imagination and to make discoveries about math and writing. The extent of "openness" may differ, but the underlying premises are that children can interact with the computer and exert at least some influence on what appears on the screen.

Logo

Logo, developed at the Massachusetts Institute of Technology,[4] is a programming language primarily for children. "Turtle geometry," a sublanguage of Logo, allows children to press keys in order to talk to a triangular "turtle" on the computer monitor or to a "floor turtle," which moves according to directions typed on the keyboard. Children can learn basic programming strategies by indicating how the turtle should move, for example, FORWARD, BACK, RIGHT, LEFT, a particular number of spaces. Ideally, children "map out" turtle movements on grids or "walk" them off on the floor before trying them out on the computer.

    Logo strengthens children's sense of number, geometry, logic, sequence, and spatial relationships and presents a specialized social context for oral language growth. Children focus their collective intellects, share knowledge and information, and discuss solutions for solving particular Logo problems. They may personify the turtle and refer to it as *you* or *him*. A kindergarten teacher writing of her students' use of Logo shared the following dialogue about the turtle in her classroom:

Daniel: I'm making him dance! See, I can make it dance! (Repeatedly making the turtle turn.)

Shannon: What are you making now, a box? What is it?

Daniel: Look! I'm making math paper. OOOOOO! What happened? (The turtle "wrapped around" the screen and disappeared as the child drew lines for "math paper.")

Shannon: No, you didn't. It's back now, down there . . . (The turtle reappears at the bottom of the screen). Look, now you made a cross.

Daniel: Oh, look. Teacher, it is a cross. This is tricky, man. Look what I did, he's gone. (The child hit the "hide turtle" key which makes the turtle invisible although its "tracks" still show.)

Michael: Mr. T! It's a big T. Now go there. Make a T.

Shannon: (pointing) That's a T but this one is too long.

Daniel: Look, he's invisible but he's still moving. Look at what you did. (Michael has pushed Clearscreen.) Poor turtle![5]

She also stated that as children grew in competence, they talked about their learning at the computer, reasoned their way through their Logo problems, and described the figures they had created.

Story Generators

Software referred to in this chapter as **story generators** range from those with as few options as *Story Machine* (Spinnaker) to much more open-ended examples such as *Storytree* (Scholastic). Unlike real word processors, story generators may limit vocabularies, reject unconventional spelling or grammar, or direct children's choices for story development.

Many story generators can be introduced to young children through a modified language experience approach. Each child sits on the teacher's lap so that he or she gets a "line of sight" view of the keyboard similar to that in shared book experiences. The teacher tells a story, types it, and reads it back word by word while pointing to the screen. Alternatively, children can dictate the story. Soon the children can type their own stories, especially if the story generator accepts invented spelling.

Story Machine is a good example of a limited story generator. Users select from a list of words, spell them correctly, use correct syntax, and must end their sentences with periods. Stories are animated on the screen and can be viewed repeatedly. For many children, *Story Machine* is too limited, especially because it will not accept invented spelling. However, second language learners or children working on standard grammar benefit from putting together and writing correctly worded sentences. *Kidwriter* has more options, including allowing children to select from an extensive list of backgrounds and objects for the illustration of their stories. Their stories, which can be written in invented spelling, can be edited during composition, saved, and revised later.

WORD PROCESSORS

Open-ended word processing has tremendous potential for early childhood education because it gives children the most control over the technology.[6] Children dictate or type their own words and see them appear on the screen in synchronization with their speech or spelling. As children's words appear on the monitor, they often touch them, count them, or measure them for length.

Word processors make it easy for writers to compose, revise, and edit text and to produce a clean copy in less time than possible with traditional writing methods. Writers tend to "take risks, to be more tentative about meaning for longer, to consider organization and word choices more freely than ever before. What this means is that children . . . can learn a great deal about language and the writing process each time they engage in writing" (Newman, 1984, p. 495). Chapters on handwriting, invented spelling, and beginning composition stressed that young writers have a lot to remember—letter formation, rules for segmentation, letter-sound correspondences, and the actual texts of stories they wish to write. When children use a word processor, they still must remember considerable information but they *do not have to remember* how to form letters. This eases their memory demands and guarantees them neat copies of their work.

Word Processing for Beginning Writers

A brief discussion of computer use in a kindergarten illustrates the potential of word processing for beginning writers.[7] The kindergarten had a strong phonics program and particularly emphasized neat handwriting. Language experience was used frequently, but no student writing was encouraged "because the children could not read." A computer had been in the class for several months when the study began. To introduce word processing, each child dictated at least one language experience story that was typed on the computer. Children sat on an assistant's or my lap so they could see the monitor and observe typing mistakes and corrections. Traditional LEA strategies were used in rereading the stories, and all stories were saved on disk. Given a printed copy, the children could read what they had dictated, and some wanted to make editorial changes to correct grammar or add or change words.

Invited to type their own stories, the children demonstrated capitalization and punctuation, and showed increasing growth throughout the study. All used invented spelling. Although abilities varied widely, no child refused to compose because he or she "couldn't spell." Some children sought help frequently, while others spent considerable time in thought before typing any words. One stated, "I have to think before I can type it," and another would sit in deep concentration between words. Some children requested help frequently; others worked independently, typing and deleting to get the desired spellings. Many nonchalantly spelled what were obviously sight words. Only one child seemed aware of this mastery as she proclaimed "Watch this—I can spell *for* and nobody taught me how." Others craned their necks to find needed environmental print.

Some children were aware of capitalization, but their information was not always accurate. Some capitalized the first letter in nouns or names or what seemed to be important words, as in: "I am a Ballerena. And I can Tern arand. I have perty Shos. I Lick Lolypops wile I am dansing. in El paso we selebrat birthdays and I am The one that Dansis." Random use of the shift key, possibly simply for the fun of it, was not uncommon. Other children avoided capitalization entirely and created thoughtful stories entirely in lower case letters. Application of vaguely formed punctuation rules was also evident. Few used commas, but most knew that periods or "dots" should be used to indicate breaks in thought.

In all cases, children could read their stories after composition and a week later on the computer and in print. Few children, however, began to "go public" with paper and pencil writing, probably because of the continued emphasis on accurate handwriting. Samples of the children's work are presented in Figure 14.2.

Word Processing for More Experienced Writers

Easy-to-use word processors such as *Magic Slate* (Sunburst) or *Bank Street Writer* (Scholastic) can have tremendous impact on classroom writing procedures. Even the simplest word processor allows writers to type in text, save it on disk, make changes easily within the body of their text, insert and delete chunks of text, and move chunks of text around. Some word processors have features that allow writers to find specific words in text, to replace *all* examples of specific words (for example, a misspelled word) with one procedure, and to load parts of text from one file to another to create new texts. Some have spelling checkers or thesauri. Printing is easy, and print options include single, double, and triple spacing. With the *Bank Street Writer* students can print a triple-spaced draft copy that looks exactly like what they have worked with on the computer monitor.

Introducing Word Processing

Word processors for children are easy to use, once an adult has demonstrated basic procedures. First, teachers should elicit a story from the group and, as in a language experience session, transcribe it on the computer. Typing errors should be corrected normally with clear explanations of procedure. Children

---

CHAPTER 14

Kindergarten writing samples

Child 1.

Woof I am a dog. Woof My Name is Sally. and I Can do tricks. Woof My Pet is a dog. I am the dog. Woof I See a Bunny Hi Bunny. Woof I Love You Kutty. I Sol a kutty

Child 2.

I wish foer a hudred dollrs to by strewoer figers I will plae with them and sher with them

Child 3.

I am gon to sevineelevun to day, pls jimmy wil you go with me to get sum bred for uor moms to day? we can git sum cande and to coc slrpes.

It is a pupe and domino is a gerl dog I love her I wont a nuther wun to day I love you mome + dad + chris dumey I hat you chris

I haf to wat all sumer to go to disne land and se the ulimpicks (Olympics) and stah at the disneland hotel I wish chris wont go to disuneland

The pocku dotid dinosooer
wuns ther livd A gerl dinusooer and her nam was jeanne berry and her culer was purple and she noo anuther gerl dinsooer cath lynnn

---

FIGURE 14.2
These stories have all been reproduced from a disk prepared in a kindergarten classroom.

will be curious about the "ends of lines" and will remark that words that "don't fit just move to the next line." Stressing that they do not have to use the "return" key as on a typewriter is important. As in LEA, the dictation should be read and possibly edited. The files should be *named, saved,* and *cleared,* so that when needed later, they can be (almost magically) called up again *from memory.*

The second step is to demonstrate revision, the real value of word processing. Teachers should prepare a file with a neutral story similar to what class members might write themselves and to those used to teach paper-and-pencil revision. Giving the children a dittoed copy of the story can be useful, too. The small group, seated in front of the computer, directs the teacher to change words and make other revisions. The teacher edits the text and explains procedures for the word processor that the children are learning to use. Children can make changes themselves because they do not totally "believe in" the computer's ability to "save" text and may fear that they will "lose" the story if they change it. To help them overcome these fears, teachers should also prepare several "stories for editing" and save them on a class disk. By "write protecting" the disk with tape, the stories cannot be erased, and children can edit and change at will. As they experiment revising these stories, they gain confidence in the word processor and their ability to use it.

Children Using the Word Processor

Teachers often wonder how everyone will be able to do word processing if a class has only one computer. Teachers need to schedule specific times for word processing but should keep blocks flexible enough so that children will not feel pressured to stop work in the middle of a composition. Word processors for children are usually "menu driven," meaning that directions and prompts appear on the screen. If children know what to look for and how to access a "help menu" to answer questions, they can work without teacher supervision. A chart of procedures posted by the computer can be a reference guide as well. Children composing together at the computer can write one story or can help each other on individual efforts.

For efficiency, before they approach the computer, children should plan their work and prepare brief notes, outlines, or maps on paper. Inasmuch as this is part of the process approach to writing, children should do this anyway. First drafts of stories that are already taking form mentally can be typed relatively quickly and printed for conferencing. Revisions can be made on the "hard copy" away from the computer, possibly even as homework. When children return to the computer, they enter their changes and write more if they wish. Alternatively, children can compose on the computer, save their efforts, and later retrieve their file for revision without an intermediate paper-and-pencil step. Teachers and children can meet in front of the computer for a conference or teachers themselves can retrieve a file and write and save their comments at the beginning of the story (using the computer as a bulletin board). The first strategy is preferable for young writers who need time to study and think about their writing. Having a paper copy of their work also gives them something to doodle or draw on, if that is part of their revision procedure.

Word processors eliminate handwriting as an obstacle to composition so that all children have clean draft copies to revise individually, share with teachers, or talk about in conference with peers. Children have a clear, graphic image to examine for errors, so it is easier to decide if something "looks wrong." Children know that revising will not require them to copy *the whole thing* over. Additionally revising allows them to play with the computer, which they see as fun. Children also know that clean and neat final drafts can be produced for publication. Teachers, of course, may want to add finishing touches to children's files before final copies are printed for official publication, just as they would make small revisions when typing them for display. Teachers should also remember that most printers accommodate ditto masters, so class books can be made easily.

COMPUTERS FOR INSTRUCTION

Teachers can use word processors like *Bank Street Writer* for individualized instruction. They can set up a file for each child or a file for separate activities, such as follow up to stories in a basal reader. If all children have files, they should retrieve their files to see what assignments their teachers have written, do the assignments, and respond on the computer. Assignments should involve reading and writing and may be as direct as questions to answer or as open-ended as suggestions for additional reading or essay topics. Because there is no page length specified, children tend to write more than they would with paper and pencil. The process of writing after reading strengthens comprehension, and with the word processor, children can easily think, answer, rethink, and change answers as comprehension deepens. Children should save their responses on the computer and can also print them out. An alternative method to computer use is to set up a file for separate activities, such as directed-thinking-about-reading (DTAR) activities. Teachers might make a file on each story in a basal reader with directions to approximate a directed-thinking-about-reading activity. Again, children answer in writing without regard for the amount of space they use. As they answer, the computer keeps "scrolling" and filling up space between questions. "Write protecting" disks eliminates the possibility of accidental erasing.

Drill and Practice

Software marketed for the early childhood years has minimal reading requirements so that young learners can work with relative independence. With the exception of word processing, there is little available to challenge beginning readers and writers. What is available is drill-and-practice software, which presents tasks that children repeat until reaching a desired level of mastery. As with worksheets and workbooks, children usually must select from several choices to indicate a letter-sound correspondence or correct spelling, complete an open sentence, specify where punctuation should be placed, or correct a grammatical error. In some software, children read short passages and answer multiple-choice questions. The software may or may not provide reasons why responses are wrong, and children can spend time repeating errors without corrective feedback.

Drill-and-practice activities may be useful *if* a child has already learned the target skills, but they will not *on their own* guarantee any more mastery than the dullest teacher-made ditto sheet. Drill and practice cannot replace quality teaching or meaningful practice through real reading and writing tasks. These children need to apply their skills in diverse, purposeful reading tasks. Software activities may be too difficult, and "the child simply muddles through with a sense of being asked to do too much too soon. Often, the child simply repeats an inaccurate response many times without a means of assisting or correcting the error" (Rosegrant, 1986, p. 132). Rather than helping, such drill and practice makes reading more confusing than ever.

Management Systems

Many commercial reading programs include a computerized management system to assist teachers keep track of children's progress. These can save time and energy and free teachers for more interaction with children. Other management systems feature computers that can evaluate children's needs and recommend software and other materials for subskill instruction and practice. One writer (Aukerman, 1984) referred to "computerized learning systems for beginning reading [that] will consist of thousands of subskills, calling for thousands of responses to multiple choices presented by the computer . . . Criticism of computers as being impersonal will be irrelevant for children who already work with computers in a one-to-one, personal relationship. Moreover, the child is in *control* of the learning process, including goals, motivation, amount, speed, degree of accuracy desired, and satisfaction derived" (pp. 531– 532). This may be true, but **reading management systems** will never negate the importance of storybook reading, language experience, and beginning writing.

Interactive Reading Programs

The first **interactive** reading program was O. K. Moore's "Responsive Environment," the so-called talking typewriter developed in the 1960s. The typewriter was programmed to say letter names as children typed them in an initial, exploratory phase of the approach. The second phase introduced letter-sound correspondences, and the third phase developed a basic sight vocabulary. In all phases, the children interacted with the typewriter as they typed to activate the voice synthesizer. Children also could dictate stories into a tape recorder, play them back, and type with no voice accompaniment.[8] Commercial production of the talking typewriter was never realized, probably because Moore's research predated microcomputers, but software such as *KidSpeak* (Apple/MacIntosh) approximates the effect with word processing and voice synthesizers.

Another computer-based early childhood reading program called *Writing to Read,* is marketed by International Business Machines (IBM).[9] It began as a computerized phonics program but now includes computer-based instructional materials, correlated student work journals for writing and daily record keeping, language development activities, and read-along tapes of children's literature. The computer aspect of *Writing to Read* finds children watching a picture on the monitor as a synthesized voice says and spells the name of the picture. Children must type the correct spelling in order to animate a scene on the monitor. Their next activity, however, is to type their own stories on a typewriter; and at this point, invented spelling is welcomed. Children also write in journals and listen to tapes while following along in children's books. Exposure to correctly spelled words on the computer and in literature is supposed to ensure the transition from invented to standard spelling. Daily practice writing on the typewriter and in journals, of course, eases the transition as well.

Educational Testing Service has evaluated *Writing to Read* for IBM and found it to be highly effective. Kindergarten participants in the evaluation study progressed more rapidly than the national norm in reading, writing, and spelling, regardless of ethnicity or economic background. Parents seemed to approve of the program, and teachers were enthusiastic. Media coverage of those sites experimenting with *Writing to Read* has extolled its virtues.

Some writers point out that most new programs usually are successful at first;[10] this is called the *halo effect*. It is easy to imagine how children would try harder and be more motivated because of their fascination with computers. (This is true with word processors, too.) Teachers, too, might place confidence in the program to teach their students and provide extra encouragement and support. While these statements are probably true, the core idea of *Writing to Read* is so sound that the program should not be dismissed as another technological gimmick. *Writing to Read* uses pictures, letters, and voice to teach sight words and then asks children to type the words themselves for reinforcement. It requires children to write, both by hand and on a typewriter (which has some of the lesened memory demands of a word processor). It also uses a form of storybook reading: the child listening to a tape may not be snuggled in an adult's lap, but he or she has clear line of sight to the print that is being read. All these elements of a whole language approach to beginning literacy contribute to the success of *Writing to Read*.

SUMMARY

There is a real place for computers in early childhood education, especially as a tool to assist children explore oral language and literacy. Just as print can produce a special kind of relationship with adults and children, computers can stimulate discussion about concepts, skills, ideas, and experiences. Computers also encourage child-child interaction, planning, and problem solving. Furthermore, if teachers were to use a computer for *nothing* more than a bridge between language experience and beginning composition, the computer would be a valuable part of the curriculum.

Computers are not going to replace early childhood teachers, nor are they going to eliminate the need for mastery of basic literacy skills. They should, though, be part of children's environment, stimulating new kinds of thinking, reinforcing emerging thinking skills, and offering challenging opportunities for a new variety of technologically enhanced "literacy events."

REVIEW QUESTIONS

1. Be sure that you can define each of these terms:
   interactive (as it relates to computers)
   reading management system
   software
   story generator
   word processor
2. In your opinion, what is the biggest advantage of using computers in early childhood education? What disadvantages might you expect?
3. What biases have you had about computers? How many have changed? What biases can you still identify?
4. Find articles about *Writing to Read* in educational journals or the popular press. If a school near you is using the program, arrange to visit. How does this approach reflect a "whole language approach" to beginning language?
5. Write a letter to a principal expressing the reasons why you would like to have a computer in your classroom. Explain how it will benefit your students and increase their learning.
6. Visit classrooms that use computers. Talk to the teachers and students to assess their attitudes. Are these what you expected?
7. View different kinds of early childhood software and prepare reviews. State your reasons for liking or disliking the software.
8. Inspect several early childhood classes that have computers and determine if the computer center is in the best place in the room, if furniture and decorations are appropriate, and if record keeping is adequate.

NOTES

1. Salinger, T. S. (1982). Unpublished final report, *Computer Use in Day Care*, YWCA Executive Director, El Paso, TX.
2. Turkle, S. (1984). *The second self: Computers and the human spirit.* New York: Simon & Schuster.
3. Ball, S., & Salinger, T. (1986). A computer in my classroom. In J. L. Hoot (Ed.). *Computers in early childhood education* (pp. 81–103). Englewood Cliffs, NJ: Prentice-Hall.
4. Papert, S. (1980). *Mindstorms: Children, computers, and powerful ideas.* New York: Basic Books.
5. Craig, A. (1986). End term report, ECED 3552, University of Texas at El Paso, used by permission.
6. Turkle, *op. cit.*
7. Salinger, T. (1985). Kindergarteners and word processing. In L. Gentile (Ed.). *Reading education in Texas* (pp. 1–5).
8. Aukerman, R. C. (1984). *Approaches to beginning reading* (2nd ed.). New York: John Wiley & Sons.
9. Aukerman, *op. cit.*
10. Aukerman, *op. cit.*

Appendix 1

Children's Books

The following lists present a sample of the many excellent books available for young children. Veatch (1968) suggested a minimum of 100 books for a permanent classroom library—and that does not include the seasonal or content-related books that "rotate" in and out of a classroom to meet immediate needs. Investing in books is perhaps the best step early childhood teachers can take toward making their classrooms literate because the investment can have long-term impact on children's attitudes toward reading and the sense of the utility of books in their lives.

Many of the books in these lists have a multicultural theme and many can be used for concept development. Separate lists for these kinds of books have not been included. Additional information about children's books can be obtained from Burke (1986) and Trelease (1985), both of which are listed in the references.

STORYBOOKS—NARRATIVE (POETIC) PROSE

Brando, M. W. (1926). *The velveteen rabbit.* Garden City, NY: Doubleday.

Brown, M. W. (1947). *Good night moon.* New York: Harper & Row (and others by the author).

Buckley, H. E. (1959). *Grandfather and I.* New York: Lothrop, Lee & Shepard (also *Grandmother and I,* 1961).

Cleary, B. (1968). *Ramona the pest.* New York: William Morrow.

Cohen, M. (1977). *When will I read?* New York: Greenwillow Books.

_____. (1967). *Will I have a friend?* New York: Macmillan.

de Paola, T. (1973). *Nana upstairs and nana downstairs.* New York: G. P. Putnam's Sons (and others by author).

Ets, M. H. (1955). *Play with me.* New York: Viking.

Flack, M. (1933). *The story about Ping.* New York: Viking.

Freeman, D. (1968). *Corduroy.* New York: Viking.

Hill, E. S. (1967). *Evan's corner.* New York: Holt, Reinhart, & Winston.

Hoban, R. (1964). *A baby sister for Frances*. New York: Harper & Row (and others in series).

Johnson, C. (1958). *Harold and the purple crayon*. New York: Harper & Row (and others in series).

Keats, E. J. (1967). *Peter's chair*. New York: Harper & Row.

Krauss, R. (1945). *The carrot seed*. New York: Harper & Row.

Leonni, L. (1966). *Frederick*. New York: Pantheon.

Lobel, A. (1979). *Frog and Toad are friends*. New York: Harper & Row (and others by author).

Mayer, M. (1968). *There's a nightmare in my closet*. New York: Dial Press.

McCloskey, R. (1941). *Make way for ducklings*. New York: Viking.

Minarik, E. H. (1957). *Little Bear*. New York: Harper & Row.

Ness, E. (1966). *Sam, Bangs, and Moonshine*. New York: Holt, Rinehart & Winston.

Raskin, E. (1968). *Spectacles*. New York: Atheneum.

Sendak, M. (1963). *Where the wild things are*. New York: Harper & Row (and other books).

Seuss, Dr. (1940). *Horton hatches an egg*. New York: Random House (and his other books).

Steig, W. (1969). *Sylvester and the magic pebble*. New York: Farrar, Strauss, & Giroux.

Steptoe, J. (1969). *Stevie*. New York: Harper & Row.

Urdy, J. M. (1961). *Let's be enemies*. New York: Harper & Row.

Viorst, J. (1972). *Alexander and the terrible, horrible, no good, very bad day*. New York: Atheneum.

Waber, B. (1963). *Rich cat, poor cat*. Boston: Houghton-Mifflin.

Yashima, T. (1955). *Crow boy*. New York: Viking.

Zolotow, C. (1963). *The quarreling book*. New York: Harper & Row.

ANIMAL AND SCIENCE BOOKS (EXCEPT DINOSAURS)—TRANSACTIONAL PROSE

Aliki, (1976). *Corn is maize*. New York: Thomas Y. Crowell.

_____. (1962). *My five senses*. New York: Harper & Row.

Arnosky, I. (1979). *Crinkleroot's book of animal tracks and wildlife signs*. New York: G. P. Putnam's Sons.

Bendick, J. (1975). *Ecology*. New York: Franklyn Watts.

_____. (1971). *How to make a cloud*. New York: Parents Magazine Press.

Busch, P. (1972). *Exploring as you walk in the city*. Philadelphia: J. B. Lippincott.

Carle, E. (1977). *Grouchy Ladybug*. New York: Harper & Row.

_____. (1975). *Mixed-up chameleon*. New York: Crowell-Collier Press.

_____. (1969). *Very hungry caterpillar*. New York: Philomel.

Chlad, D. (1982). *Matches, lighters, and firecrackers are not toys*. New York: Children's Press.

Crews, D. (1982). *Harbor*. New York: Greenwillow Books.

_____. (1981). *Light*. New York: Greenwillow Books.

_____. (1980). *Truck*. New York: Greenwillow Books.

de Paola, T. (1980). *The cloud book*. New York: Holiday House.

_____. (1978). *The popcorn book*. New York: Holiday House.

_____. (1977). *The quicksand book*. New York: Holiday House.

Gans, R. (1964). *Icebergs.* New York: Thomas Y. Crowell.

Ginsberg, M. (1981). *Where does the sun go at night?* New York: Greenwillow Books.

Holl, A. (1965). *Rain puddle.* New York: Lothrop, Lee, & Shepard.

Hutchins, P. (1974). *The wind blew.* New York: Macmillan.

_____. (1970). *Clocks and more clocks.* New York: Macmillan.

Komori, A. (1983). *Animal mothers.* New York: Philomel.

Lauber, P. (1979). *What's hatching out of that egg?* New York: Crown.

Selsam, M. E. (1963). *Greg's microscope.* New York: Harper & Row.

_____. (1972). *Is this a baby dinosaur and other science puzzles?* New York: Harper & Row.

_____. (1976). *Popcorn.* New York: William Morrow & Co.

Showers, P. (1975). *Hear your heart.* New York: Harper & Row.

_____. (1967). *How you talk.* New York: Harper & Row.

_____. (1980). *No measles, no mumps for me.* New York: Harper & Row.

Wulffson, D. (1981). *The invention of ordinary things.* New York: Lothrop, Lee & Shepard.

Zims, H. S. (1952). *What's inside me?* New York: William Morrow & Co. (and other books by author).

DINOSAUR BOOKS

Aliki (1981). *Digging up dinosaurs.* New York: Harper Trophy.

_____. (1985). *Dinosaurs are different.* New York: Harper Trophy.

_____. (1972). *Fossils tell of long ago.* New York: Harper Trophy.

_____. (1971). *My trip to the dinosaurs.* New York: Harper Trophy.

Jacobs, F. (1982). *Supersaurus.* New York: Putnam.

Most, B. (1978). *If the dinosaurs came back.* New York: Harcourt Brace Jovanovich.

Sattler, H. (1984). *Baby dinosaurs.* New York: Lothrop, Lee & Shepard.

_____. (1981). *Dinosaurs of North America.* New York: Lothrop, Lee & Shepard.

ALPHABET BOOKS

Alexander, A. (1971). *ABC of cars and trucks.* New York: Doubleday.

Anno, M. (1974). *Anno's alphabet: An adventure in imagination.* New York: Thomas Y. Crowell.

Barry, K. (1961). *A is for everything.* New York: Harcourt, Brace and World.

Beisner, M. (1981). *A folding alphabet book.* New York: Farrar, Strauss, & Giroux.

Brown, M. (1974). *All butterflies.* New York: Charles Scribner's Sons.

Duvolsin, R. (1952). *A for the ark.* New York: Lothrop, Lee & Shepard.

Elting, M., & Folsom, M. (1980). *Q is for duck: An alphabet guessing game.* New York: Clarion Books.

Emberley, E. (1978). *Ed Emberley's ABC.* Boston: Little, Brown, & Co.

Feelings, M., & Feelings, T. (1974). *Jambo means hello: Swahili alphabet books.* New York: Dial Press.

Isadora, R. (1983). *City seen from A to Z.* New York: Greenwillow Books.

Kitchen, B. (1984). *Animal alphabet.* New York: Dial Press.

Lear, E. (1965). *Lear alphabet—Penned and illustrated by Edward Lear himself.* New York: McGraw-Hill.

Lobel, A. (1981). *On Market Street.* New York: Greenwillow Books.

Montresor, B. (1969). *A for angel: Beni Montresor's ABC Picture Stories.* New York: Alfred Knopf.

Musgrove, M. (1976). *Ashanti to Zulu: African traditions.* New York: Dial Press.

Niland, D. (1976). *ABC of monsters.* New York: McGraw-Hill.

Parish, D. (1969). *A beastly circus.* New York: Macmillan.

Provensen, A., & Provensen, M. (1978). *A peaceable kingdom: The shaker ABECEDARIUS.* New York: Viking.

Sendak, M. (1962). *Alligators all around: An alphabet book.* New York: Harper & Row.

Tallon, R. (1969). *An ABC in English and Spanish.* New York: The Lion Press.

Tudor, T. (1954). *A is for Annabelle.* New York: Rand McNally.

Yolen, J. (1979). *All the woodland early: An ABC book.* Collins.

WORDLESS PICTURE BOOKS, PREDICTABLE BOOKS, AND BOOKS THAT FEATURE LANGUAGE PLAY

Wordless

Alexander, M. (1970). *Bobo's dream.* New York: Dial Press.

Carle, E. (1971). *Do you want to be my friend?* New York: Crowell-Collier.

Cristini, E., & Puricelli, L. (1983). *In my garden.* Picture Book Studio.

_____. (1984). *In the pond.* Picture Book Studio.

_____. (1983). *In the woods.* Picture Book Studio.

Knobler, S. (1974). *Tadpole and the frog.* New York: Harvey House.

Krahn, F. (1974). *Flying saucers full of spaghetti.* New York: E. P. Dutton.

Mayer, M. (1977). *Oops.* New York: Dial Press.

Predictable Books

Becker, J. (1973). *Seven little rabbits.* New York: Scholastic.

Carle, E. (1969). *The very hungry caterpillar.* Cleveland: Collins World.

Keats, E. J. (1971). *Over in the meadow.* New York: Scholastic.

Martin, B. (1970). *Brown Bear, Brown Bear.* New York: Holt, Rinehart & Winston (and others by same author).

Mayer, M. (1968). *If I had . . . .* New York: Dial Press.

_____. (1975). *Just for you.* New York: Golden Press.

Preston, E. M. (1978). *Where did my mother go?* New York: Four Winds Press.

Language Play

Einsel, W. (1972). *Did you ever see?* New York: Scholastic.

Emberley, E. (1967). *Drummer Hoff.* New York: Prentice-Hall.

Gwynn, F. (1973). *A chocolate mouse for dinner.* New York: E. P. Dutton.

_____. (1972). *The king who rained.* New York: Windmill.

Parish, P. (1963). *Amelia Bedelia.* New York: Harper & Row.

Spier, P. (1971). *Gobble, growl, grunt.* New York: Doubleday.

_____. (1972). *Crash, bang, boom.* New York: Doubleday.

Appendix 2

Parents As Partners in Emerging Literacy

Parents are children's first teachers and should remain instructional partners throughout the early childhood years. A student's response to an exam question that asked her to write a letter explaining this partnership conveys the importance of the parents' role very well.[1]

An Explanatory Letter

Dear Parents:

The duties of parents today may seem at times overwhelming. Most households necessitate both husband and wife working outside the home—a great pressure in itself. The routine household duties we face may sometimes seem endless. We need to make sure that our children are well equipped to deal with our sometimes violent world, and for many families being able to provide adequate physical comforts may be an ongoing challenge. The list seems to go on forever. Now, on top of everything else, educators want you to be "teachers" in your home to help prepare your children for success in school. What can parents do?

The ideas proposed here are new and not-so-new. The point is not for parents to actually "teach" as we know it, but to facilitate, to stimulate. There are ways to modify homes, conversations, and interests to help children in the complicated task of learning about literacy without adding yet another pressure to parents' already long list of tasks.

One current way of thinking is that children themselves can take command of literacy and indeed should be supported in doing so. Does this mean that you as parents should leave your children alone so they can "take command" of their learning? Not exactly. You do need to create an environment which will encourage children to wonder, to discover, to learn about, and to become interested in knowing more about reading and writing. This is called a "literate environment." The name itself may cause you to gasp for air, but it is much more simple than it sounds. A literate environment is one that is alive with print: signs, labels, books, junk mail, anything that contains print. The type of print is not important, nor is the price of what is being displayed. A literate environment also demonstrates how and why people use writing and reading skills and provides opportunities for individuals to talk about literate behaviors.

In a literate environment, children play with beginning skills. These beginning reading and writing behaviors are known as "emerging literacy." Children begin to be aware of literate behaviors and practices and develop a sense of how reading and writing "feel." Emerging literacy begins with parent-child interaction—between you and your child. This is an important bond: parents and children talking about reading and writing. These discussions, however brief and spontaneous, are called "literacy events." Children also develop a sense of literacy from seeing people around them reading and writing as part of routine activities, for information, and for pleasure.

You can demonstrate writing to your children by taking a minute or two to tell them what you are writing and why, by letting them look over your shoulder as you form letters and numbers, and giving them opportunities to do their own writing. It is important to let children know that there are many purposes for writing: communicating with letters, paying bills, making lists, writing reminders. Long before they can actually form letters correctly, children will want to try out their emerging writing skills. Parents' task here is to encourage experimentation by suggesting that children write their own grocery lists or letter to relatives, write messages on art work, fill out order forms on junk mail, or even write out their own "checks" while a parent pays bills. Letters to relatives should be mailed and other writing can be displayed around the child's room. Children may want adults to "read" what they write or to transcribe their ideas into conventional print. Parents provide models and explanations about writing when they "play along" with these behaviors.

Parents encourage reading behavior by displaying, pointing out, and talking about print. You may already have many articles with print in your home. Articles such as printed grocery items you keep exposed, cross-stitched phrases or names on throw pillows, welcome signs, "reminder" notes tacked in the bathroom or on the refrigerator, t-shirts, lists of chores to be done—these are part of the printed world. The next step is to go a step further and expand on these materials. Call them to the attention of your children. Chances are they can already "read" or identify many things around them. Children develop this initial reading skill from seeing and asking about signs and labels—so-called "environmental print." An example of how you can build on environmental print would be as follows: when you buy a package of Oreo cookies, your child might take it from you and trace the word "OREO"; while he says it, do not dismiss this as a fluke. Instead, take a moment to praise him and perhaps call his attention to the "O's" in the word while you say "OREO" and stress the long-o sound. This is a reading literacy event; the entire interaction would only take a few seconds but has planted a seed for later thought.

Reading to children is widely recognized as an important way parents can help children acquire an interest in reading. Books should be chosen carefully and read lovingly. Parents and children should snuggle down together *with enough time allowed* for pleasant interaction. Parents should read with normal tone and inflection and should discuss stories and pictures to help children become familiar with terms like *title* and *author* and with the basic organization of storybook narration. Children must recognize that story and pictures go together, that stories may be about a wide variety of topics, and that they are *allowed* to like some stories more than others. Children's books should be left conveniently in sight for youngsters to "read" themselves, and parents should encourage them to participate in reading them orally.

Parents' job is to build subtly on children's emerging literacy. Remember that children learn best in an environment rich with opportunities to explore interesting objects and ideas. For that reason, children can never be exposed to this type of environment too early. Parents must also remember that they have already been good teachers as they have supported their children's oral language growth. Did you ever marvel at the amazing way children learn to speak? In 3 years or so, a child acquires more language than adults could ever hope to obtain given the same amount of time. Language development has been the beginning of children's journey toward literacy, the biggest hurdle in learning to communicate; and you have helped your child cross it! Helping your children didn't cost you any extra time or effort; it just happened—is the job of helping children acquire literacy seeming any easier?

The question, of course, is whether we should concentrate all our efforts on pushing ABCs and 123s, thus robbing our children of their childhood. This is certainly not what is meant. As a matter of fact, much learning about literacy comes from play: children will play with books, paper, writing equipment, story lines, and actual reading and writing behaviors just as they play with toys, blocks, art materials, and other equipment. They reproduce their impressions of literate behaviors when they "play school," take phone messages, or "pay bills." Making paper and writing tools available encourages this play and helps children refine their ideas.

Children will reenact the stories you have shared with them and may even make up new ones. Encouraging this behavior—by asking for it and by listening—motivates children to learn more about reading. Parents usually can appreciate the value of these charming reenactments, but may be less sure how to respond to beginning writing efforts. Children want to write, but the process may start with a mere scribble. Even though there is no letter-sound correspondence as in conventional spelling, parents should welcome these first efforts. The words children write are those they really want to know because they come from within themselves. Many times you may not be able to read your children's words yourself, but the spelling is their own and eventually will develop into what we can actually recognize. In time, children begin to correlate letters and sounds and produce spelling that looks more and more correct. What a change from the traditional method of teaching spelling from the outside with repetitions, reinforcement, and corrective feedback. Writing has taken on a whole new meaning for young children. As they begin to write, even with nonconventional spelling, they are also beginning to read. This is an important stage, as children's confidence increases with every step they take toward literacy. Mistakes should not be corrected any more than nonstandard oral usage was corrected; encouragement and even challenges make children reach even farther.

Your role as parent "teachers" need not be a burdensome one. You can enhance children's love for learning early on by sharing your adult literacy behaviors with your children. As you become aware of the slight adjustments needed to make in your lives to engage in literacy events and to make your home a literate environment, you will almost effortlessly produce literate children in your homes.

Many thanks for your concern.

Sincerely,

A Final Point

The student who wrote this letter offers a solid, well-planned, early childhood curriculum to the children she teaches. Her explanation of her program would give parents insight into the way they can help support what she does in her own classroom. The final point that must be stressed for parents is that, while they can indeed be excellent teachers of their young children, they need to look for and demand quality early childhood experiences in the daycare centers, preschools, and early primary classes their children attend.

Just as they want to establish a literate environment in their homes, they want to find one in their children's schools and to encourage their children's teachers to adopt the same strategies for literacy growth.

NOTES

1. Letter written by Rae Mowad Martinez, Midterm, ECED 3455, used by permission.

Bibliography

Allen, E. F. (1986). Literacy instruction for LES children. *Language Arts, 63,* 51–60.

Aukerman, R. C. (1984). *Approaches to beginning reading* (2nd ed.). New York: John Wiley & Sons.

Aulls, M. W. (1986). Activity teaching main idea skills. In J. F. Baumann (Ed.). *Teaching Main Idea Comprehension* (pp. 96–132). Newark, DE: International Reading Association.

Baghban, M. (1984). *Our daughter learns to read and write.* Newark, DE: International Reading Association.

Ball, S., & Salinger, T. (1986). A Computer in My Classroom: Teacher Concerns. In J. L. Hoot (Ed.). *Computers in early childhood education* (pp. 81–103). Englewood Cliffs, NJ: Prentice-Hall.

Beers, C. S., & Beers, J. W. (1981). Three assumptions about learning to spell. *Language Arts, 58,* 573–580.

Bernstein, B. B. (1972). A critique of the concept of compensatory education. In C. B. Cazden, V. P. John, & D. Hymes (Eds.). *Functions of language in the classroom* (pp. 135–151). New York: Teachers College Press.

Bettelheim, B., & Zelan, K. (1982). *On learning to read.* New York: Vintage.

Bissex, G. L. (1984). The child as teacher. In H. Goelman, A. Oberg, & F. Smith (Eds.). *Awakening to literacy* (pp. 87–101). Portsmouth, NH: Heinemann Educational Books.

Bissex, G. L. (1980). *Gnys at wrk: A child learns to write and read.* Cambridge, MA: Harvard University Press.

Bloom, L. (1970). *Language development: Form and function in emerging grammars.* Cambridge, MA: MIT Press.

Bloom, L. & R. Lahey, P. (1978). *Language development and language disorders.* New York: John Wiley.

Bondy, E. (1984). Thinking about thinking: Encouraging children's use of metacognitive processes. *Childhood Education, 60,* 234–238.

Britton, J. (1970). *Language and learning.* Harmondsworth, England: Penguin Books.

Brown, R. A. (1973). *A first language: The early stages.* Cambridge, MA: Harvard University Press.

Brown, R., & Bellugi, U. (1970). Three processes in the child's acquisition of syntax. In R. Brown (Ed.). *Psycholinguistics* (pp. 75–99). New York: The Free Press.

Bruner, J. (1984). Language, mind, and reading. In H. Goelman, A. Oberg, & F. Smith (Eds.). *Awakening to literacy* (pp. 193–200). Portsmouth, NH: Heinemann Educational Books.

Buckley, M. H., & Boyle, O. (1983). Mapping and composing. In M. Myers & J. Gray (Eds.). *Theory and practice in the teaching of composition* (pp. 59–66). Urbana: National Council of Teachers of English.

Burg, K. (1984). The microcomputer in the kindergarten: A magical, useful, expensive toy. *Young Children, 39* (3), 28–33.

Burke, E. M. (1986). *Early childhood literature: For love of child and book.* Boston: Allyn & Bacon.

Burris, N. A., & Lentz, K. A. (1983). Caption books in the classroom. *The Reading Teacher, 36,* 872–875.

Butler, D., & Clay, M. (1979). *Reading begins at home.* Exeter, NH: Heinemann Educational Books.

Calkins, L. M. (1981a). Children learn the writer's craft. In R. D. Walshe (Ed.). *Donald Graves in Australia: "Children Want to Write."* (pp. 65–72). Rozell, New South Wales: Primary English Teaching Association.

———. (1981b). When children want to punctuate: Basic skills belong in context. In R. D. Walshe (Ed.). *Donald Graves in Australia: "Children Want to Write."* (pp. 89–96). Rozelle, New South Wales: Primary English Teaching Association.

Caplan, R., & Keech, C. (1980). *Showing writing: A training program to help students be specific.* Berkeley: University of California/Bay Area Writing Project.

Carratello, P., & Carratello, J. (1984). *Let's investigate computers.* Sunset Beach, CA: Teacher Created Materials.

Cazden, C. B. (1983). Adult assistance to language development: Scaffolds, models, and direct instruction. In R. P. Parker & Frances A. Davis (Eds.). *Developing literacy* (pp. 3–18). Newark, DE: International Reading Association.

———. (1981). Language development and the preschool environment. In C. B. Cazden (Ed.). *Language in early childhood education* (Rev. ed.) (pp. 3–16). Washington, DC: National Association for the Education of Young Children.

Chenfeld, M. B. (1985). Words of praise: Honey on the page. *Language Arts, 62,* 266–267.

Chomsky, C. (1969). *The acquisition of syntax in children from 5 to 10.* Cambridge, MA: MIT Press.

———. (1970). Reading, writing, and phonology. *Harvard Educational Review, 40,* 287–309.

Church, J. (1961). *Language and the discovery of reality.* New York: Vintage.

Cicourel, A. V., & Boese, R. J. (1972). In C. B. Cazden, V. P. John, & D. Hymes (Eds.). *Functions of Language in the Classroom* (pp. 32–66). New York: Teachers College Press.

Clay, M. M. (1979). *Reading: The patterning of complex behavior.* Portsmouth, NH: Heinemann Educational Books.

———. (1976). *What did I write?* Portsmouth, NH: Heinemann Educational Books.

Cochran-Smith, M. (1984). *The making of a reader.* Norwood, NJ: Ablex.

Cullinan, B. E. (Ed.). (1974). *Black dialects and reading.* Urbana, IL: National Council of Teachers of English.

DeFord, D. (1981). Literacy, reading, writing, and other essentials. *Language Arts, 58,* 652–658.

BIBLIOGRAPHY

Donaghue, M. R. (1985). *The Child and the English language arts* (4th ed.). Dubuque, IA: William C. Brown.

Dore, J. (1977). "Oh Them Sheriff": A pragmatic analysis of children's responses to questions. In S. Ervin-Tripp & C. Mitchell-Kernan (Eds.). *Child discourse* (pp. 139–163). New York: Academic Press.

Dunn, R., & Dunn, K. (1978). *Teaching students through their individual learning styles.* Reston, VA: Reston Publishing.

Durkin, D. (1984). Is there a match between what elementary teachers do and what basal manuals recommend? *The Reading Teacher, 37,* 734–745.

_____. (1981). Reading comprehension in five basal reader series. *Reading Research Quarterly, 16,* 515–544.

_____. (1972). *Teaching young children to read.* Boston: Allyn & Bacon.

_____. (1978–79). What classroom observations reveal about comprehension instruction. *Reading Research Quarterly, 14,* 451–533.

Dyson, A. H. (1984). Who controls classroom writing contexts? *Language Arts, 61,* 618–625.

Eckhoff, B. (1983). How reading affects children's writing. *Language Arts, 60,* 607–616.

_____. (1986). *Writing in a bilingual program: Habia una vez.* Norwood, NJ: Ablex.

Ferreiro, E. (1979). The relationship between oral and written: The children's viewpoints. In Y. Goodman, M. Haussler, & D. Strickland (Eds.). *Oral and written language development research: Impact on the schools.* Urbana, IL: National Council of Teachers of English.

_____. (1984). The underlying logic of literacy development. In H. Goelman, A. Oberg, & F. Smith (Eds.). *Awakening to literacy* (pp. 154–173). Portsmouth, NH: Heinemann Educational Books.

_____. (1978). What is written in a written sentence? A developmental answer. *Journal of Education, 160,* 25–39.

Ferreiro, E., & Teberosky, A. (1982). *Literacy before schooling.* Portsmouth, NH: Heinemann Educational Books.

Fishman, J. A. (1977). A model for bilingual and bidialectal education. In W. F. Mackey & T. Andersson (Eds.). *Bilingualism in early childhood* (pp. 11–17). Rowley, MA: Newbury House.

Fryburg, E. L. (1974). Black English: A descriptive guide for the teacher. In B. E. Cullinan (Ed.). *Black dialects and reading* (pp. 190–196). Urbana, IL: National Council of Teachers of English.

Furth, H. G. (1970). *Piaget for teachers.* Englewood Cliffs, NJ: Prentice-Hall.

Furth, H. G., & Wachs, H. (1979). *Thinking goes to school: Piaget's theory in practice.* New York: Oxford University Press.

Garcia, E. E. (1982). Language acquisition: Phenomenon, theory and research. In B. Spodek (Ed.), *Handbook of research in early childhood education* (pp. 47–64). New York: The Free Press.

_____. (1980a). Language switching in bilingual children: A national perspective. In E. Garcia & M. S. Vargas (Eds.). *The Mexican-American child: Language, cognitive and social development.* Tucson: University of Arizona Press.

_____. (1980b). Bilingualism in early childhood. *Young Children, 35,* 52–66.

Garvey, C. (1977). Play with language and speech. In S. Ervin-Tripp & C. Mitchell-Kernan (Eds.). *Child discourse* (pp. 27–48). New York: Academic Press.

Geller, L. G. (1985). *Wordplay and language learning for children.* Urbana, IL: National

BIBLIOGRAPHY

Council of Teachers of English.

Genishi, C., & Dyson, A. H. (1984). *Language assessment in the early years.* Norwood, NJ: Ablex.

Gentry, J. R. (1981). Learning to spell developmentally. *The Reading Teacher, 34,* 378–381.

Gentry, J. R., & Henderson, E. H. (1978). Three steps to teaching beginning readers to spell. *The Reading Teacher, 31,* 632–637.

Gibson, E. J., & Levin, H. (1975). *The psychology of reading.* Cambridge, MA: MIT Press.

Gleason, J. B. (Ed.). (1985). *The development of language.* Columbus, OH: Merrill.

Gonzalez, G. (1979). *The development of curriculum in L1 and L2 in a maintenance bilingual program: Language development in a bilingual setting.* Los Angeles: National Dissemination and Assessment Center.

Goodman, K. S. (Ed.). (1979). *Miscue analysis.* Urbana, IL: ERIC.

Goodman, Y. M. (1984). The development of initial literacy. In Goelman, H., Oberg, A., & Smith, F. (Eds.). *Awakening to literacy* (pp. 102–110). Portsmouth, NH: Heinemann Educational Books.

_____. (1985). Kidwatching: Observing children in the classroom. In A. Jagger & M. Smith-Burke (Eds.). *Observing the language learner* (pp. 9–17). Newark, DE: International Reading Association.

Graves, D. H. (1978). *Balance the basics: Let them write.* New York: Ford Foundation.

_____. (1975). An examination of the writing process of seven year old children. *Research in the teaching of English, 9,* 227–241.

_____. (1983). *Writing: Teachers and children at work.* Portsmouth, NH: Heinemann Educational Books.

Gumperz, J. S., & Hernandez-Chavez, E. (1972). Bilingualism, bidialectalism, & classroom interaction. In C. B. Cazden, V. P. John, & D. Hymes (Eds.). *Functions of language in the classroom* (pp. 84–108). New York: Teachers College Press.

Hansen, J. (1983). Authors respond to authors. *Language Arts, 60,* 970–976.

Harste, J. C., Woodward, V. A., & Burke, C. L. (1984). *Language stories and literacy lessons.* Portsmouth, NH: Heinemann Educational Books.

Healy, M. K. (1980). *Using student response groups in the classroom.* Berkeley: University of California/Bay Area Writing Project.

Heath, S. B. (1982). What no bedtime story means: Narrative skills at home and school. *Language in Society, 11,* 49–76.

Henderson, E. (1985). *Teaching spelling.* Dallas: Houghton-Mifflin.

Herr, S. (1982). *Learning activities for reading.* (4th ed.) Dubuque, IA: William C. Brown.

Hickman, J. (1983). Classrooms that help children like books. In N. Roser & M. Frith. (Eds.). *Children's Choices: Teaching with books children like* (pp. 1–11). Newark, DE: International Reading Association.

Holdaway, D. (1979). *The foundations of literacy.* Sydney: Ashton Scholastic.

_____. (1986). Guiding a natural process. In D. R. Tovey & J. E. Kerber (Eds.). *Roles in literacy learning* (pp. 42–51). Newark, DE: International Reading Association.

Horner, V. M., & Gussow, J. D. (1972). John and Mary: A pilot study in linguistic ecology. In C. B. Cazden, V. P. John, & D. Hymes. *Functions of language in the classroom* (pp. 155–194). New York: Teachers College Press.

Keller-Cohen, D., & Gracey, C. A. (1979). Learning to say *NO:* Functional negation in discourse. In O. K. Garnica & M. L. King (Eds.). *Language, children, and society* (pp. 197–212). Oxford: Pergamon Press.

BIBLIOGRAPHY

Kernan, K. T. (1977). Semantic and expressive elaborations in children's narratives. In S. Ervin-Tripp, & C. Mitchell-Kernan (Eds.). *Child discourse* (pp. 91–102). New York: Academic Press.

Klima, E. S., & Bellugi-Klima, U. (1971). Syntactic regularities in the speech of children. In A. Bar-Adon & W. Leopold (Eds.). *Child language: A book of readings.* Englewood Cliffs, NJ: Prentice-Hall.

Kutzer, M. D. (1981). Children's literature in the college classroom. *College English, 43,* 716–723.

Labov, W. (1972). *Language in the inner city: Studies in black English vernacular.* Philadelphia: University of Pennsylvania Press.

_____. (1970). *The study of nonstandard English.* Urbana, IL: National Council of Teachers of English.

Leichter, H. J. (1984). Families as environments for literacy. In H. Goelman, A. Oberg, & F. Smith (Eds.). *Awakening to literacy* (pp. 38–50). Portsmouth, NH: Heinemann Educational Books.

Lindfors, J. W. (1980). *Children's language and learning.* Englewood Cliffs, NJ: Prentice-Hall.

Mason, J. M., & Au, K. H. (1984). Learning social context characteristics in prereading lessons. In J. Flood (Ed.). *Promoting reading comprehension* (179–203). Newark, DE: International Reading Association.

McKenzie, M. G. (1985). Classroom contexts for language and literacy. In A. Jaggar & M. Smith-Burke (Eds.). *Observing the language learner* (pp. 232–249). Newark, DE: International Reading Association.

Menyuk, P. (1970). Language theories and educational practices. In F. Williams (Ed.). *Language and poverty* (pp. 190–211). Chicago: Markham.

_____. (1969). *Sentences children use.* Cambridge, MA: MIT Press.

Moffett, J., & Wagner, B. (1983). *Student centered language arts and reading, K-13: A handbook for teachers.* (3rd ed.). Boston: Houghton Mifflin.

Monson, D. (1982). The literature program and the arts. *Language Arts, 59,* 254–258.

Montessori, M. (1967). *The absorbent mind* (C.A. Claremont, Trans.). New York: Holt, Rinehart & Winston.

_____. (1964). *The Montessori Method* (A.E. George, Trans.). New York: Schocken Books (original work published 1912).

Morris, D. (1980). Beginning readers concept of word. In E. H. Henderson & J. W. Beers (Eds.). *Developmental and cognitive aspects of learning to spell. A reflection of word knowledge* (pp. 97–111). Newark: DE: International Reading Association.

Myers, C. (1983). Drawing as prewriting in preschool. In M. Meyers & J. Gray (Eds.). *Theory and practice in the teaching of composition* (pp. 75–85). Urbana, IL: National Council of Teachers of English.

Nelson, K. (1973). *Structure and strategy in learning to talk.* Chicago: University of Chicago Press. Monograph of the Society for Research in Child Development, Series No. 38.

Newkirk, T. (1982). Young writers as critical readers. *Language Arts, 59,* 451–457.

Newman, J. M. (1984). Language learning and computers. *Language Arts, 61,* 494–497.

Pearson, P. D., & Johnson, D. D. (1978). *Teaching reading comprehension.* New York: Holt, Rinehart & Winston.

Pease, D., & Gleason, J. B. (1985). Gaining meaning: Semantic development. In J. B. Gleason (Ed.). *The development of language* (pp. 103–138). Columbus, OH: Merrill.

Pelligrini, A. D. (1985). The relations between symbolic play and literate behavior: A review and critique of the empirical literature. *Review of Educational Research, 55,* 107–121.

———. (1984). The effects of classroom ecology on preschoolers' functional uses of language. In A. D. Pelligrini & T. D. Yawkey (Eds.). *The development of oral and written language in social contexts* (pp. 129–141). Norwood, NJ: Ablex.

Piaget, J. (1955). Language and thought of the child (M. Gabian, Trans.). Cleveland: World Publishing.

Powell, M. (1973). Acquisition of a reading repertoire. *Library Trends, 22,* 177–196.

Ramirez, A. G. (1981). Language attitudes and the speech of Spanish-English bilingual pupils. In Duran, R. P. (Ed.). *Latino language and communicative behavior.* Norwood, NJ: Ablex.

Raphael, T. E., & Womnancott, M. (1985). Heightening fourth grade students' sensitivity to sources of information for answering comprehension questions. *Reading Research Quarterly, 20,* 282–296.

Rosegrant, T. J. (1986). Using the microcomputer as a scaffolding for assisting beginning readers and writers. In J. L. Hoot (Ed.). *Computers in early childhood education* (pp. 124–143). Englewood Cliffs, NJ: Prentice-Hall.

Russell, D. (1984). Teacher assistance for children learning how to learn to spell. In McVitty, W. (Ed.). *Children and learning* (pp. 65–71). Rozelle, New South Wales: Primary English Teaching Association.

Sachs, J. (1985). Prelinguistic development. In J. B. Gleason (Ed.). *The development of language* (pp. 37–60). Columbus, OH: Merrill.

Salinger, T. (1985). Kindergarten word processing. In L. Gentile (Ed.). *Reading Education in Texas 1,* 1–5.

Sardy, S. (1985). Thinking about reading. In T. L. Harris & E. J. Cooper (Eds.). *Reading, thinking, and concept development* (pp. 213–229). New York: College Board.

Schmidt-Mackey, I. (1977). Language strategies of the bilingual family. In W. F. Mackey & T. Andersson (Eds.). *Bilingualism in early childhood* (pp. 132–146). Rowley, MA: Newbury House.

Searle, D., & Dillon, D. (1980). Responding to student writing: What is said and how it is said. *Language Arts, 57,* 776–780.

Skinner, B. F. (1957). *Verbal behavior.* Englewood Cliffs, NJ: Prentice-Hall.

Smith, F. (1984). The creative achievement of literacy. In H. Hoelman, A. Oberg, & F. Smith (Eds.). *Awakening to literacy* (pp. 143–153). Portsmouth, NH: Heinemann Educational Books.

———. (1979). Conflicting approaches to reading research and instruction. In L. B. Resnick & P. A. Weaver (Eds.). *Theory and practice of early reading, Vol. 2* (pp. 31–43). Hillsdale, NJ: Lawrence Erlbaum.

Smith, N. B. (1965). *American reading instruction.* Newark, DE: International Reading Association.

Sowers, S. (1981). Kds cn rit sunr thn we thngk. In *Donald Graves in Australia: "Children want to write."* Rozelle, New South Wales: Primary English Teaching Association.

Spache, G. D., & Spache, E. B. (1977). *Reading in the elementary school.* (4th ed.). Boston: Allyn & Bacon.

Squire, J. R. (1983). Composing and comprehending: Two sides of the same basic process. *Language Arts, 60,* 581–589.

Stauffer, R. G. (1980). *The language experience approach to the teaching of reading* (2nd ed.). New York: Harper & Row.

Stein, N., & Glenn, C. (1977). An analysis of story comprehension in elementary school children. In R. Freedle (Ed.). *Multidisciplinary approaches to discourse comprehension.* Hillsdale, NJ: Lawrence Erlbaum.

Stever, E. F. (1980). Dialect and spelling. In E. H. Henderson & J. W. Beers (Eds.). *Developmental and cognitive aspects of learning to spell* (pp. 46–51). Newark, DE: International Reading Association.

Stewig, R. (1980). *Read to write: Using children's literature as a springboard for teaching writing.* (2nd ed.). New York: Holt, Rinehart & Winston.

Strong, W. (1976). Close-up: Sentence combining: Back to basics and beyond. *English Journal, 56,* 60–64.

Sulzby, E. (1985). Children's emergent reading of favorite storybooks: A developmental study. *Reading Research Quarterly, 20,* 458–481.

Tager-Flusberg, H. (1985). Putting words together: Morphology and syntax in the preschool years. In J. B. Gleason (Ed.). *The development of language* (pp. 139–171). Columbus, OH: Merrill.

Taylor, D. (1983). *Family Literacy: Young children learning to read and write.* Portsmouth, NH: Heinemann Educational Books.

Tchudi, S. N., & Tchudi, S. J. (1983). *Teaching writing in the content areas: Elementary School.* Washington, DC: National Education Association.

Teale, W. H. (1984). Reading to young children: Its significance for literacy development. In H. Goelman, A. Oberg, & F. Smith (Eds.). *Awakening to literacy* (pp. 110–121). Portsmouth, NH: Heinemann Educational Books.

Temple, C. A., Nathan, R. G., & Burris, N. A. (1982). The beginnings of writing. Boston: Allyn & Bacon.

Tiedt, I. M., Bruemmer, S. S., Lane, S., Watanabe, K. O., & Williams, M. Y. (1983). *Teaching writing in K-8 classrooms: The time has come.* Englewood Cliffs, NJ: Prentice-Hall.

Time Magazine, *126*(1), July 8, 1985. "Final destination" (pp. 36–39); For learning or ethnic pride (pp. 80–81); growth of a nation (pp. 34–35).

Tizard, B. (1981). Language at home and at school. In C. B. Cazden (Ed.). *Language in early childhood education* (Rev. ed.). (pp. 17–27). Washington, DC: National Association for the Education of Young Children.

Tizard, B., Cooperman, O., Joseph, A., & Tizard, J. (1972). Environmental effects on language development: A study of young children in long-stay residential nurseries. *Child Development, 43,* 337–358.

Trelease, J. (1985). *The read-aloud handbook* (Rev. ed.). New York: Penguin.

Turkle, S. (1984). *The second self: Computers and the human spirit.* New York: Simon & Schuster.

Veatch, J. (1968). *How to teach reading with children's books* (2nd ed.). New York: Richard C. Owen.

Venezky, R. L. (1980). Spelling instruction and spelling reform. In U. Frith (Ed.). *Cognitive processes in learning to spell* (pp. 9–30). New York: Academic Press.

Vygotsky, L. S. (1962). *Thought and language* (E. Hanfmann & G. Vakar, Trans.). Cambridge, MA: MIT Press.

Wall, E. S. (1984). *The computer alphabet book.* New York: Avon.

Walshe, R. D. (Ed.). *Donald Graves in Australia: "Children want to write."* Rozelle, New South Wales: Primary English Teaching Association.

Weir, R. H. (1970). *Language in the crib.* The Hague: Mouton.

_____. (1966). Some questions on the child's learning phonology. In F. Smith & G. A. Miller (Eds.). *The genesis of language* (pp. 153–168). Cambridge, MA: MIT Press.

West, B. E. (1983). The new arrivals from Southeast Asia: Getting to know them. *Childhood Education, 60,* 84–89.

Wilkinson, A., Barnsley, G., Hanna, P., & Swan, M. (1983). More comprehensive assessment of writing development. *Language Arts, 60,* 871–881.

Willert, M. K., & Kamii, C. (1985). Reading in kindergarten. *Young Children. 40*(6), 3–9.

Index